Leaving A Legacy

An Inspirational Guide To Taking Action and Making a Difference

JIM PALUCH

FOREWORD BY MARK VICTOR HANSEN

JP Horizons
INCORPORATED

Leaving a Legacy

Published by
Executive Books
206 West Allen Street
Mechanicsburg, PA 17055
717-766-9499   800-233-2665
Fax: 717-766-6565
www.executivebooks.com

ISBN: 0-937539-32-5

Printed in the United States of America

2000

10 9 8 7 6 5 4 3

Cover/book design:

BARRY EDWARDS • 2350 HAMILTON AVE., CLEVELAND, OH 44114
216-241-6695 • HTTP://WWW.EN.COM/USERS/INTEGMD

~ <u>To All of My Aunts and Uncles</u> ~

You've Inspired My Life and Left a Legacy

Jim Paluch

ACKNOWLEDGEMENTS

Many people could be thanked, as a book is always a group effort, but the following are those that played an important part in making this book become a reality.

Barry Edwards for his design and creativity

Rita Hamley, whose editing made it an enjoyable read

Nick DiBenedetto for reading the manuscript and getting excited

Charlie "Tremendous" Jones for always giving excellent advice

Alton Maiden for allowing me to use THE DASH

My sons, *Jim* and *Andrew* for a constant source of inspiration

My wife *Beth,* whose unselfish support makes everything possible.

Leaving A Legacy

Foreword

by Mark Victor Hansen

The wisdom of the ages is found in books like <u>Leaving A Legacy</u>, and since wisdom is something we never seem to have enough of, there is always a grateful sigh when we can lay a book down and know a little more about ourselves. Wisdom comes when all the knowledge we store in our mind mingles and assimilates with actual experiences to become "magically" transformed into real life applications. And so, a life changing book can be full of all the things we already know, but need to be reminded of over and over again. When it becomes your personal quest to build a better you and to break through the barriers that may be blocking your highest potential, then the reading of a single book can often become a turning point and a catalyst for your future.

The classic motivational books are written with the similar purpose of the ancients passing tales from one generation to the next, sharing stories of what they've learned in life with the hopes of helping another. They tell about the things that matter in living successful lives. . . of building our belief systems, nurturing a positive attitude, understanding our individual poten-tial, valuing the importance of honesty and character, and most importantly, learning to appreciate and add to the lives of those around us.

It is the helping of others that sustains life and gives us purpose, and we don't have to look far to find a cause we can commit ourselves to. Whether it's the need to reforest the earth, feed a hungry world, revitalize our schools, help the American Red Cross replenish its supply of blood, or battle against illiteracy, we can all feel compelled to help in some way.

When you begin to read this wonderful book called <u>Leaving A Legacy</u>, it first appears that its cause is to appreciate the value of our "old people," this group of individuals that should be revered and looked to for their wisdom, rather than forgotten or set aside by our society.

The biggest message we learn from this book, however, is that growing older is not a curse, but a blessing, and if you take the wisdom that comes with all of life's experiences and use it to improve yourself and those around you, then each of us, young and old, can truly "flower." The real cause behind <u>Leaving A Legacy</u> is that everyone possesses the knowledge to make a difference in the world, and all that we know becomes wisdom bearing beautiful fruit when we have the courage to take action.

Whether you are seventeen or seventy, I challenge you to take the wisdoms found in this book, in other books, and most importantly, found in your life and the lives surrounding you, and allow them to motivate you to take action for the betterment of humanity.

- Mark Victor Hansen

Co-author, New York Times #1 Best-selling
"Chicken Soup for the Soul" series

⇌ INTRODUCTION ⇌

SIMPLE QUESTIONS. . .

It is amazing what a simple question can lead to. "What do you do out there in your part of the world, Uncle Joe?" His part of the world was Los Angeles, California, and it seemed like another world away from the campfire in the middle of a peaceful woods at my home in Northern Ohio. It was more than just trying to make conversation with my uncle at a family reunion several summers ago; I really wanted to know what his world was like. His answer was given with the level of detail that only seems to be possible after a certain age is passed and the element of time, especially in a conversation around a campfire, doesn't matter.

"Well..." he began. "I get up every morning and make some toast to take with me to McDonald's because I don't like the English Muffins they use on their sandwiches. Then I wrap it in a napkin to take with me and meet with my buddies at McDonald's and we sit and talk all morning about anything we want to...."

His words painted a picture that grew continually in my mind. Our nation's old folks sitting in fast food restaraunts, malls and parks around the country, waiting. Waiting... with knowledge acquired through life's experiences that is going virtually untapped. What would this world be like if this untapped precious resource was inspired to take action and make a difference... to turn their knowledge into wisdom... to leave a legacy?

Unfortunately Uncle Joe died shortly after our time around that campfire.

He did not get the opportunity to read this book or even really know that his answer to my question was the inspiration for this book. Leaving a Legacy is a fictional story that I believe could be true not only in Los Angeles, but in cities and towns around the world. I want Leaving a Legacy to be a book that inspires the old people to continue living until there is no more life left in the body. Even if just one more person cares enough to take action and make a difference, then the world will become a better place.

All of this brings up yet another question. When does a person become old?

I have witnessed 92 year olds with the vitality and wit of a teenager, and teenagers with the ambition and drive of a bedridden nursing home patient. When does a person become old? It is never too early or too late to begin taking action and leaving a legacy. The ability to make a difference lies within each of us. Leaving a Legacy is not a book written for old people or young people. It is written for the people desiring more for themselves and all the world around them, regardless of their age.

My thoughts now go to you and another question. You've purchased this book or someone has given it to you thinking you would benefit. What are you going to do with it? There are several possible answers to this question. You can stop reading now and miss the potential that lies on the pages ahead. This option really has no benefit to anyone and is hopefully not the one you'll choose. You can read and be entertained. This is a great option. You will be introduced to a variety of characters that will make you laugh and cry and there will be some you may possibly even relate with. Some are fictional characters that have become so real to me and my family that they seem like family themselves. Some of the characters are real people from famous Hollywood actors, to a Vienna psychologist placed in fictional settings to help the story unfold. Reading to be entertained is a wonderful option to pursue.

You may also read to think and to learn. Some of the greatest books I've read have caused me to set them down, take a walk, and come back to read the pages I'd just finished. They caused me to think, and in thinking I learned. What you have the potential to think and learn about in Leaving A Legacy revolves around the seven wisdoms that the main characters will introduce you to....

MAKING THE BEST USE OF YOUR TIME

KEEPING THE DESIRE TO SMILE

SEEING LIFE AS IT REALLY IS

FACING THE DRAGON WITHIN

APPRECIATING THE VALUE OF HARD WORK

FINDING INSPIRATION IN EVERYTHING

HAVING THE COURAGE TO TAKE ACTION

Yet another option is to read to be inspired. Every book can inspire its reader as long as the reader has the desire to be inspired. At the close of this book you'll find a list of "Books That Inspire." The books on this list inspired me because they combined the entertainment that kept my attention, and the content that caused me to think and learn. When these elements combined with my desire to be inspired, I closed the back cover of each knowing I was a better person for reading it. That is what I hope Leaving a Legacy will do for you, make you feel like a better person for reading it. If you set it down inspired, then your own inner potential is rekindled and you are that much closer to taking action and making a difference... leaving your legacy.

There seems to be yet one more question to ask. This is undoubtedly the most important question of all, because it relates directly to you, the person caring enough to hold a book like Leaving a Legacy in your hands. It is important because the answer might very well direct the remaining course of your life and touch the lives of every person you come in contact with. The question is simply this....

"What will you do out there in your part of the world... ?"

~ PROLOGUE ~

The white lights were nearly blinding Joe Yamka as he tried to squint past them through the darkness to the thousands of people gathered in the Los Angeles auditorium. Sitting in the solitude of the shadows cast deliberately on the stage, he was not alone. Beside him were the five men that had served with such commitment, dedication, and purpose that, if not for their efforts, this moment would not have been possible. The murmur of the crowd began to increase in antici-pation of the occasion and the speech that would soon be delivered. Joe's gaze went to the faces of those men sitting beside him, the Board of Directors.

He studied their faces and, although they were now drawn with the lines of age, he could still see a youthful enthusiasm fueled by the thrill of accomplishment that only a relatively short time ago would not have seemed possible. He reflected on the wisdom of the group gathered beside him. It was wisdom that had been bought with the price of years, yet covered up by the fear of what those same years would bring, the end of life. Until a short time ago none of them had ever looked at the good side of growing old… the gift of wisdom. This gift would have been lost if not for the collective realization that there is life right up to the grave, as long as we choose to live it. Joe's eyes fell on the empty chair at the end of the stage. The one that was missing. How much he would have enjoyed this moment. The American flags lining the stage behind them, the red, white, and blue streamers hanging from the ceiling, and the bands playing would have thrilled the patriot who should have been occupying the seat at the end.

Joe's thoughts were jolted back to the present as the crowd of people let out a cheer and "Hail to the Chief" began to play. The Board of Directors rose to their feet as they had been instructed to do at the rehearsal, their faces glowing with pride and excitement as they watched the Secret Service secure the aisle leading up to the side of the stage; the President of the United States of America stepped onto the same platform that they were now occupying. As the President stopped and threw an enthusiastic wave that raised the cheering to a resounding pitch, Joe glanced back over his shoulder once again at his colleagues, whose eyes shone with tears that had broken loose and fallen down their rugged faces. Joe knew he was experiencing success as he stood basking in accomplishment, sharing *this moment with those he cared about beside him.*

The President turned his attention away from the crowd and moved toward the men at the opposite end of the stage. Breaking away from the protocol that had been presented in the rehearsal, he extended his hand to Joe Yamka and with a hearty grasp gave a warm "thank you" that thrilled Joe to the center of his being. He could hardly comprehend that he was shaking hands with the President of the United States, who warmly greeted each of the Board of Directors and then, moving past the empty chair, stopped, as if he were picturing the one who should have been there. He turned, throwing up a wave to the crowd, which again brought thunderous cheers as he moved to the podium at center stage. The deafening roar fell to a spellbinding silence as the crowd awaited the President's message. The power and impact of the occasion forced Joe's thoughts back three and a half years to the very beginning of this moment.

⮞ CHAPTER 1 ⮜

THE BOARD OF DIRECTORS

The wind-up Westclox Little Ben was sending out its clanking message to start the day. Joe walked out of the bathroom and picked it up to shut it off. He looked at the once-white face of the clock and noticed that the yellowing brought on by age was slowly eroding the twelve Roman numerals. The glass covering was scratched from being knocked to the floor more than once, and there was even a dent on the casing. He smiled, not able to remember why he had thrown it against the wall.

"For thirty-eight years you've been clanking like that and for thirty-eight years I've always been up before you. Thirty-eight years... where has the time gone?"

He set it back on the old nightstand next to his already made bed and went back into the bathroom to finish his shave. Looking in the mirror he hesitated, set the electric razor back down, and just stared. He could see that time had taken the same toll on him as it had on his clock. It had eroded his face and his entire being. "Old age has quietly crept up on you and is here to stay," he told himself.

"All that is left is death, and then age will have won." He watched in the mirror as the words fell from his lips.

It had been thirty-eight years since Joe had finished his travels and arrived in Los Angeles and forty years since a car accident that took his wife and daughter. Joe had never been sure if he felt lucky or not, being thrown from the car before it went over the mountain and burst into flames. The agony of that scene playing over and over in his mind had to be more painful than death itself could be. For two years after the tragedy, he'd wandered the country, living on odd jobs and looking for something. Whatever it was he was looking for, he was sure he'd never found it. And now here he was, seventy years old, standing in front of the bathroom mirror half shaven, talking to himself and his alarm clock. The full head of hair that he had once enjoyed had vanished to just a few gray strands strategically placed, in an attempt to cover up the baldness that only his Angels hat could fully disguise. He still stood pretty straight for seventy, but that military physique he'd once known was long gone. As he hit the last of the stubble with the razor, he was reminded of another brush with death. He glanced at the scars on his chest that marked the triple bypass he'd had four years earlier. Lucky? Joe really couldn't decide.

Putting on his usual slacks and shirt, he walked out of the bedroom with anticipation for a productive meeting. He went to his desk to continue his morning ritual. Sitting down, he called the weather service to decide on his means of transportation to the morning meeting, took a quick glance at yesterday's mail, and reviewed the news headlines, which he was certain would come up sometime in the meeting today. He picked up his little note pad, a habit he had nurtured for many years, and took a new pen out of a package in the lower right-hand desk drawer. Placing the others back in the drawer, he glanced at the hundreds of little note pads filling the drawer, some turning yellow with age just like the clock. He quickly shut the drawer and wondered why he'd ever taken the notes in the first place. He'd never looked at them since.

Glancing at his watch, Joe realized he would have to hurry or be late, and if there was one thing he wasn't up to today, it was the hard time he'd receive for being late to a board meeting. One more quick stop in the kitchen and his morning ritual would be complete. He reached into the bread drawer and pulled out two pieces of rye and placed them into the toaster. Moving to the counter and picking up his medicine container, he lamented, "Man, I forgot again. Well, I'll take yesterday's dose now and catch up with today's dose tonight."

Downing the heart medicine with a swig of grapefruit juice, he removed the toast from the toaster and wrapped it in a paper towel before placing it in his coat pocket and moving toward the door. He then stopped to pick up a picture and smiled down at the two memories smiling back. He had completed his morning ritual and headed out to the street. Smiling, he wondered why he called the weather service every morning, because he always walked to the "office."

The parking lot was full as he turned the corner and moved toward the building entry. The building was buzzing with people and infused with the familiar aroma of coffee. Over in the corner the board had already gathered in their usual meeting spot. Melvin always arrived an hour before anyone else to secure the spot. Stepping up to the table, he saw that the other six were already there and ready for business. He glanced at his watch and was relieved to see it was only 7:25; he wasn't late for the 7:30 start.

"Have a seat," said Howard. "Hoover's check must have come in and he was feeling generous this morning. He ordered for you. I think he's wanting a favor."

"No favor. Why do you think I'm always wanting a favor? It was just crowded and I didn't want to hold the meeting up waiting for him to get his stuff."

"Ain't never bought for any of the rest of us before," barked Sammy through his usual stone face.

"Ain't never wanted to," returned Hoover.

"Come on, you two. If you get started we might as well forget it for the day," snapped Roadie as he adjusted his head-band and looked over his round wire-rimmed glasses.

"Hey, let me tell you somethin'.... "

"No, let me tell you how it really is," piped Leo. "We never get anything discussed here because you two.... "

"You're always tryin' to tell us how it 'really is,'" Hoover countered, "but, the fact is you don't know noth.... "

"Can we get started here?" Melvin quietly asked, stopping the conversation and hoping it might head in a different direction. He hated confrontation of any kind. "Joe, would you please have a seat?"

"Yeah, Joe, I got your usual. Sausage Egg McMuffin and a small coffee. This one's on me, don't worry about it."

Joe sat down, shaking his head and smiling, and then thanked Hoover for his generosity. "Why should this morning be any different from the rest?" he thought to himself. Taking the toast from his pocket, he carefully placed it on the table next to the Egg McMuffin. Opening both packages, he removed the top English muffin from the sandwich and in one swift motion flipped the remainder onto the piece of rye toast. Next he removed the other muffin and placed it with the first half on the paper towel. His next step was to remove the now exposed piece of sausage from the sandwich and place it on the wrapper. The remaining piece of rye toast was carefully placed on top of the sandwich, skillfully aligned with the bottom piece, and then set onto an extra napkin, freeing the paper towel to systematically wrap both English muffins, and the wrapper to fold up the sausage. Each was then placed in a separate coat pocket for later use. Next he removed the lid from his coffee, blew twice, took a sip, and then set it back on the table. The meeting was officially under way.

"Ain't never gonna figure out why you do that," growled Sammy.

For nearly three years this ancient group of misfits had been meeting at the same McDonald's, eating the same thing, at the same table, talking about the same subjects, and accomplishing the same results... NOTHING. They called themselves the Board of Directors.

"Why do you do that, Joe?" asked Hoover, not trying to be imposing.

"Do what?" Joe asked back, taking another sip of his coffee and biting into his newly modified sandwich.

"Take your sandwich apart and bring your own toast, and take the sausage home in one pocket and muffins in the other. That's strange, man. You're doin' some strange stuff there, man...." Sammy crossed his arms, shook his head, let out a large disgusted sigh, and stared out the window.

"Yeah, but let me tell you what is really weird," piped in Leo.

"Oh, man, here we go, the expert's 'bout ready to speak. Here we go." Sammy just kept looking out the window, disgusted with the skateboarders rumbling through the parking lot and enjoying the early morning Los Angeles sun. "Them kids goin' to break their necks."

"What is really weird, Leo?" asked Melvin, trying to keep peace.

"I heard on the news last night, the people in Washington are gonna cut our medical benefits more. I can't make it now, how am I gonna make it after that?"

"You're always worrying about yourself. It's always I, I, I...." Hoover added with the hope that the complaining would stop. "Just once you should think about what you might do for someone else."

"DO? Do for someone else! Listen who's talkin'!" Roadie laughed, taking a long drag on his cigarette. "You're the one that's wanting someone to do for you. You're needing a place to stay, aren't you? That's why you bought Joe's breakfast. You ain't foolin' nobody."

Howard had finished the last bite of his pancakes when he said, "You ought to do something for yourself there, Roadie, you smoke so many cigarettes... keep it up and you won't be around for too many more of these meetings."

"Hey, I don't need your opinion. My mother died a long time ago, okay? I do what I want. You got that, four eyes?" Roadie did not like anybody talking about his smoking.

"Come on, guys," Melvin said in his calm monotone. "We never get a chance to have any kind of discussion here because it always ends up in an argument. Why don't we try and find something good to talk about?"

"Huh! Ain't nothin' good to talk about," said Sammy, still staring out the window. "Those stupid kids gonna break their necks. I tell ya, that board with wheels on it should be against the law. Look at 'em. Somebody gonna get hurt. KIDS!!!!"

"Well, for once I agree," said Leo. "There isn't anything good going on

18

for people when they get to be our age… Wife is gone, family is scattered, money is slim. Let me tell you how it is: the most exciting part of my day is coming to this stupid McDonald's and meeting with all of you, and frankly I can't stand doing this."

"Well, maybe we can't stand you," said Roadie, lighting up another cigarette.

"Come on, if we keep at this we'll all walk away mad again and nothing good will come from it," said Howard.

"Why should today be any different?" Hoover said with an uncharacteristically sad look coming across his face.

Melvin noticed the look on his face. "Hey, Hoove, don't worry, everything will work out. It always does."

"It always works out for the bad," said Sammy. "Ain't never gonna be any good for people like us."

"Oh, that makes us all feel real good," said Leo. "Why don't you add some more cheer to this meeting?"

"Man, I don't care much for you and your know-it-all ways," said Sammy, bringing his attention from outside back to the table and getting out of his seat.

"Hey, sit down and take it easy!" said Hoover. "You're drawing attention to us from the whole restaurant. And you're bothering Joe here."

"Watch out, Joe. He's really trying to get on your good side," said Roadie. "I know he's needing a place to stay."

"Hey, Joe, you doing okay?" asked Melvin. "You're being awfully quiet. You feeling okay? Heart's not acting up, is it?"

Joe couldn't even speak. He just surveyed the cast of characters sitting around the table. Over the past three years this group had been haphazardly assembled for what seemed to be no purpose except to come together and hate life. He looked at each person thoughtfully.

Hoover, sitting next to him, seemed to be a ten-year-old kid caught in a seventy-year-old body. His bald head and features reminded Joe of "Curly" from the Three Stooges. Hoover was a Midwestern farm boy who'd spent most of his life trying to sell farm machinery in the Midwest but had never had much success. He'd moved to Los Angeles to start a little lawncare business twenty-five years earlier but couldn't keep it going. He'd been fired from almost every job he'd ever had and now, at seventy-two, was out of money, out of work, and soon to lose an apartment. He had a hard time admitting to all of this and never talked of any family. As far as Joe knew, he had never been married. The bright eyes and smile that Hoover had only a few months ago had been replaced with the worry and uncertainty of a bleak future.

Joe's eyes went to Roadie sitting next to Hoover. How could he not notice Roadie? There he sat with a cloud of smoke around his head from the chronic habit of chain smoking. Yellowed fingers, broken blood vessels across his face, and a constant cough were sure signs that this habit hadn't started just yesterday. He was the newest member and probably the youngest of the board, having been around only for six months. His long gray hair was held in place with a red bandana head-band, and the John Lennon wire-rimmed glasses set him apart from the other members. His emptiness and apparent uncertain future, however, tied him to the group. Joe wasn't sure, but he had heard that Roadie had spent his life as a stage hand for many rock and roll bands during the fifties, sixties, and seventies. Roadie said himself that he'd spent a year traveling with Elvis and his bands in 1952 when Elvis was just getting started. At times he would also mention Janis Joplin, Jimi Hendrix, Otis Redding, and some band called Bachman Turner Overdrive. Rumors of his time spent riding with motorcycle gangs were supported by his daily uniform of jeans, boots, a Harley Davidson T-shirt, and a chain hooked to his belt leading to a wallet. Under this mysterious and, at times, intimidating facade, however, was the hint of humility and caring that time had forgotten.

Next to Roadie sat Howard, trying to avoid the secondary smoke that was starting to circle his head. Joe knew that Howard would never complain about the smoke. He was too meek and reserved. Howard would always show up at the meetings with a thin black tie, a white shirt with sleeves rolled up, and several pens in his pocket; he'd been an accountant and had a promising career until sometime in the early sixties, when a scandalous charge was brought against the firm that he was a senior executive with. Joe thought he remembered reading about it. After being blamed for the whole incident and spending a short time in prison, he was released, but never able to reach the prominence he'd once known. No one was really sure, but Joe thought Howard had been set up and just never defended himself. He was the only member of the group who was still married, and his wife spent most of her time cleaning homes for people while Howard spent a little time doing bookkeeping and tax returns for several small companies. Joe always felt like Howard was a man who had been robbed of a life and a career. What might he have done if things had only gone a little differently?

At the end of the table sat Melvin. No one loved the United States of America more than Melvin. He had been a Marine in World War II, and though his Marine physique was slightly lost under the presence of fifty or sixty extra pounds, his flat-top haircut and patriotism still showed evidence of his high standards. The irony of Melvin's life was that sometime during the war he'd been discharged. Joe was not quite sure of the reasons or the details but thought it had to do with a cowardly act that cost the lives of several men. The discipline of the Marines had remained with Melvin, or maybe it was just the fact that he had always been an early riser as a child growing up on a Kansas farm. In the three years that they had been meeting, Melvin was always the first person there and always tried to bring out the positive side of every issue. His wife had died more than twenty years ago after a long battle with cancer, his four children were scattered around the country, occasionally sending a birthday card or greeting. Melvin came to California in the sixties and sold flags and banners for a company back East. He had made enough to live on, but never really got ahead. One thing that Joe recognized in Melvin was that the deadline for complaining was yesterday, and he would never waste his time doing it.

This was certainly a different philosophy than that of the person sitting next to Melvin. Leo Horowitz was a complainer. Even when Joe met him twenty years ago in the jewelry store where Leo worked, he had been complaining. Leo's balding head and ring of gray, curly hair just over the ears, along with his big nose and large eyes, made him a person you couldn't help but smile at. Yet, the many years of habitual negativism had forced his face into a constant frown. He wore a gold necklace and bracelet and several rings, all memories from his days in the jewelry business. He was the Casanova of the Jewish Home for the Aged where he now lived, and nearly every statement he made was prefaced by the words, "Let me tell you how it really is." Leo was quietly respected, at least Joe thought so, by the other members of the board because he had survived some of the toughest concentration camps in WWII. Joe was never really sure why Leo showed up at the board meetings, but he hadn't missed one since they had started.

The only person in the world that was more sour than Leo was the individual sitting next to him, Sammy Johnson, who had once again turned his attention to the activity going on outside the window. He seldom, if ever, would allow himself to be drawn into the meeting, nor was he able to look at anyone else at the table. One thing that Joe was sure of was that he had never seen Sammy smile. Short and stocky with a stooped walk, he'd spent fifty-seven years of his life shining shoes at the Los Angeles airport. His large hands and twisted fingers were a testimony of the many shoes he'd polished and shined. Sammy never took off his old blue sailor's hat with the turned-down rim. His curly, gray-black hair was barely able to be seen sticking out from under the hat, and his look was completed with a matching mustache. Sammy's eyes were cold and dark, almost as if a tear could fall from them at any time. Even though Sammy's very presence brought a chill to the meeting, Joe couldn't imagine a meeting without him. Perhaps this was because his sad countenance was symbolic of the lost hopes and perceived future of every member of the so-called Board of Directors.

"Well what about it, Joe, what are you thinking?" Melvin questioned again. "What's on your mind today?"

Joe slowly stood up and gulped down the last of his coffee. He cleared his throat and addressed the six blank stares gazing up at him. "You guys are dead and I am dying," Joe sighed, shaking his head. He placed the empty cup back on the table and slowly turned, his head and eyes cast to the floor. Without another word the lonely figure headed for the door.

Once outside Joe could hardly believe what he had done. No one had ever walked out of a board meeting, no matter how bad it got. Now he'd just walked out on the only friends he really had. He wanted to go back inside, but something told him not to. He could almost feel the six sets of eyes staring through him from the other side of the windows. He decided to move forward; besides, his next appointment would be waiting for him.

⌒ CHAPTER 2 ⌒

SEE THE MAGIC

As Joe rounded the corner onto Horizons Drive, he saw the familiar little picket fence that had first attracted him to his next stop. As he walked closer, he could see the tiny figure running toward the street. When he arrived in front of the house where the fence met the sidewalk, the little dog was nearly jumping over the four-foot barrier.

Joe moved to the corner of the lot where the little dog was already waiting. Reaching in his pocket, he pulled out the wrapper that contained the sausage. To the greeting of thankful yelping from the little mixed breed, he gave the sausage a toss; the grateful recipient grabbed it in midair and had it gone before he'd hit the ground again. Then, just as he had done every day for the past three years, he began to lap the little postage stamp front yard as fast as his four legs would carry him. One, two, three times around, and then up on the porch, jumping over all four steps and right beside the little boy, whose thrill of running could only be carried out in the joy of watching his little dog. The pup ran behind the wheelchair and then back to the front of it, lying down at his master's feet. As he had done every day in the past, Joe let out a laugh and raised a hand to the boy in the wheelchair, who slowly raised his hand and gave a smile. Always the bright spot in Joe's day this event took less than a minute. Now, with it over once again, he slowly turned to go back to the loneliness of his apartment and a life that made him wonder why it ever was.

Joe stopped immediately. He hadn't moved a single step when the color caught his eye. Memories of his childhood in West Virginia began to flood his mind. How much he had enjoyed seeing this sight when he was a child. It let him know that spring was on the way. He would always pull out his old rusty pocket knife, cut off a few branches, and then run the blossoms home to his mother. Joe could feel the memories of his mother's hug almost sixty-five years earlier as she would thank him for the wonderful gift and put the branches in water in the center of their makeshift kitchen table. Joe always enjoyed her smile when she would see him running up the lane with the blossoms of a redbud tree. He hadn't seen a redbud in years. They didn't grow in California. So, what was this one doing here? And it was obviously an old tree. Why hadn't he noticed it in the past three years of making this stop?

"Ernest," Joe whispered to himself. He could hear the words of Ernest.

"JoJo, would you like to know the magic of redbuds?"

That's what Ernest used to call him, "JoJo." Joe couldn't remember where he had come from, he just seemed to show up in town. Joe's mother never liked him even talking to Ernest.

"Don't you be with that hobo. He ain't no good and you'll be no good bein' around him."

She didn't realize the emptiness for a nine-year-old boy of Eastern European descent in the hills of West Virginia without a father and with very few friends. It was lonely. Joe had known loneliness all of his life. Ernest filled both roles, father and friend, and it was always a great day when he would appear. Joe was never sure where he came from or where he went. He was only around for a year or so. He had a "home" in a run-down mine shack on the other side of Oak Hill. It was as though he would show up almost magically about once or twice a week. Joe would hear stories about riding on trains and traveling across the country. He learned more about the United States listening to Ernest than he ever did in school. His history lesson was listening to Ernest tell about his own father, who fought in the Civil War, and of Teddy Roosevelt and the Rough Riders storming San Juan Hill. Ernest had been right there with them as they made the charge. That was how he'd gotten the scar on his face. A Spanish bayonet just missed a direct hit as Teddy Roosevelt fired a shot into the heart of the Spaniard, throwing off his aim and saving Ernest's life.

Besides the scar, the other thing that Joe remembered was his limp. Ernest couldn't walk very fast. Thrown from a train years before, his left leg was twisted and bent. Ernest told the little nine-year-old every detail of that incident. Perhaps it was to strike fear in Joe to go to school and try and make something of himself. Or, maybe it was Ernest just wanting this little boy to see that every life has some meaning. No matter how seemingly insignificant, there was meaning. Ernest told Joe how a conductor had caught him sleeping in a cattle car in Ouray, Colorado. The conductor told Ernest that it would be too cold for him in the cattle car as they would be going through the mountains and kindly offered a spot in the mail car if he promised to get off at the end of the line and never get back on. Ernest thanked the conductor and slept quietly in the spot given to him. Sometime during the night the conductor and two other men, all smelling of alcohol, jerked Ernest out of his sleep, and with the light of a lantern shining brightly in his eyes, the conductor swore and screamed, "HEY, Scarface, you ain't never gonna ride any train again."

In the glow of the lantern the three men began to beat Ernest with clubs, laughing, spitting, and cussing. They hit him until he fell to the floor, and then each took several turns kicking and stomping until they were sure life was gone from the victim of their own hate and drunkenness. Without a thought, they picked up what they presumed was a lifeless body and walked over to the door in the side of the car, slid it open, and threw their evening's work out into the cold of the Rockie Mountains. With a big whoop they shut the door. Ernest was left for the wolves.

"How I got out of that mountain, JoJo, I'll never know. But I do remember lyin' there, being able to look up and see the moon. I could feel the pain in this here twisted leg and knew it was broken. But some way I was able to smile. Imagine that, JoJo, almost dead and still smilin'. I told myself that I had to go on. I felt there was a reason to live. I wanted to help someone. I laughed out loud. I was lyin' there at what I thought was the end of my life and I wanted to help someone. I promised myself that I would help someone if I made it out of those mountains. You know what, JoJo? That gave me life. Wanting to do something for someone will give life to a person, even one near dead as I was. Well, I don't know how, JoJo, but I made it. Some old miners found me and left me at a hospital. I got better and now here I am. That was a long time ago, JoJo, and now I have life because I'm here, maybe to help you. What do you think of that, JoJo?"

Joe was mesmerized by each word that fell from the lips of his old friend. He noticed the deep wrinkles and heavy eyebrows over the coal black eyes of this ancient story teller.

"How old are you, Ernest?" asked Joe, knowing what the answer would be.

"Ohhh, I'm real ooolllddd," came the reply, just as it had every time Joe had asked the question.

"Well, are you a hundred?"

"Not real sure anymore. I don't think so, but I could be."

"I hope I get to live to be a hundred. I really do." Joe said, staring deeply into the eyes, and possibly through to the soul of his hero sitting next to him on the log.

"JoJo, maybe you're the person I was supposed to help. Maybe you're the reason I wasn't dinner for wolves back there in those mountains. You think that might be the truth, JoJo? You think I'm here to help you?" Ernest let a warm smile form on the leathery face as he waited for the young boy's reply.

"I don't know, Ernest. How you gonna help me? I'm just a boy. What am I gonna do?"

"You plan to get older, don't ya? Maybe I can tell you somethin' that will help you get older. I'll tell you what. You meet me at my old shack tomorrow and I'll show you some magic, JoJo. The magic of redbud trees. Now go on, git. Your ma is gonna start wonderin' where you're at. Go on, I'll see you tomorrow."

Tomorrow couldn't get there soon enough. Right after breakfast Joe stopped in the kitchen and filled his pocket with leftover biscuits, knowing that if his mother saw him and realized that he was going to see Ernest, especially with food, she would get a switch and whip him. Out the door and jumping off the back porch, he was running bare-footed toward the old mine shed. His mind raced, wondering what the magic would be that Ernest was going to share with him.

As he came around the big oak tree and over the hill he could see Ernest standing in front of the shack.

"Ernest!!!" he yelled, "What's the magic?"

Ernest just smiled and waved as he saw the little boy come running down the dirt road toward him.

Barely able to get the words out when he stopped, he looked up at Ernest and asked again between gasps, "Ernest, what's the magic?"

"Now, young man, you just better slow down and catch hold of your breath. We want you to get old, remember?" Ernest couldn't help but let out a laugh as he watched the eagerness grow in his young friend.

"I'm here to see the magic. I couldn't hardly wait till mornin' got here, Ernest. You're still gonna show me that magic you were talking about, ain't ya? I gotta see it."

"Well, I can show you magic, JoJo. But it isn't the showin' of magic that's important. What matters is if you can see the magic. Do you think you can see magic, JoJo?"

"Oh, Ernest, I don't know. I think I can. I know I want to, anyway. What do I have to do to see magic? Will you tell me so I can make sure I see it?" Joe was almost begging.

Ernest just smiled and sat down on the old crate that was the only piece of furniture outside his shack. "To see magic, JoJo, you got to look past what you believe. If you just think everything is the way it seems or the way you think it is, you'll never see the magic. We don't get in trouble in life until we start thinking that life should be the way we want it to be. Life is never the way we want it to be... life is the way it is, and if we look past our beliefs, then we can see the possibilities that life has for each of us. That is magic,

JoJo, seeing the possibilities of life."

Ernest looked straight into the eyes of his little friend and realized this wasn't quite making sense to his young mind.

"You don't understand too good yet, do you, JoJo?"

"No, Ernest, I'm afraid I don't understand too good at all, and now I'm afraid I won't be able to see any magic. Will I, Ernest? Will I be able to see any magic?"

Ernest could see the fear in Joe's eyes. He knew that the little boy desperately wanted to know more, and with this he would be able to teach him the lesson. "Here, JoJo, let me show you just exactly what I mean." He reached down and broke a chunk of wood about two inches long and a half-inch wide off the dusty old crate he was sitting on.

"JoJo, do you think this piece of wood could turn into something else besides a piece of wood?"

"What do you mean, Ernest? How could a piece of wood turn into something else besides a piece of wood? What do you mean? What else could it be? I don't understand."

"Remember what I said about magic, JoJo. It is looking past what we believe and seein' the possibilities. If you don't believe that this wood can turn into something else, say a pocket knife, then maybe it can't, but… if you can look past your beliefs, then magic can happen, JoJo. Let me show you."

Ernest held up the piece of wood between the thumb and pointer finger of his right hand, about two inches from the nose of his young audience. Joe's eyes were locked onto the piece of wood, and his heart seemed to skip a beat at the moment Ernest held up his left hand in a tight fist. Bringing his left hand slowly toward the right and the chunk of wood, they met again, inches from Joe's face. Ernest slowly pushed the wood lengthwise into the thumb end of his fist until it completely disappeared into his left hand.

Holding his left hand now slightly above both of their heads so that they had to look up to see it, he quietly whispered, "This is it, JoJo. This is where magic takes place. Can you look past what your eyes saw and what your mind believes and what your head is telling you, and see the magic of the possibilities in life?" Ernest turned his head slowly away from the fist and looked at the little boy staring up in wonderment. A tear fell down Ernest's face as he again asked, "Can you look past it, JoJo, and see the magic?"

Without taking his eyes off the raised fist, Joe answered with the confidence of a new-found courage and whispered back, "I can, Ernest. I can see the magic."

Ernest slowly lowered his fist back down in front of the boy's face once more. With the gentleness of a flower opening, his fingers lay back to reveal a pocket knife where the wood should have been. Even though the knife was covered with age it appeared as a jewel to Joe. He looked at the knife and then up at his hero, who had now grown multitudes in stature in the heart and eyes of this young boy.

"I seen it, Ernest," first in a whisper and then in a shout. "I seen it! I seen the magic! It happened! The wood is a knife. And a beautiful knife it is. Where'd ya get it? Ernest, where did you find that knife?"

"It was way down in the mine," Ernest said with a smile, pleased at the joy it brought to the face of his friend. "But, it was magic that brought it here. Magic because you were able to see the possibilities, JoJo. And because you could see it, now you can have it."

Ernest held out the knife to Joe, whose hand slowly reached out and took a possessive grip on the treasure. Looking up with glistening eyes he breathed, "Do you really mean it, Ernest? I can have it? For keeps? My very own knife. Ernest, thanks. Thanks."

"You're welcome, JoJo. It's yours. That's how magic is. Sometimes it happens fast, right before our eyes like that wood turnin' into that knife. But, other times, JoJo, it may take a lifetime. And that is when we really need to look past our beliefs to see the possibilities. That is the magic I really want to tell you about today, JoJo, the magic that may take the rest of your life to see. Come on, follow me."

Joe put the knife into the good pocket of his bib overalls and hurried along to follow after Ernest. He stayed about three steps behind his mentor and studied every step he took. Following down the rutted, dusty, dirt road that led over the hill to the Johnson pasture, Joe observed everything about the man in front of him. His limp was slightly more noticeable as they started up the hill. He was stooped with age and the long, stringy, gray hair seemed to add to the beauty of his character. Even though Ernest was small in stature, he seemed as big as one of the West Virginia mountains surrounding them. His faded clothes were patched and worn, and the boots he wore barely stayed on his feet. Yet, Ernest seemed to be happy, even though life had not given him reason to be. "I wonder if magic ever happened to Ernest?" Joe thought to himself, as they wandered along in silence. "It doesn't seem like it has, but maybe this is the magic Ernest has been waiting for. Maybe he's been waiting all his life for magic."

Joe seemed to feel older all of a sudden; grown-up thoughts were coming into his mind as he walked along, feeling for his new pocket knife every five seconds. He was realizing that he, too, would one day become old. His life would not always be as a nine-year-old boy. One day he would be old, maybe even as old as Ernest.

"See there?" Ernest said as they came over the crest of the hill that looked down on Johnson's pasture.

"I see 'em, Ernest, the Johnsons' two cows and three old sheep. I see 'em," Joe said, pulling his hand out of his pocket and turning his attention from his new knife to the animals.

"No, JoJo," Ernest said in a serious tone. "Look beyond the obvious. Look to those beautiful trees beyond the pasture."

"Yeah, Ernest, I see 'em. Mother calls them pinks. She loves those kinda trees. She says it tells us that the cold winter is behind us and spring is on its way."

"She's right, JoJo, they send a special message. The name that they go by is redbud... a redbud tree. Scientists and what you call a botanist call them Cercis Canadensis. No matter what you call them, they are a special tree that can teach us a special lesson. Remember yesterday I told you I was going to show you the magic of redbud trees? Well, that's just what I'm going to do. Come on, we have to look closer."

Ernest took several steps and then turned around and motioned to Joe. "Come on, JoJo, I'm going to show you the magic of growing old."

Joe put his knife back into his pocket and once again began to follow Ernest. Joe's mind was swirling. He was excited about the magic that brought him his new prized possession but wasn't sure what he would find looking at trees. Joe just wished Ernest would tell more about the wars and his travels around the country, not some tree that some person calls a "circus cannon" and that his mother likes. "What fun is there in something that your mother likes?" Joe thought to himself.

"See there, JoJo, they're in full bloom. There is nothing more beautiful or wiser than a redbud tree. If only more people knew it." Ernest was in a world of his own as he looked back down at his little companion and continued, "Maybe you will be able to tell more people about their magic, JoJo. One day you'll understand it and then you will know how to tell people that old wood flowers. You see, that's the magic of redbuds, JoJo, the old wood flowers."

Joe was just staring up at Ernest while his right hand held tightly to his knife in his pocket, as if he was afraid it would disappear if he was not able to understand this strange thing Ernest was talking about.

"You don't understand, do you, JoJo?"

Joe just quietly shook his head.

"Of course you don't, son. How could you? You couldn't possibly understand as a child. Most people never understand. We allow ourselves to grow old, and when we get older we think we're worthless and all that is left is to die, and then when we die no one ever even remembers that we were alive. You see, JoJo, my young friend, no one ever looks at the good side of getting old... wisdom. WISDOM!"

Ernest shouted it with such feeling that it even made the Johnsons' old cows and sheep look up for a moment.

"Do you know what wisdom is, JoJo?"

Joe was part of a moment in time that he didn't understand. He thought he should be happy and enjoying this magic that Ernest was sharing with him. But he wasn't; it was scary and confusing. What was he doing here with this man? There were so many things in life he didn't understand and now Ernest was telling him about being old and something called wisdom and how he might need to tell others about this magic. Joe felt tears coming to his eyes and, even though he didn't want to show his fear in front of Ernest, he began to cry.

"I don't understand, Ernest. I don't want to get old, and I don't know nothin' about wisdom and flowers and I'm not sure I know nothin' about even myself."

Ernest smiled a warm knowing smile and placed his hand on the little boy's shoulder. "Don't let it scare you, JoJo. There ain't nothin to be scared of. You'll understand it. Here, have a seat on this log over here where we can get a good look at these beautiful redbuds and I'll explain it all to you."

"JoJo, do you see that hornet's nest hanging from that old maple over yonder?"

"Yeah, Ernest, what about it?"

"Well, I would like you to go knock it down real quick and bring it back over here to me. Hurry up and get it."

Joe looked at the nest, back to Ernest, and then back to the nest again, noticing all the excited and busy hornets swarming around it. "Ernest, you don't mean it, do ya?"

"Course I do. Now, hurry and go get it."

"But, Ernest, those hornets will sting me and you, if I stayed alive long enough to bring it back over here to ya."

"How do you know they'll do that?" asked Ernest, still looking seriously at the nest.

"Cause when I was six years old I was out climbing in a tree and found me a nest even bigger than that one. I thought it would be fun to knock it down and take it back home to my mother. Well, I got stung so many times that the doc in town thought I was going to die. That's why I don't want to mess with no hornet's nest, Ernest. Tell me you ain't serious."

Ernest just slapped his knee and let out a big laugh like he always did when something struck him really funny. "You know what that is, JoJo? That's wisdom, son. That is wisdom. You see, wisdom is when we can make a choice based on something that has happened to us in the past. All of us have things that happen to us every day. Some of it is going to be good and some of it may not be good. Like you and that hornet's nest a couple years ago. But, through all of these life experiences we gain knowledge, and when you use knowledge it becomes wisdom."

"You just used your knowledge and experience of a hornet's nest, and that shows wisdom. That is what's so great about growing old, JoJo, we'll have lots of experiences to gain knowledge from. But, if we don't use that knowledge then the wisdom is lost. In fact, JoJo, if we don't use that knowledge we are fools."

Ernest sat silently as if he were contemplating his own words. Trying to sort through their meaning, JoJo took the knife out, turned it over in his hand and placed it back into his pocket, looking at his aged friend. The silence seemed to be connecting generations of time. A slow, warm smile came to Ernest's face and then he spoke.

"Do you know what a legacy is, JoJo?"

JoJo just quietly shook his head and whispered, "No."

"It is the passing on of wisdom. It is caring enough to take action to do something and make a difference." Ernest stood up and seemed to be talking to an audience of people filling Johnsons' pasture. "We leave a legacy by caring enough about the people who may not even be born yet, to use our wisdom in a way to make the world better because we were here. We can leave a legacy. No one is too young and no one is too old."

Ernest's attention came back to the present with JoJo and the redbud tree. "That is where the magic of the redbud tree comes from, JoJo. The magic of the redbud is that it's the only plant on this earth that puts out a flower on its old wood. Do you know what that means, JoJo?"

Joe was suddenly feeling a little more sure of himself, having been shown that he possessed wisdom and that it was possible to gain more wisdom as each day came and went. This time he answered with confidence, "No, Ernest, I'm not sure what flowering on the old wood means. But I can learn."

Ernest smiled, knowing that his lesson wasn't being wasted. He was satisfied with the hope that what he was telling this little boy would grow and one day possibly make a difference in this world, making his own life worthwhile.

"Well, good, JoJo, let me explain. See that wild rose over there? It has probably been around as long as this group of redbud trees. And the same for that old apple tree on the other side of the pasture, and those forsythia bushes leading up to the Johnsons' house along their lane. All of those trees and bushes are goin' to flower. And they will be beautiful flowers, too, but what makes them different from these magical trees that we're sittin' by is that they'll only flower on this year's new growth. Only on the young part of those plants will flowers appear. Only on the young. But, look here on the redbud, JoJo, see this branch?   It is older than you and maybe even older than me, but look at the beautiful flowers lining that branch. That is the magic of redbuds and the magic of life, JoJo, old wood flowers."

"You see, most people think that you have to be like that rose or the apple tree. They think only the young ones and the new wood can put out a flower or do anything that would be helpful to another person. But it's not true, JoJo. In life old wood can flower. An old person has gained knowledge through experience, and if they will apply that knowledge, then the wisdom they have gained through the years will show as beautiful as these redbuds we're looking at here today. The sad thing, JoJo, is that not many people realize this magic. Maybe you can teach it to them. What do you think?"

Joe's head was spinning. How could he teach anyone anything? He was just a country boy deep in the hills of West Virginia. Getting old and getting out of there seemed like a long ways away.

"Ernest, I'm just a boy. Who is going to listen to me about anything? And who am I going to tell it to? The only people I really know is you and my mother and Chuckie Sturgill over the hill, who don't much listen to me anyway. I don't think I'll be teaching anyone anything, Ernest, but I sure appreciate you tellin' me this magic anyway."

"JoJo, you will be old one day. It will be here before you know it. And I believe a lot of people will be listening to you. Maybe even everyone across the country will listen to you. If a piece of wood can turn into a knife, don't you believe that same magic can work in your life, JoJo?   This magic just takes longer. You will no doubt forget our talking beside these redbuds, JoJo, because lots of things will happen to you, some good and some bad. That's where your wisdom will come from and the memory of this day may be pushed aside. But, one day you'll remember, and when you do, you too will flower on old wood."

"Now, listen to me, JoJo." This time Ernest cast a look at Joe like he'd never done before. It was one of seriousness, almost as if life depended upon it. "Do you remember me telling you about lying along them railroad tracks, making a promise to help someone if I lived to see another day? Well, I'm helping someone right now, JoJo. I believe you're the reason I didn't die there in those mountains. You are the person I was supposed to help. You are my legacy, JoJo...." Ernest's voice broke with emotion on those words and he once again smiled his warm smile. "You may not understand it all now but one day you will. You'll be old, too, and all that I ask of you is that you don't die until you're dead. Live out every day of your life even after the years have crept up on you. Keep living. Be willing and ready to help another person. It may be possible that you can help thousands of people. Keep in your heart, JoJo, the magic of the redbuds, remembering that old wood flowers. And when it is time, it will all make sense and you will be leaving your legacy."

"Now it's time for you to get on home. Your mother is going to skin you if she finds out you're spending so much time with a crazy old hermit. Go on, get out of here now."

Joe stood up from the log that had been his classroom. Looking into the eyes of his best friend he smiled, "I'll see ya, Ernest. Oh, here, I almost forgot! I brought some biscuits we had left over." Joe took the biscuits from his pocket and placed them beside Ernest on the log. "And thanks for the knife. I'll keep it forever."

Somehow Joe knew he was saying goodbye forever. He turned and took a few steps down the road. "Thanks for the magic, Ernest." So his friend wouldn't see him crying again he quickly turned around and took off running toward home.

"Thank you, JoJo. Now run, JoJo. Run, JoJo. Run...."

☞ CHAPTER 3 ☜

IF YOU HAD YOUR LIFE TO LIVE OVER AGAIN. . .

"JoJo, run here! Run up here now! JoJo, come! Come, JoJo! JOJO!"

Joe was brought back to reality once again by the persistent barking of the little mixed breed.

"JoJo, come here. JOJO!"

Joe turned around to see a beautiful young woman in a night shirt coming from the front door of the house and stepping off the porch. Her blond hair was tangled and blown and her red puffy eyes made it evident that she might not have been done sleeping yet, or maybe hadn't even begun. Her walk seemed more like a stagger as she stepped off the porch and moved toward Joe and the yelping dog.

Clearing the hoarseness from her throat she again called in a raspy voice, "JoJo, come here. Come here now!"

Joe was shocked. How did this woman know who he was? "How do...? Why...? How do you know my name...?" Joe asked in a rather tongue-tied fashion.

"JoJo, come here," continued the woman. "What? Know whose name?" came the reply as she started coughing and tried to pull the hair back out of her eyes.

"JOJO, would you SHUT UP!" she finally yelled. The dog immediately ceased its barking and made a run back up to the porch, circled behind the wheelchair, and settled again at its companion's feet.

"That stupid mutt," said the woman in disgust as she turned back around and started to stumble back to the porch. Both the little boy and the dog watched her with hopes that her attention would turn to them.

"Is that the name of your dog?" Joe asked, feeling a little timid and shy talking to such a young woman, especially one in a night shirt. "That's my name too."

"What did you say?" the woman asked, turning back around with a look that said she had more important things to do than talk to an old man.

"Is your dog named JoJo?"

"Yeah, it's JoJo. My son named him that. I could call him a few other names most of the time. I don't even like dogs... he's just good company for Mikey." The woman again acted as if she wasn't willing to waste her time talking to their uninvited guest and moved toward the porch.

"That was my name, too." Joe heard the words blurt out of nowhere. He couldn't believe he was trying to carry on a conversation with this woman.

"What?" came the impatient reply.

"My name was JoJo when I was a boy," Joe said. "I had a good friend that used to call me JoJo. My real name is just Joe."

The woman stopped again and shook her hair back as she put her hands on her hips and turned. She let her eyes observe the lonesome figure standing at the corner of her yard the same way she had seen him stand for the past three years. She cleared her voice again and this time through what seemed to be tears she said, "Well, Just Joe, I'm glad to meet you, I'm Just Jessie. Now I have to get back in the house."

"Is that the boy's name?" Joe asked, hoping he was not stretching her patience too far.

"What?" came the forced response.

"Mikey, is that the little boy's name? Mikey?" Joe pointed and nodded toward the porch and the little boy who was now leaning forward in his wheelchair with the hint of a smile, slowly waving again when Joe pointed in his direction.

"Yeah, that's Mikey. The one and only... Mikey."

Mikey's face lit up when he saw that his mother was directing her attention his way.

"I've really got to go," she said, not wishing to take up any more of her morning in the yard with an old man and idle conversation. She turned and walked back up onto the porch, looking at her son as she climbed the steps. Suddenly she stopped and turned in time to see Joe lowering his head and walking away. Glancing quickly at the front door of her house and at the front windows she shouted out, "HEY! Just Joe, would you like to meet Mikey?"

Joe's heart jumped into his throat as he turned and looked first at the woman and then at her son. The little boy had become one of his most treasured friends and they had never even spoken. Joe looked at the smiling face that, even from a distance, was showing two big front teeth with a few missing beside them. The two dark eyes almost hidden behind his thick glasses were shining brightly in anticipation that Joe would say yes.

"Yes. Yes, I would love to meet him," came Joe's thankful reply. "But the real question is, does Mikey want to meet me?"

"How 'bout it, Mikey, would you like to meet Joe?" asked his mother.

Mikey began clapping his hands as his eyes became even brighter. "JOOBAA! JOOBAA BA JOOBAA!"

Jessie's smile seemed to erase the puffiness and harshness in her face and eyes. "Well, come on up onto the porch, JOOBAA, or Just Joe. Mikey would love to meet you, too."

Joe moved through the little white gate in the picket fence. JoJo stood up and barked as soon as he stepped through the gate.

"JoJo," said Jessie, "It's okay, lie down." The little dog gave one more quick yelp and then lay back down, wagging his tail.

"Who is Jooba?" asked Joe as he moved up the little sidewalk.

"JOOBAA BA JOOBA!" squealed Mikey again.

"Joobaa Ba Jooba," said Jessie "That's you."

"Joobaa Ba Jooba?" asked Joe, stepping up onto the porch.

"Yeah. I don't know where he came up with that name. Don't feel bad, he used to call you POOP!" she said with the slightest giggle. She glanced with concern toward the front door and then back to observe the special moment occurring on her front porch.

Joe and Mikey were looking at each other but saying nothing. Joe knelt down as well as his stiff legs would allow and was looking Mikey in the face. The neatly combed hair and bright red windbreaker set off his pale complexion and freckles. Joe could see his own reflection in the thick glass that Mikey's warm brown eyes were looking through. They both gave a big smile at the same time, causing JoJo's tail to wag, beating a rhythm against the spokes of the wheelchair.

"Hi, Mikey, I'm Joe." Joe extended his hand toward his friend, who slowly brought his own hand up and over the tray on the wheelchair, which was covered with paper and markers, and placed it into Joe's. As Joe experienced the warmth and softness of the little hand, he felt certain he could never let go of either it or the moment.

"Mikey and Joe," came a slow labored response from the little boy. "Mikey... and Joe... and JoJo... fun." Joe's eyes were moist as he looked up at Jessie. She was leaning alternating against the porch post with her arms crossed, biting on her lips and exchanging glances between the front door and the meeting taking place in front of her. Looking back down at the two her eyes met Joe's. Unable to maintain the hard exterior and rough voice that had been her image to this point, she asked with a quiver in her voice, "Did you see his pictures on his tray?" She pointed toward the papers and markers on the wheelchair tray and then returned her stare toward the front door.

Joe slowly stood up and moved behind the wheelchair, where he could look over Mikey's shoulder. He was amazed at what he saw. There in front of Mikey were several sketches made with the array of colored markers scattered across the tray.

The one on top was of a man standing next to a tree. "He's an artist," Joe said. "Mikey, you're an artist." Joe's soft pat on the little boy's back was returned with a warm and labored "thank you."

Jessie turned her gaze back to Joe and Mikey. "Yeah, not bad for an eight-year-old retarded boy," Jessie said, not being able to hold back the one lone tear that left her eye and fell down her cheek before she could wipe it away. "People say I should get him lessons. He's a natural, they say. Art lessons, that would be something. He needs a lot of things. A new wheelchair, doctor's bills, clothes, care, sure I should get him art lessons. Art lessons fit right into a danc... I mean a waitress in a club's wages. Yeah, art lessons fit right into the budget. I'll probably send him to Berkeley when he gets older, and we can summer in Europe to broaden his talents. Yeah, he's a natural... too bad for him."

Joe could see the tension and anger growing in the young woman as she clenched her fists and again folded her arms tightly across her chest. She rocked back and forth against the porch post, looking nervously toward the front door. It was a sad scene and Joe felt deep pain as the porch grew quiet and no one knew what more to say.

He returned his attention to the sketches. "That's a redbud!" Joe said as he saw the bright reddish pink of the tree was captured perfectly on the paper by his young artist friend. "And that's me... Mikey, you're a natur..." Joe caught himself before he said the words that he knew might upset the desperate young mother. Instead he focused his attention on the tree.

"That's a redbud tree, Mikey. They're magical. There is magic in redbuds." Joe grew silent as his thoughts quickly went back to the daydream he'd just had of Ernest and the redbuds, which had lasted long enough for this talented little boy to catch the moment on paper. He realized he had not thought of that moment in years, even though it had been the most special day of his life. That is, until possibly today. Joe wondered what was happening. All the memories and the magic of this moment were swirling in his head. Where was it all leading?

"Well, that tree is sure magical," Jessie said, with her glance still intent on the front door. "My mother stays the evenings and nights here watching Mikey. She said about a week ago an old man came along and planted that tree in the corner of the yard. It was just a twig when he put it in. He said the city was planting them as a beautification project. Then he also added that these trees will keep the wolves away. Isn't that the craziest thing you've ever heard? Besides, it's the only one I see on this street, and if it keeps growing like that it's going to take over the whole yard. It's magical, all right."

Joe could see the tension still growing as Jessie wrenched her hands and again crossed her arms and leaned back against the post. "An old man planted it?" questioned Joe as he considered the strange coincidence, and quickly put it out of his mind as impossible. " Well, they are magical all right, and that is the most beautiful redbud I've ever seen. It has been forty years since I've seen one. They don't grow in California but they grew wild back in West Virginia. I used to love to pick the flowers and take them to my mother. They are a magical tree." Joe returned his glance to the soft stare of Mikey, who was listening intently to every word and probably wishing the moment would never end.

"Well, I don't know anything about redbud trees," Jessie said. Her voice seemed to be growing more strained from nervous anticipation. "The only redbud I know about is the kind the creeps smoke before they come into the club… and that's no magic at all." Her glance returned to the two friends on the porch and the smile that tried to come across her lips was quickly interrupted.

"JESSIE!" The harsh yell of a man's voice from inside the house caused her to move from the post and leap toward the door. "JESSIE, WHERE ARE YOU, GIRL? YOU BETTER GET IT BACK IN HERE! GET IN HERE NOW! JESSIE!"

Her hands came up and gripped her head, pulling the long snarled blond hair back as she spun around and looked at Joe. Once again taking on the rough image that he'd seen in the yard, she said, half pleading and half ordering, "Okay, the party's over, old man, you better get out of here. Mikey, you stay out here for Mommy, OK?"

"JESSIE!"

"Hey, look, I gotta go," she said, glancing at Joe with a look that clearly said "There is no such thing as magic," and she disappeared into the house.

Joe knew he'd better go whether he wanted to or not. He stepped down from the porch and turned back to his friend. Mikey's eyes were glued to him, as they had been for the past ten minutes. "So long, Mikey. I'll come by tomorrow. You and JoJo are the bright spot of my day. And I know JoJo couldn't make it without his morning sausage. See ya." Joe turned to walk away.

"Joe," came the slow, soft voice of the little boy. Joe turned to see Mikey holding the picture he had drawn that morning in his outstretched hand. "Bright spot too, Joe. Redbud… magic."

Joe took the drawing from his young friend, again looking in amazement at the wonderful talent.

"Thank you, Mikey."

"Welcome, Joe. Tomorrow?" he asked with a hopeful grin.

"Tomorrow, Mikey. Tomorrow." Joe could still hear the rhythm of JoJo's tail against the wheelchair as he walked the several paces down the sidewalk and through the white picket fence.

"Old wood flowers," he said out loud as he walked toward the little apartment he'd allowed to become his prison over the last several years. Joe stopped in his tracks as a startling question went through his mind, "Where are your flowers?" Joe closed his eyes and slowly shook his head as he realized that there were none. There was no magic in his life because he had not made the effort to put any there. He was just as bad as what he'd accused the board members of being that morning: "dead and dying."

Joe found himself whistling as he came through the door of his apartment. He hadn't whistled in a long time and liked the way it felt. He carefully placed Mikey's drawing on his desk and began to examine it in detail. "That's amazing. That little boy is a natural. He caught the colors and the feelings of the moment with incredible accuracy." Joe was delighted to have the picture and planned to frame it and put it on his wall. He also replayed the comments of Mikey's mother. "Not bad for a retarded kid." Joe thought it was sad that she would say it that way. The whole situation was sad: her apparent occupation, the mental and financial drain that Mikey would be on her, the needs that he would have, and the voice coming from inside the house. He felt sorry for them and wished he could help. "Hey, you're an old man, what can you do to help? You can barely help yourself," Joe said to himself as he turned from the desk and moved toward the television.

He picked up the remote and pointed it in the appropriate direction. Hitting the well-worn power button, he took his place in front of the box that had become his companion, his escape. "What now?" he groaned, pushing the button again and again with no response. "It must be the battery," Joe said to himself, walking over to hit the power button on the set. This action produced the same result… nothing. He quickly checked the plug and then the cord, no problem there. Back to the power button… nothing. He would have to check inside the set. If there was one thing Joe Yamka knew about,

40

it was electronics. He moved back to the desk to get his tool kit out of the lower left-hand drawer. Giving a pull on the drawer he was surprised to find it locked. "How did that get locked?" Joe said out loud. "This is really turning out to be quite a morning."

Joe knew the key was located in the lower right-hand drawer, so he reached across, found the handle, and yanked it open. Leaning over to look in the drawer, a strange feeling came over him. "The research," he said. Almost reverently, he reached in and touched the little spiral-bound note-books that numbered more than a hundred and had been stored in that desk drawer for over thirty years. Each contained records of the research that Joe had conducted years ago. He was going to write the book that would somehow help the world, but there it all sat, aging and useless in a desk drawer. What was the purpose of it all?

Joe leaned back in the desk chair and stared at the contents of the drawer. "That television wasn't supposed to work," he whispered to no one. "I was supposed to be reminded of these books." He looked again at the artist's drawing he'd received that morning. "The beautiful tree... its magic," he thought. He then looked at the picture of Lucille and Becky sitting on his desk. Their smiles were identical... both beautiful, so full of life. Joe hurt as much that instant as he had so many years ago when he buried them side by side. "Why?" Joe said to himself, "Why?" Why had his life seemed to play out so cruelly? Pain, loss, and loneliness seemed to be all he had ever known. What would Ernest think of him today? Joe felt he had not lived up to Ernest's expectations. Ernest would never know the impact he'd had on Joe. His talks and tales and discoveries of magic and wisdom had caused Joe to want to learn. In the serenity of the moment Joe Yamka's life seemed to replay before his eyes.

He never missed a day of school after the summer that Ernest left. He carried the knife in his pocket every day as a reminder of the magic that is out in this world if we only look past our own beliefs. He graduated from the Oak Hill High School with such good grades that the University of West Virginia offered him a scholarship, making it possible for him to attend college that fall. It was 1938 and he was leaving home and his mother, liter-ally for the first time.

Joe had worked hard in college, holding many jobs to help him through school. One job had him working at a grocery store where he met a young cashier between his junior and senior year. He had never had a girlfriend before, but the instant he saw her he was hooked. They planned to marry right after graduation, but the United States had entered the war and, like so many young men, Joe felt a duty to defend his country. He enlisted and the marriage was delayed. Joe remembered the letters he got from Lucille almost

41

every day as he served his country well in the South Pacific. She always wrote of the future and how great it was going to be when they were married and had children, and she could even imagine the day that they would have grandchildren. Her letters kept him strong and true.

It was on a month's leave back home in the States that Joe asked Lucille to marry him. He had another year of duty but didn't want to wait any longer, so they found a Justice of the Peace one evening in Morgantown, West Virginia, and on June 21, 1944, they were married.

Nine months later, while Joe was in a tent with the ugliness of war and a torrential rainstorm raging all around him, he'd read the letter that told him of the birth of his son. As they had decided, his name was Ernest. Joe remembered the pride and happiness he had enjoyed that night as he read the letter. Later, lying in the darkness, he made the same promise to himself that Ernest had made in the mountains of Ouray, Colorado. If he could only get out of that tent and back to the U.S., back to his family, he would work to help someone.

That was the last time he remembered ever thinking about Ernest and the memories of his childhood. The next letter that Joe received from home was delivered by his sergeant. It was marked special delivery and urgent. Joe thought it was probably pictures, but knew by the look on the sergeant's face he was mistaken. The tear-stained letter told how young Ernest hadn't made it through his third night. He just quietly died in his sleep. Joe was devastated. He had lost a son that he would never see or hold. The sergeant told him that provisions had been made for his tour to end two months early. He would be going home in three days.

Back home, Lucille's strength and courage made it possible for both of them to make it through the loss and to begin to build their life together. Joe had found a great job in Cincinnati with General Electric in their aircraft engine division as an electronics engineer. They enjoyed their time together in Cincinnati, and Joe was making more money than he ever thought possible. In the spring of 1949 Lucille gave birth to Becky, and Joe was so enthralled by his daughter, he could hardly wait to get home each evening to see her. The three of them were great friends, enjoying every moment together. Joe thought back to all the pets, and silly games, and Becky learning to ride a bike, and tea parties with stuffed animals, and hide and go seek, and bedtime stories, and laughing, lots of laughing. The years flew by and when Becky entered the first grade she was an exceptional student. Her daddy had promised her that if she earned great marks on the final report card, they would all take a vacation through the mountains.

Joe slowly picked up the picture of his wife and daughter and wondered how many times he'd regretted that promise. As the tears streamed down his face, he closed his eyes and remembered once again.

On June first they loaded up the station wagon and headed for Lookout Mountain, Tennessee, singing all the way. On the third day of their vacation Becky wanted to go to the top of the mountain for a picnic. It was a perfect idea and a perfect day for it, yet fate intervened, and they never made it. Coming around a curve, Joe had to swerve to miss a truck that was going too fast and was way left of center. He hit a guardrail on the passenger side and bounced off, hitting the back of the truck, which caused his door to fly open and hurl him miraculously into a ditch. The car flew off the truck and rolled over the guardrail. Joe watched in horror as the whole scene unfolded before his eyes. The car seemed to stop in midair and he could see the terrified looks on the faces of both his wife and daughter. He remembered the scream that seemed to tear out of his throat as the car continued to roll in midair and then began its long descent down the mountainside. He arrived at the guardrail in time to see the car hit bottom and burst into flames. His mind twisted as he fell back against the guardrail. Blood and sweat were mingled, running frantically down his face and onto his chest; his heart was beating uncontrollably. As far as he was concerned, his life had just ended. In a single instant everything he really cared about was gone.

After a short memorial service in Cincinnati, Joe went home and put a "for sale" sign in the front yard of their home. He sold everything the little family had owned, and on July 4, 1956, boarded a bus headed north to "anywhere." Filled with loneliness that he couldn't even fathom, Joe stepped off the bus in Newark, Ohio, the next morning and stepped into his new, uncertain future. Feeling like all he could do was walk, he ended up in the center of town and was greeted by a classic country square complete with a big county courthouse, ancient trees, and park benches. Joe observed the old people perched on the benches, some smiling, some frowning, some looking completely indifferent. He watched the hustle of people going to work. There was such a difference in the way they walked. Some seemed happy to be alive, while others seemed burdened. What separated them, he wondered, and what would their park bench attitude be one day? Even in his own devastating circumstances, he somehow knew that thoughts and feelings were more than chance. Certainly some of the people that passed him were experiencing heartbreak and loss, and yet they went on with life. In Joe's own quiet desperation to understand life and find a purpose to go on, he stood on that town square and decided he would find out. He wanted to talk to people, lots of people, and he had to start then. He walked over to a little drug store on the far corner of the square, and grabbed a little spiral bound notebook and a blue ballpoint pen. As he paid for them, he looked the druggist in the eye and said, "I'm going to write a book." The druggist just smiled and said, "That's nice."

Joe slowly turned to walk away and then asked, "Tell me, if you had your life to live over again, what would you do differently?" He opened the notebook and began to write the response. Thanking the druggist, he walked out of the little store toward the people sitting around the courthouse.

That question became Joe's driving passion for the next two years. Feeling almost obsessed to get answers, he set a goal to talk to at least fifteen people each day. He never had a problem getting someone to respond to the question, "If you had your life to live over what would you do differently?" He traveled the United States, living from his savings and odd jobs, gathering his research. He stopped in small towns as well as large cities, seeking every opportunity to ask older people his question and record their answers. As he filled notebook after notebook, he knew he'd write a book one day that would help others get more out of life. Holding onto the belief that he would actually be helping others, Joe continued.

At the end of two years, he found himself in Salt Lake City, Utah, and his calculations showed that he had talked with more than 10,000 people. The briefcase he was using was now full of the little notepads of research, yet Joe was sitting in a two-dollar hotel room still looking for answers. As rain spattered against the windows and Joe took in his dingy surroundings, he decided it was time to begin questioning himself. What could he possibly put into a book? And what made him think he could write a book anyway? Joe was still feeling the incredible loss of his family and felt the past two years were just a way of trying to escape the pain, but he didn't escape it. It was always there, gripping his heart and tearing at his mind. The picture of the car in mid-air over the guardrail woke him in a cold sweat every night, no matter where he slept.

Now, sitting in a hotel room in Salt Lake City, he was out of money, hopes, and direction. At midnight he walked up to a hill above the State Capitol with a beautiful panoramic view of the entire city. Joe silently looked down on the twinkling lights and knew he had two choices. He could quit running from the past and begin building a new life or end the misery of this life right then and there. His hand went into his pocket and found the knife that he had carried with him since his childhood. Blinking back the tears, he smiled and realized it was just as rusty as the day it was given to him. Opening the blade, he held the knife in the palm of his hand. The moonlight reflecting off the sharpness of the blade made it look mystical, powerful. The time had come, he was tired of living the life he'd been living, and it had to end. Joe rolled the old knife over in his hand and gripped the handle, and as the sweat running down his forehead mingled with the tears on his cheeks, he folded the blade and slid it back into his pocket. He would move on.

Placing the picture carefully in its spot on the desk, Joe let out a long, deliberate sigh. "And here I am," he said. "Thirty-eight years later, still looking for answers and wondering. If I had it to do over, what would I do differently? What is the answer to that question?"

He looked once again at Mikey's drawing, then to Lucille and Becky, and then to the drawer. One by one he began pulling the notebooks out and placing them in chronological order on the desk. With each one in place, he glanced again into the drawer and saw the abandoned knife. It had been a long time since he believed in its magic or even wanted to. Joe slowly leaned over and reached to the back of the drawer. Picking it up, he once again opened the blade and ran his finger along its sharp edge. It was the first time it had been opened since that night in Salt Lake City. He remembered how many redbud flowers had been cut with that knife. What he did next was almost instinctive as he tossed the knife up in the air over the desk. He watched it slowly rotate to the ceiling and come falling straight back down, finding its mark as it stuck firmly in the book numbered "1 - July, 1956." "It's time for this 'old wood' to start flowering," Joe said out loud, as he removed the knife from the book. He folded the blade and placed it into his pocket as he had done more than sixty years before. Getting up from his desk and nearly running to the bedroom, he returned with his old Smith Corona type-writer. Placing it on the desk amongst the notebooks, he adjusted the lighting coming through the blinds, situated Mikey's drawing, gave Lucille and Becky a wink, and opened the first notebook to begin a job that was four decades overdue.

⪜ CHAPTER 4 ⪛

MAKING THE BEST USE OF YOUR TIME

*J*oe's morning routine was broken. The old Little Ben alarm clock had certainly served its purpose waking him at 5:00, which was a challenge, considering he hadn't stopped working until after 1:00 the night before. He had been so absorbed in sorting through the information found in the notebooks that he hadn't stopped for lunch or dinner. Yet Joe was up with more energy and enthusiasm than he remembered having in a very long time. It was great to have a reason to get out of bed. He hadn't felt this way in… in longer than he could remember. It was as though the events of the day before had given meaning to his life again, and though it seemed he'd waited forever for it, he was grateful for the long overdue excitement he now felt.

"Some people wait a lifetime and never find a sense of purpose," he said to himself as he systematically placed the notebooks back into the drawer. "I can't believe it, Joe. You put that task off for thirty-eight years and all it took was one good day. A long day, but a good day. All of the people I talked to during those two years were right… it's all about TIME." Joe smiled as he realized he was talking to himself and enjoying the conversation. "It's a sad man, my friend, who lives in his own skin and can't stand the company. For the first time in a long time you can stand the company. It feels great to feel great about yourself."

After a shave and a shower he was in the kitchen popping in his usual toast and moving toward his daily dose of medicine. Joe felt a greater desire to take it this morning, perhaps because he felt a greater desire to live. He grabbed the toast, wrapped it in a paper towel, and then moved toward the door. This was going to be a board meeting like never before. "I almost forgot it," Joe said, stopping in his tracks. Jogging back to the bedroom he bent down and grabbed the old chunk of wood on his nightstand. It was the same piece that Ernest had used to show Joe his magic trick that day outside his little shack. It had been sitting on the log next to Ernest when Joe had set the biscuits down. Why or how he kept it for this long was a mystery, yet it had traveled with him everywhere the knife had throughout the years. Joe had practiced Ernest's magic trick for hours the night before, and that magic was going to be an important part of the meeting today.

As he passed the desk on his way out, he paused to smile at the precious picture. For the first time in many years Joe felt a warmth throughout his being, one that allowed him to appreciate the happy times they had shared rather than resent the loss. With a new purpose and a spring in his step, he left his apartment and stepped out into the early morning sunshine.

"Man, I feel great," he said, as he whistled his way to the meeting.

As he entered the building Joe saw Melvin waiting at the head of the table, just as he had been doing for the past three years. Everyone knew that Melvin would save the usual spot for the rest of the board. Joe approached the table like a man ready for business and placed his old briefcase in the center, catching Melvin's attention.

Nearly falling from his seat, Melvin gasped, "Joe, what are you doing here?"

"Melvin, you're acting like I died or something. What do you mean, what am I doing here? I'm always here, aren't I?"

"Yeah, sure, Joe, it's just... well, you know... You walked out on us yesterday. Nobody has ever walked out of a meeting. Most of the board members thought you weren't coming back. A few of 'em were pretty mad, Joe. They thought you said some pretty tough things, you know, about being dead and dying. And what are you doing here so early?"

"Melvin, I got more energy today than I've had in decades. And I got more to tell all of you than I know where to start. I'm going to tell you about magic today, Melvin. The magic of redbuds. I'm going to tell all of you about it along with some other secrets I've found. That is, if you'll listen, and I know you'll listen. I'm not going to give any of you a choice but to listen."

Barely pausing for a breath, he continued, "Hey, I gotta get some breakfast. Do you want anything? Hoover gets here early, too, doesn't he? I'll be right back. Sure I can't get you anything?"

"No, uh, no, Joe, I'm all set here. You, you go right ahead. I'll watch your stuff here for ya...."

Melvin was shocked by the energy and enthusiasm radiating from his fellow board member and hoped the others wouldn't take the wind out of his sails. They were all pretty mad when the meeting broke up yesterday and vowed to give Joe a piece of their minds if he ever showed up again. Melvin shuddered as he looked toward the door and saw Hoover coming in.

"Well, at least Hoover will be okay," Melvin convinced himself. In fact, he would be glad to see Joe. It was quite apparent that Hoover was looking for a place to stay with his funds running out and a danger of losing his apartment.

"Hi, Hoove," Joe said with a chuckle, returning to the table with breakfast. "Hey, I'm returning the favor, Hoove. Pancakes and sausage, right? And a large coffee. Here you go."

Hoover just stared. Joe looked different somehow this morning. Melvin wasn't sure if he was just trying to make up for yesterday or what, but he definitely knew something was different.

"Thanks, Joe. Thanks...."

Joe assumed his position at the table. Taking the toast from his pocket and carefully placing it on the table next to his Egg McMuffin, he began his breakfast ritual. With each step completed and the English muffin and sausage tucked away into his coat pockets, he removed the lid from his coffee, blew twice and took a sip. Setting it back on the table, he sighed, "Man, that coffee tastes good this morning."

"Sammy's going to be disgusted that he missed seeing you do that, Joe," Hoover said with a half smile.

"Sammy's always disgusted," came a voice and a cough from behind Joe. "I've never seen a person who stays more disgusted than him." Roadie lit up another cigarette from the last one and sat down with his large coffee and carton of milk.

"Well, welcome back to the morgue, Joe. Couldn't find anyone else to hang with this morning so you came back to be with the dead. Well, I'm sure glad to have you back. Gonna have any more inspiring words of wisdom for us today or will you just keep poking again with the same sharp stick?"

Joe didn't sense much humor in Roadie's words. He could tell it was his way of saying he didn't appreciate Joe's performance the day before. Joe looked through the smoke that was starting to gather around Roadie's head, past the wire-rimmed glasses and right into the eyes of this ancient hippie. "When was the last time you saw some magic, Roadie?"

The question caught Roadie off guard and the quizzical, almost comical, look that came across his face softened the hardness from the beard, headband, and Harley Davidson T-shirt.

"What do you mean, magic? What does that have to do with anything?" Roadie huffed as he shook his head and took another long drag and a drink of coffee. Joe just responded with a smile and a wink that made Roadie sit back in his seat and listen with guarded anticipation.

From the corner of his eye, Joe spotted Howard and Leo approaching. As they walked up and found their places at the table, Howard just gave a short "Hello, Joe" and then a quick greeting to the rest of the board. Leo sat down with a grunt and looked down at his breakfast. Joe decided to let the silence do the talking and waited. It seemed like hours, but only a few

49

seconds actually passed before Leo, with all eyes on him, stood up once again and looked right at Joe with penetrating eyes. Joe slowly raised his head and swallowed the last bite of his sandwich. Leaning back in his seat he looked at the little man with the big nose and curly hair. His gold chain and bracelet glistened brightly in the sun. Joe could always tell that Leo was real nervous or real mad when he began pulling on his nose with his right hand and then his left. This morning the action was so frantic that Joe thought Leo would hurt himself. He tried not to laugh as he watched him and glanced at the others' stares that were transfixed on the man who was obviously about to deliver a lecture like one that had never been delivered before.

Somehow, before the words came out, Melvin, Hoover, Roadie, and Howard, who all knew what would be said, blurted out in unison and with exact precision, "LET ME TELL YOU HOW IT REALLY IS...."

The outburst broke Leo's concentration for a moment and had Joe's insides shaking from unreleased laughter. With a determined yank to the nose Leo was able to recapture his thoughts and anger and blurted out his message.

"Let me tell you how it really is," he began, with his finger shaking directly in Joe's face. "I'm not dead, I'm living. And I've lived through things that you wouldn't know anything about. I've hurt and I've lost and I've suffered to be living here today, and let me tell you I'm not dead. Do you understand me? And I'm not ready to die... or want to die... or want to be old or even close to dying."

Emotion caused Leo's voice to break. He fell back into his seat and through the tears in his voice he finished. "I'm afraid of old age, Joe Yamka. I'm afraid of death. And I'm even afraid of being reminded of it. There is nothing left for people like us. . . nothing but death." Leo buried his head in his hands and tried to hide the sobs. The faces around the table were stunned. The words had an enormous impact, and the emotion cut through every barrier and tore at the heart of each and every person. Leo looked up with moist eyes and then back in Joe's direction.

"I'll tell you how it really is. Life is cruel. The whole process of life. Each of us has lived more than seven decades. What have we got? Nothing! You can go to any fast food joint or mall around the country and find the same worthless situation. Old people. . .with nothing left but death. We don't need to be reminded of it, we know it. That's why your words yesterday stung so bad, Joe. We all know it. It's like we're flowers after a frost. The life is gone, there's no beauty left and death is only the next frost away. Then the flowers will have died."

Joe felt the heaviness of Leo's words and the sincerity with which they were delivered. It made the message he wanted to share with the board even more appropriate. Joe allowed the silence after Leo's message to have its full effect on everyone. Little did they know, that same silence was creating a bond that would never be broken.

Joe quietly spoke, knowing his comment would bring the unified stares of his associates. "That is exactly why I'm so excited, Leo." His words were interrupted by Sammy, who had been standing back away from the table listening and absorbing the whole scenario. All eyes turned to him as he approached the table, everyone wondering what would be said. Sammy's stone face revealed nothing new, yet the old blue hat seemed to be pulled down a little lower today. He moved to his usual seat and slowly, purpose-fully sat down, swiveling into position to stare out the window toward the parking lot. Folding his arms and lowering his chin to his chest, Sammy spoke, "Look at them stupid skateboarders. Them kids gonna kill themselves, or somebody else."

Joe smiled inside as Sammy made his message clear as only Sammy could. His actions said, "You ain't nothin'. Your words and comments don't make any difference. Today is like yesterday and tomorrow will be like today and there isn't anything that anyone says or does that's going to change it." With everyone present Joe could now feel a twinge of nervousness as he considered the challenge at hand.

"What do you mean, 'that's why you're so excited,' Joe?" Melvin asked with sincere interest and a feeling that this morning's meeting had the poten-tial to be different from any in the past.

"Gentlemen," Joe said, looking around the table, "how would you like to learn the magic of redbud trees?" Joe could tell he had their attention as each set of eyes, with the exception of Sammy's, focused on him. Joe knew he had his attention, though, when his chin was no longer buried in his chest. Roadie even took the cigarette he was about to light out of his mouth and put it back into the pack, bringing a smile of relief to Howard's face.

Joe realized it was now time to move. He slowly stood up for effect and stepped away from the table. Looking over his shoulder as if to see if anyone was listening, he turned back to the Board of Directors and asked in a hushed tone, "You all believe in magic, don't you?" The quizzical stares made him smile as he thought to himself, "If only Ernest was here...." The thought made him look around mysteriously. He caught a glimpse of a man with gray hair and a noticeable limp walking across the street and around the corner of the bank. "It couldn't be," Joe whispered out loud.

"Couldn't be what, Joe?" Hoover asked, wondering where Joe's mind had slipped in the last few seconds.

"Huh? Oh, nothing," Joe said, giving another quick glance across the street and then back to the men gathered around him. "Would you like to see a magic trick?" Joe knew by the silence and the intensity of the stares that he had their permission to continue. "Well, I can show you magic. But it isn't the showing of magic that is important; it's if you can see the magic that matters. Do you think you can see magic?"

Joe knew exactly where those words had come from. They were the same words Ernest had spoken to him. He was excited about the magic of the whole moment and he could feel his excitement growing.

"Hey, you just do it," Roadie said. "We'll be able to see it."

"Yeah, Joe, we'll see it. I think we will anyway," Hoover broke in. "What do we need to do though, just in case?"

Joe could see the others were glad that Hoover had asked that question and remembered the words that were spoken to him. "To see magic, gentlemen, you've got to look past what you believe. If you just think everything is the way it seems or the way you think it is you'll never see the magic. We don't get into trouble until we start thinking that life should be the way we want it to be. Life is never the way we want it to be. . . life is the way it is and if we look past our beliefs, then we can see the possibilities that life has for each of us. That is magic, my friends, seeing the possibilities in life."

The words came from Joe's lips as if he'd been waiting a lifetime to say them. "You don't quite understand what I'm getting at yet, do you?"

"Well, it is a little early in the morning, Joe," Melvin concluded, trying to make everyone feel more comfortable with the conversation to this point. "Maybe if you just continue we'll understand a little better."

"Yeah, Joe, just keep going," Howard added.

"Here, let me show you just exactly what I mean." He reached down into his pocket and slowly brought out the chunk of wood that had grown brittle with age. "Gentlemen, do you think this piece of wood can turn into something else besides a piece of wood?"

"What do you mean, Joe? How could a piece of wood turn into something besides a piece of wood?" Leo was now getting caught up in the spirit of the moment. "What do you mean? What else could it be? I don't understand. Tell us how it really is."

Joe smiled at Leo recognizing the privilege to tell them "how it really is."

"Remember what I said about magic? It's looking past what we believe and seeing the possibilities. If you don't believe that this wood can turn into something else, say a pocket knife, then maybe it can't, but. . . if you can look past your beliefs, then magic can happen. Let me show you."

Joe could feel the nervousness growing inside him. He had practiced the magic trick so many times before, but never with an audience.

He held up the piece of wood between the thumb and pointer finger of his right hand just as he had seen Ernest do years before. All eyes were locked on the wood; anticipation grew as Joe held up his left hand in a tight fist. Bringing his left hand slowly toward the right, they met as eyes grew wider. Joe slowly pushed the wood lengthwise into the thumb end of his fist until it completely disappeared into his left hand.

Holding his left hand now slightly above their heads so they had to look up to see it, he quietly whispered, "This is it, men. This is where the magic takes place. Can you look past what your eyes have seen, what your mind believes, and what your head is telling you, and see the magic of the possibilities in life?"

Joe's eyes surveyed the table. Each man's gaze was now locked on his outstretched left hand. He thought of the wisdom that was gathered around the table. If numbers were to be put to it, their lives would probably total over five hundred years of experience, and with all those years of experience came an abundance of wisdom. Joe was finally able to grasp the words that Ernest had shared with him years ago. "Wanting to do something for someone will give life to a person, even one as near death as I was."

Joe felt energized as he looked at the men sitting around the table. He wanted to help them. He wanted them to realize the good side of getting old and to believe that old wood flowers. The feeling was so strong that Joe felt tears fall down his face. He again asked, "Can you look past it, men, and see the magic?"

Without taking their eyes from the raised fist, they answered in precise unison. "We can see it."

He slowly lowered his fist back down to eye level. In the same fluid motion that he remembered witnessing years ago, his fingers lay back with the gentleness of a flower opening and revealed a pocket knife where the wood should have been.

The silence was rewarding. Joe knew he had captivated his audience.

"How did you do that?" Roadie asked, pulling out another cigarette and then, for some reason, placing it back in the pack.

"What are you getting at, Joe?" asked Melvin, as the others exchanged glances and quizzical looks up and down the table.

"What's your point?" asked Leo, this time without a hint of sarcasm.

"Well, Leo, ol' buddy, maybe I can tell you, tell you all, how it really is."

Joe once again looked around the table and knew he had their attention. This group had been assembled for a reason. What that reason was he was not quite sure of yet, but he knew there was a reason.

"Gentlemen," Joe began, "when I was about eight or nine years old in the hills of West Virginia, an old hobo...."

This group that had been so hungry for something of significance to be talked about in their morning gathering, was spellbound by Joe's every word. He told them every detail of his visits with Ernest and how he'd taught him the magic of redbud trees. He talked about the good side of getting old, the gift of wisdom, a gift he had forgotten until his magical day yesterday. Tears were shed as he told of the accident in which Lucille and Becky were lost, and everyone leaned forward as he began to tell of his two-year journey across the country with the little notebooks.

"Why?" asked Howard, almost out of character and hoping he didn't disrupt the meeting by butting in. "Why did you travel around the country like that? What were you trying to find?" All eyes turned back toward Joe.

"I'm not sure, Howard. I think at first it was because I was trying to lose something. I was wanting to lose the hurt and the loneliness and the loss of that accident, but lying in bed my first night out on the road I knew the only thing that would help would be time. Just like grass covers the scars of a battlefield. So when I woke up that morning in Newark, Ohio, and walked down to that town square and saw people sitting around, the idea came to me that if I talked to enough people I might just get some insight into life. Insight that would help me endure what I was going through."

"That is why I came up with the question, 'If you had your life to live over, what would you do differently?' I thought that with all the answers I would get I might even write a book. That became a burning desire over most of those two years. I really thought I would write a book."

"So, where's the book?" Sammy asked, looking at Joe and then resuming his stare out the window.

"Yeah, Joe," added Hoover. "How come we never saw your book?"

Joe slowly shook his head and with a wistful smile said, "It's like so many good intentions I've had in my life. The initial idea seems so exciting and then I start looking at all the work that needs to be done and it becomes frustrating. That frustration removes the motivation to act. When the motivation to act is removed then discouragement starts to set in. I can remember thinking, 'I'll never be able to write a book.' Or 'Who would read what I had to say?' I noticed the more discouraged I got the more cynical I became about my goal of writing a book. I started feeling like it was a stupid idea or would end up being a waste of time. The frustration, discouragement and cynicism won out. One night in Salt Lake City I decided to bag the whole idea. The next day I was on a bus to L.A. When I arrived I dumped the notebooks in a desk drawer and there they stayed. I never looked at them again... until yesterday that is."

Joe looked around the table. He knew he had been wrong yesterday. These men were not dead. He could see the spark of life in their eyes. It had needed only to be ignited. His story of magic, wisdom, loss, and travel had helped do that. Joe could also see that the change in conversation was good for the meeting. Even though the McDonald's was full and busy for breakfast, the complete concentration of his six board members was on his presentation... even Sammy's. Joe gratefully returned the smile of each individual as he looked around the table and hoped one of them would ask the question.

Howard spoke up again; his analytical mind had to know. "What did you find, Joe?"

"What's that, Howard?" Joe asked hopefully and for effect.

"What did you find to be the answer to your question? How did all those people answer?"

"I'm glad you asked that question, Howard," Joe said as he stood up and opened his briefcase. Walking around the table he handed each person a 3x5 index card and a new black felt tip pen.

"What's this for?" Hoover asked, holding them both up and then laying them on the table.

"I'm going to ask each of you that same question and I want you to write your answer on this card. Be careful not to let anyone see your answer til we're done. Are you ready? Here it is, 'If you had your life to live over, what would you do differently?'" Joe could see the wheels begin to turn. He knew some hadn't thought about a philosophical question in a long time and was relieved when he saw them begin to write. First Melvin, which would have been Joe's prediction, then Hoover, Leo, Howard, and Roadie, who picked up the pen and acted as if he hadn't used one in years. Finally Sammy turned in his chair and focused his entire attention on his 3x5 card, not what was going on outside the window. Joe felt a twinge of nervousness in his stomach as they began to lay their pens down. He hoped his hunch would be right and a little bit of wisdom could be shared.

"Okay, gentlemen, who wants to answer first?" Looking around the table, Joe knew everyone was too shy to volunteer. "How about you, Hoove, what did you write?"

Hoover slowly turned his card over, "Make better use of my time."

Joe smiled, almost relieved. "How about it, Roadie, what would you do?"

Roadie cleared his throat and reached for his shirt pocket and the pack of cigarettes, then drew his hand away and put it on the card. "You know I'm not very good at spelling things, Joe, but that is what I said, too. Make better use of my time." Roadie's card was covered with scribbles that were barely legible, but somehow the only thing that looked like a word was the word time spelled, 'tiemm'. Joe appreciated his courage.

"Great, Roadie, thanks. You're next, Howard. What did you write?"

Howard turned his card over, "Three in a row, Joe, make better use of my time."

"All right." Joe could feel the smile growing on his face. "Melvin?"

"Me, too, Joe. Make better use of my time."

Now came the most challenging side of the table. Leo and Sammy. Both of them were sitting poker-faced but moving a little in their seats as if they could hardly wait to keep the streak going.

"Leo," Joe said with a smile. "Your turn, tell us."

"Well, Joe, I'll tell you how it really is. I thought hard about this and I took my answer very seriously and I thought about the possibilities, but my mind kept coming back to the same answer." He flipped his card over and read it out loud. "Make better use of my time."

Everyone smiled and all eyes turned to Sammy. He didn't even wait to be asked. Flipping his card into the middle of the table, he repeated the same words: "Make better use of my time."

Everyone looked around the table and then seemed to simultaneously look to Joe. He could tell by their stares that they wanted to know what it all meant. They had been given more to think about today than they probably had in years. Good, positive things.

"Gentlemen," Joe said again. "Would you believe me if I told you that this is exactly what ten thousand people over a two year period told me? They would make better use of their time. Their answers over thirty-eight years ago are the same as yours here today. Amazing."

Joe again stood up and reached into the old leather briefcase, pulling out a bag from the copy center around the corner. In the bag was a stack of papers, one for each board member. Joe had typed the document himself and had it copied onto thick, important-looking paper with a border. It was a document he hoped each person would keep.

"In my interviews everyone said they would make better use of their time, and with a little more coaxing they were always able to add a way that they would accomplish that. This is what I present to you this morning. The wisdom that I bring to this table is that we need to make better use of our time, and what you have in your hand is how to do that."

Joe looked at each of the board members as they sat a little taller in their seats after being handed something that was printed and copied for them to keep. He also felt something very important happening inside of him. No longer just sitting with a group of guys who had nothing else to do, he felt for the first time that he was actually sitting with a group of friends. Even though the group was diverse, there was an incredible bond being established by the sharing of a wisdom. "This cannot end today," Joe thought to himself.

"Gentlemen, do you mind if I read these thoughts to you?" Joe hadn't planned to do this but felt it was necessary. After seeing Roadie's writing skills, he figured his reading skills weren't much better.

Everyone agreed, and so standing there at the head of the table with all the commotion of an early morning McDonald's, Joe began to read with the conviction and belief of a great orator delivering a famous proclamation. Every ear was opened and every head began to nod as he read the words he'd discovered decades before...

"MAKING THE BEST USE OF MY TIME"

If you had your life to live over, what would you do differently?

* I would make the best use of my time by finishing every project or task that I started, knowing this habit would lead to great things.

* I would make the best use of my time by not worrying about matters that may never occur, causing me to miss opportunity and gain.

* I would make the best use of my time by striving to do things right the first time, giving importance and care to every job I began, knowing that when it is finished it is correct.

* I would make the best use of my time by never partaking in actions or habits that would knowingly damage my health.

* I would make the best use of my time by never wasting a moment complaining about things I can't change.

* I would make the best use of my time by adding value to each cent that I earned through wise spending and saving.

* I would make the best use of my time by knowing my family more than just by name, sharing every victory and defeat, each sorrow and joy, each hope and goal.

* I would make the best use of my time by not allowing it to be lost in idle tasks brought about by the fear of doing the things that I must.

* I would make the best use of my time by never fearing failure, setback, or defeat, knowing that they lead to great victories in time.

* I would make the best use of my time by never allowing discouragement and doubt to frustrate me, and lead to cynical thoughts that defeat.

I WILL MAKE THE BEST USE OF MY TIME.

Not much more needed to be said when he finished reading the last line. He looked around the table and realized that what he had read really made sense. The six heads bobbing in agreement confirmed it. He knew each could relate with one, if not all, of the ideas presented; they had hit very close to home.

"That's good stuff, Joe," Hoover said, breaking the silence. "You know, you should write that book."

Everyone turned, stared silently at Hoover and then started to laugh. Melvin threw his wadded-up sandwich wrapper and bounced if off Hoover's head. "That is what this is all about, Hoove. He wanted to but didn't!"

Roadie coughed and then laughed again, "He's still trying to butter you up, Joe. I bet he will be sleeping at your apartment before the week's over."

"Hey, Joe," Hoover said, looking a little embarrassed, "I do need to talk to you about a little problem."

"Glad you brought that up, Hoove," Joe said. "I made a little stop on the way here this morning to see a fellow I know who used to come by the gas station when I worked there. He said he might like to meet you. Here's his card. Call him."

It was easy to see that Howard was pleased with the meeting because he didn't very often smile a full smile. "Thanks, Joe, for telling us all you told us this morning. You certainly shared a lot."

"You didn't share what you do with that sausage you always put in your pocket." Sammy was sitting just as stone faced as ever, without even the hint of a smile.

Joe somehow knew that even though it didn't sound like it, Sammy was kidding and he was glad the subject had come up.

"Hey, Sammy, thanks for bringing that up. I almost forgot. Come on, men, we are going to take a walk."

"What, what do you mean a walk?" "How far are we going?" "Where to?" "Why?" "Where?" "WHAT?" "HUH?" Joe really had them going now. It was not enough that the meeting was different, now he was going to disrupt their routine after the meeting. It was almost more than any of them could handle, yet they felt an excitement that most of them had not experienced in a long time. It was obvious that the change had the potential to do them good.

"Come on, trust me," Joe said as he headed for the door. The enlightened group of aged men got up, and with a youthful enthusiasm began to bump and trip over each other as they hurried to keep up with Joe. The entourage looked like a cross-section between a fashion show for an early

1970s garage sale and a preschool class going on a field trip. Joe just looked back over his shoulder and smiled as he opened the door and entered the parking lot.

"Hurry up, I'm going to show you what I do with the sausage."

JoJo was nearly jumping over the fence when the group turned down Horizons Drive. Joe's story and lesson that morning caused the meeting to run a little longer than usual, and the little mixed breed knew his morning snack was behind schedule. Joe led his friends to the front of the house and sent a slow wave and smile, and then for the first time in three years he spoke to the little boy sitting on the porch.

"Hi, Mikey." Joe heard his voice crack as the greeting left his lips. Yesterday's few minutes with this little boy had given him life again.

"Hi, Joe," came the warm response with an even warmer smile and labored wave of his left hand. Mikey was relieved to see Joe back. If the little boy had any consistency in his life it was this three minutes every morning. "Look, Joe... Redbud... Magic." Mikey's wave pointed into the corner where his little dog was anxiously waiting for his treat. All eyes turned in the direction of the redbud.

"Wow! It's twice as big as yesterday." Joe was pulled past the front gate. His hand rested on the little picket fence as he took a few steps toward the corner and his daily stop. Reaching into his pocket he instinctively gave the sausage a flip into the air without taking his eyes off the tree. As usual, JoJo caught it in mid-air and had it gone before he hit the ground. He began his run, stopping first to give one quick bark at the unusual group of extra visitors, then around the yard, up on the porch behind the wheelchair and at his master's feet, followed by one more quick bark and then silence.

The silence seemed to stretch across the entire city. Joe just stood there, looking up into the tree that was nearly twice as big as yesterday. "What is happening?" he quietly whispered to himself. "They are magical, Ernest."

"What is, Joe? " Leo said, being the only one forward enough to break the silence. "Tell us, Joe, what is it?"

"It's a redbud."

"Well, you were right, Joe," added Melvin. "They're certainly beautiful trees."

"This is a magical tree, Melvin," Joe whispered again, still having his eyes fixed upon the branches of the tree which were covered with beautiful pink flowers in full bloom. "Even more magical than I first told you about. Do you see all these flowers along the branches? That is what I mean by the magic of redbud trees. It is flowering on the old wood. We have that same opportunity, gentlemen. Even though we are old in years, we can still find a way of flowering. We need to find a way to add beauty to our surroundings, not distract from them. That is the magic of redbuds… the old wood flowers. But this particular tree is more magical."

"How's that, Joe?" Roadie said, giving his throat a clearing and adjusting his head-band. "What makes this tree different from any other redbud?"

"It's twice as big as it was yesterday, Roadie. And it wasn't even here a couple of days ago. Something magical is happening and I think it's just beginning." Joe turned his attention from the tree and looked at the faces of each man standing next to him. He saw a glimmer of hope for the first time since knowing any of them. It was present in the way they stood, listened, and gazed up into the branches of this magical tree. "Gentlemen, something great is going to happen."

"You gotta be kiddin' me!" came a raspy voice from the front porch. "Hey, Just Joe! What's with the crowd? Kinda like feedin' raccoons, isn't it, Just Joe? If you be nice to one, a lot of them show up. Why don't all of you get back to the Salvation Army shelter?"

Joe's heart sank as he looked at the figure on the porch. He saw her stumbling through the door and then catching herself on the railing before almost falling down the steps. Mikey's wide smile quickly turned to fear as he laid his head on his tray and covered it with his arms.

"Jessie," Joe said in a kind voice his companions had never heard before. "We just stopped to…."

"You just stopped to be a nuisance. That's all any of you are good for. You're a nuisance. All old people are a drag, especially old men. You probably stopped by for a show. Is that it, Just Joe, you want a show? Well, you're not getting one here. I usually get paid to work. And I'm sure none of you have enough money to make it worth my time."

As she finished her last words her foot slipped and she fell to the bottom of the steps, landing on the sidewalk but trying to pick herself up quickly. The scene nearly caused Mikey to fall out of his wheelchair and brought JoJo to his feet barking.

"Jessie!" Joe heard himself yell as he darted past the six men who were standing open-mouthed and wide-eyed at what was taking place. First of all, they couldn't believe Joe was on a first-name basis with someone as young as the woman standing on the porch in her nightshirt talking about performing shows, not to mention someone with such a degrading view of older people. They stood in awe as their leader ran through the little white gate and into the yard to help this woman.

"JOJO! SHUT UP!" Jessie screamed as she tried to get the little dog to settle down from all the commotion. "Just shut up!" She then turned to the old man standing in front of her, who was unsure of whether to offer her a hand or to gather his friends and leave. She stared glassily into Joe's eyes. For the first time she could remember, Jessie didn't feel hatred toward herself as she looked at a man. She saw warmth and caring, something she hadn't experienced in a long time.

"Sorry, Jessie. I just brought them by to see Mikey and JoJo and that redbud tree, and Sammy over there really wanted to see what I did with the sausage every morning. Well, hey, I'm sorry we bothered you. I won't do it again. I just, well, something is happening here. That tree, it is, well like all redbuds, it's magical. We were just talking this morning about old wood flowering. I just wanted to show them. We didn't want to bother you." Joe wasn't sure if she was hearing him or not. He did notice that the puffiness her eyes had yesterday was accented by a bruise on her left cheek and chin.

"Jooba's Joe?" came the beautiful voice from the porch, bringing the moment back into perspective. Both Joe and Jessie turned their attention to Mikey.

"Joo Ba Ba Jooba's Joe?" Mikey questioned again as he slowly pointed toward the six old men standing outside the fence.

Both Jessie and Joe looked toward the Board of Directors and then back to Mikey, whose voice had now brought a smile to both of their faces.

Joe was relieved to see her smile and asked, "What does he mean by Joo Ba Ba Joobas?"

Jessie brushed her hair back out of her face, looked at Joe and then to the six men. "I think it's his word for old men, Joe."

"Joobas Joe…?"

Joe looked over his shoulder at the six, then smiled at Jessie and looked up at Mikey. Laughing out loud he said, "No Mikey… Poop."

Both Jessie and Mikey laughed and broke the tension of the strange confrontation. "Hey, Just Joe, I'm sorry. I'm really sorry. I just had a bad night… really bad." Jessie's harsh voice had been softened by Joe's friendliness and the kindly, confused look of the six men standing on the other side of her fence. "I know I look terrible. It was just a bad night. Do you want to spend some time with Mikey?"

Joe wanted to say yes, but wisdom told him it was probably best to leave well enough alone. It allowed him to leave with hopes of spending some time later when it seemed more appropriate. "Thanks, Jessie, but we'd better be going." He then looked up at the boy and added, "Mikey, I gotta get these

Jooba's back to the shelter. I'll see you and JoJo tomorrow."

Turning back to the young mother he said, "Jessie, things are going to be okay. I know it. That tree is magical, we just have to wait and see what happens."

"Sure, Joe," came her reply with a hint of the hard exterior showing again. "I wish all it took was a magical tree to make things better, but I have my doubts. You will take that group with you?"

Joe was disappointed in her response but hoped it would just be a matter of time before she saw the magic. "Yeah, I'll take them. So long, Mikey."

"Hey, Just Joe," she added as Joe went through the gate. "Thanks. Thanks for making Mikey smile." She turned and ran into the house, touching Mikey's arm as she passed.

Joe shut the gate, making sure it latched, and walked past the Board of Directors, who didn't know what to say even if they could have talked. He then moved over to the redbud. Reaching up, he gently pulled seven of the small, delicate, reddish-pink flowers off the tree and walked back toward the six. Joe carefully placed a flower into the hand of each board member. One by one they looked at it, and then back to the man who was trying to wake them from decades of sleep.

"Gentlemen, we are in a situation that happens to every person that reaches our age. Only a fortunate few, however, ever take advantage of it. We can choose right now to take advantage of our years of experience and use the wisdom we have acquired, or we can let it lie dormant and wasted. I choose to use it. I don't know how yet, but I'm going to use it. We are all old wood, but I know we can flower just like this tree. I shared my discovery with you today about making the best use of your time. What I want to know now is, who's going to share their wisdom with us tomorrow?"

Joe looked at their faces. Knowing his question made each one of them feel uncomfortable, Joe also knew it was needed to move them all forward.

The silence was deafening as the little group stood together under the redbud. Then floating through the air came the deep, unexpected words, "I'll do it." All eyes quickly turned to Sammy and then back to Joe, whose smile now covered his face. A train whistle was heard in the distance as the six men filed down the sidewalk.

⮜ CHAPTER 5 ⮞

THE DESIRE TO SMILE

Joe was full of energy as he moved around his tiny apartment the next morning. The events of the past two days had brought about a renewed interest in living, an interest that had been lost for so many years. He knew that whatever was taking place in his life and the lives of the other members of the board was big, bigger than they could imagine, and he also knew that whatever it was, he was ready for it.

Once again he was up long before the alarm clock went off. He moved to shut off the clanking of the Little Ben, looked at it, and reflected on the wisdoms he had shared with the board the day before.

"Making the best use of my time," he quietly said to himself. "All we have is time and it doesn't matter if we are seven, twenty-seven, or seventy-seven, we never know how much is left, so why not use it up? From now on, if I'm going to kill time I'll do it by working it to death." Joe smiled, catching himself talking once again to the old alarm clock.

Proceeding through the morning routine, Joe again wrapped the toast, gladly took his heart medicine, and stopped for a moment to gather in the warmth of the smiles coming from his favorite picture. Beautiful sunshine greeted him when he stepped out the door. He walked down the steps of the apartment building and stopped to take in the freshness of a new morning. He felt himself stretch a little longer than he had in the past, and as he brought his hands down to his side he heard a train whistle in the distance. Now there is nothing very peculiar about a train whistle unless there are no train tracks in the immediate area. Joe wasn't sure, but he also thought he had heard it yesterday standing by the picket fence with the board members. His hand went into his pocket and felt the knife once again. It felt just like it did sixty-five years ago when he was following Ernest to Johnson's meadow. He somehow thought he was still following Ernest, even today, on his way to see the magic of the redbud trees.

Several blocks away in a tiny but well kept little gray house with only the hint of a yard, a few scattered red petunias, and some of the best looking tomato plants in town, was Sammy. He had been pacing the floor since 3:00 a.m., wondering how he was going to share his wisdom with the board members that morning. He couldn't believe he had even volunteered. Several times throughout the early morning hours he had considered just not showing up. But the words on Joe's paper reminded him that he had to make the best use of the time he had left.

Sammy felt that he had let a lot of time slip away, time that would never come back. He knew that the only thing he could do now was to make the best of what time he had left, this might just be his big chance. He paced into the living room and stopped before his "wall of fame." He had brought home all the pictures and memorabilia gathered over a half-century of shining shoes at the Los Angeles International Airport. He had placed them all back up on the wall, just as they had hung for many years at his shoe shine shop at the airport, and now they hung as a testimony to his life and the people he had met. From the day that he had shined his first shoes on the returning GI, October 16, 1943, he guessed he had shined nearly a million pairs of shoes. But that first one would always stick in his mind.

The young soldier was returning home after a year overseas. As he reached into his pocket to find the two quarters to pay for the shine, he also dug out an extra quarter. "Here's the fifty cents for the shine," the young boy said, "and here's a quarter for the smile. Been gone a long time and haven't seen a smile come close to yours. Haven't seen a smile at all. Your smile... it... it just makes being home that much greater. Thanks." He flipped the quarter high into the air and it landed perfectly in Sammy's hand. He picked up his duffle bag and looked back at Sammy, "Keep smiling, the world needs it." Sammy watched him fade into the crowd.

Sammy took a little jar from the shelf that held nothing but that quarter. "Well, I still have the quarter, but where is the smile?" Sammy thought to himself. "How am I going to tell those men about the importance of smiling?" From that first shoe shining and continuing throughout the years, Sammy had the privilege of meeting some of the most famous, interesting, and influential people in history; but he not only met them, he became friends with them. As he scanned the wall of pictures and letters from the famous people of the forties, fifties, sixties, and seventies, he could hardly believe whom he'd met and what he'd done. It wasn't bad for a poor boy from St. Louis.

The first movie star he remembered meeting was Jimmy Cagney. It was sometime in November, 1943. Sammy had always tried to save a little out of his tip money to get out and watch a movie. Movies and the mystique of Hollywood were what brought him to Los Angeles in the first place. It was just the night before that Sammy went to see Jimmy Cagney in "Yankee

Doodle Dandy." He had danced and whistled nearly all the way home after the movie, and he was still whistling an incredible rendition of the theme song when Cagney walked in.

"Hey kid," came a familiar voice and Sammy thought he must be dreaming. "Hey kid, if you can shine as good as you can whistle, then my shoes should look pretty good. Whatta ya hear? Whatta ya say?"

Sammy couldn't believe it when he looked up and was staring right into the face of Jimmy Cagney. "You bet, Mr. Cagney, I can shine 'em. Got a seat open for you here."

"Hey, call me Jimmy. What's your name, Whistler?"

"I'm Sammy, from St Louis."

"Well, Sammy from St. Louey, you sure got a smile. How did you learn to smile like that?"

"Just came about it naturally, Mr. Cag... I mean Jimmy. Always had this smile."

"Well, you can whistle, shine, and smile with the best of 'em, Sammy. Here's fifty cents for the shine and how about a fiver for the smile. See ya around. Hey, how 'bout another chorus of that whistling?" he asked with a wink and then a little tap dance. Sammy whistled the best he could through nervous lips. "Thanks, kid, keep smilin'."

Cagney would stop back every couple of months over the next twenty years with that familiar "Whatta ya hear? Whatta ya say?" and leave with a little tap to Sammy's whistle.

As Sammy continued to scan the wall, his eyes fell on one of his favorite pictures. It was a thrill the first time Bob Hope and Bing Crosby came to his shop.

Hope and Crosby had just enjoyed another successful release of one of their "Road to" movies. They were coming through the airport and, as Sammy remembered, were hurrying to get to the country club for a round of golf that afternoon. Hurrying into the shop, both jumped up into the chairs talking a mile a minute. Sammy had his back to the chairs when they walked in, but the smell of pipe smoke turned him around. He could hardly believe his eyes. It looked like a movie poster right there in his shoe shine chairs. Bing was sitting there with a gray sweater on. His golf hat was angled slightly on his head, and he puffed smoke into the air from a long-stemmed pipe. To his right sat a wide-eyed, excited, jabbering Bob Hope. His trademark ski slope nose was tanned, as were his high forehead and protruding chin. Sammy just stopped and stared. Minutes seemed to pass before both stars turned and simultaneously looked at the proprietor of the little shoeshine shop.

"WOW!" came a simultaneous exclamation from Sammy's two larger-than-life patrons.

"Great HEAVENS, Mr. Hope," Bing Crosby exclaimed, "can you tell me when you have seen a brighter, happier, or warmer smile than the one we're seeing now? This fella sure can't remember one!" Bing had removed the pipe from his mouth and was nearly standing in his seat.

"I can, Mr. Crosby!" came Bob Hope's reply. "I can remember one such smile."

"Well, please inform me of it, my dear friend, because I can't recall such a smile," his partner responded as he placed the pipe back into his mouth and released another puff of smoke.

"Oh, you wouldn't have seen it," Hope grinned. "It was on your face."

"My face, Mr. Hope? I couldn't possibly put out a smile such as the one we are privileged to be witnessing at this point in time."

"I can tell you the exact spot you did it, Bingo. The exact spot."

"Please tell then, my dear friend," came Bing's now curious voice. "You definitely have my ears."

"Why would I want your big ears?" quipped Hope.

"To match that big nose, my friend, to match that big nose. Now, how about recalling that smile?" Bing continued.

"I saw you smile like that the time I caught you looking through the keyhole of Dorothy Lamour's dressing room door when we were shooting Road to Morocco in 1942. Yes sir, you were smiling just like that when I tapped you on the shoulder and caused you to jump up and turn around. If I remember, I found you there several times, Bingo." Hope's wink to Sammy let him know that he was just trying to get a little reaction from his partner and friend. Sammy couldn't believe he was a part of this conversation.

"Oh, you have an imagination, Mr. Hope. Quite an imagination. Besides, her dressing room door didn't have a key hole or a lock on it." Bing then turned his attention to Sammy. "Can we get a quick shine, Son? We tee off in an hour."

"Right away, Mr. Crosby. Right away."

Sammy couldn't recall how many times Bob Hope and Bing Crosby stopped at his stand over the years, but he was amazed at the friendship that grew out of that first visit. They said it was because his smile brightened every situation. Over the years Sammy had golfed with them, dined with them, and gone to many parties, all because they loved having him around.

"We need your smile," Bob Hope would always tell him.

The picture of Hope and Crosby riding an elephant was now hanging on his wall signed "We're always on the road to Sammy's... Bob Hope and Bing Crosby."

The memories were almost unbelievable as he scanned the wall of photos and notes.

"Sammy, thanks for your smile and friendship." - Jerry Lewis.

"Sammy, You're on First" - Bud Abbott and Lou Costello.

Sammy remembered how the two comedians had spent six hours in his shop one day writing and practicing the "Who's on First" routine before taking it to the writers for their next movie.

"Sammy, the only smile better than Mickey's" - Walt Disney

"I Love Sammy" - Lucille Ball.

She would always be poking her head in just to say "Hi," and "Hey, doll, flash me a smile."

"Sammy, your smile saved me" - Frank Sinatra.

Sammy used to shine Sinatra's shoes about once a month after his first visit in 1952. Sinatra had been dropped by MCA after his vocal chords hemorrhaged and everyone thought his career was over. He was coming through the airport on his way back east and stopped in. After five minutes with Sammy, Sinatra was smiling again. He credited Sammy's smile for putting life back into perspective and helping him do whatever it took to keep his career going.

"Keep smilin', Pilgrim" - John Wayne.

"Next to Bonzo, your smile's the best" - Ronald Reagan.

Sammy had met Reagan in 1952 after his movie Bedtime for Bonzo was released.

"From a dancin' Sammy to a smilin' Sammy" - Sammy Davis, Jr.

The two Sammys had spent a lot of time together before drifting apart in the late sixties. Sammy could never remember why, but he had just quit coming around.

As his eyes continued to scan the wall, Red Skelton's photo popped out. Even today that picture could bring a smile to Sammy's face. It was a picture of Skelton as Clem Kadiddlehopper. That goofy smile and messed-up hair were special to Sammy.

It was a slow day in 1959 and Skelton had been a regular for two or three years. Sammy was shining and telling about growing up in St. Louis when they somehow started discussing a character that used to be the janitor at the little city school Sammy attended. Sammy didn't have a father and this man would always try to give Sammy a minute or two of his time, telling him funny stories and making him laugh. As he described his toothless grin, his sloppy clothes, and his messy hair, Skelton was up out of the chair imitating the character. They both laughed hysterically as Skelton added more and more emphasis to the character.

"What was this old boy's name?" Skelton asked, breathless from laughing as he flopped back into one of the shoe shine chairs.

"I don't know for sure," Sammy said, standing up and putting his shine kit away for the day. "He always told me his name was Clem."

"Clem?" laughed Red.

"That's right. He said his name was Clem Kadiddlehopper. He made me laugh and even the thought of him today keeps this smile on my face."

Skelton stood up, messed his hair with both hands, and then put his hat on sideways, flattening it a little. "Well," he said, wiping tears of laughter from his eyes, "it's time for Clem Kadiddlehopper to get out of here. Thanks for the smiles, Sammy, and here's a couple of dollars for that freeloader Skelton's shoe shine. I don't know what happened to him, I think his real name is Freddie the Freeloader."

He turned, stage tripped out the door, and waved back, "See ya in a couple weeks, Sammy. I think I'll go and watch the seagulls a while."

That idea of Clem Kadiddlehopper was the reason that Sammy was standing in his little gray house. Red Skelton had bought it for Sammy and his wife in 1962 for their tenth anniversary. Red wouldn't take "no" for an answer. He said the idea of Clem, Freddie the Freeloader, and eventually the two seagull characters, Gertrude and Heathcliff, were all a result of spending time with Sammy in his shop. He was the only one that ever paid for ideas and advice. He was also the only one of his famous friends that came to his wife's funeral after the shooting in 1965.

On the picture was written, "Because of you Clem lives and many people laugh. May God Bless, Red."

Perhaps Sammy's most endearing memories of his shoe shine career, however, were of the starlet whose beauty was apparent in each of the three photographs she signed for him over the years. He first met her in early 1946. It was the first time a woman had ever come into his shop for a shoe shine.

Sammy was struck by the woman's beauty, and she was taken with his smile. She told him she was on her way to New York and had been invited to come and follow up on an interview that could help enhance her new

70

modeling career. It was her first time leaving Los Angeles and she had never been on a plane. The two of them hit it off so well that she nearly missed her flight.

Paying quickly and rushing out, she looked at Sammy and asked, "Would you like to be the first?"

Sammy was generally pretty articulate with his clients, but this time he was speechless.

The peach complexion of his new customer turned a little red as she giggled, seeing how her question had been misinterpreted. "OH, no, I mean would you like to be the first to get my autograph?" She again let out a giggle and reached into her carry-on bag to pull out an 8x10 glossy. "They took this of me and sent it overseas as a morale booster for the soldiers. The agency said the boys really liked it. That's why they're asking me to come to New York. They think I have a chance as a model. Would you like my first auto-graphed one?"

Sammy's dark brown complexion got a little darker, making that ever-present smile even brighter. "Sure, it would be a privilege to have your autograph on that picture. I'll hang it up here on my wall. Sign it to Sammy, that's me."

"Okay, Sammy, here you are. How does this sound, 'To Sammy, I wish I had your smile. Love, Norma Jean.' Norma Jean, that's me. It was okay to sign 'love,' wasn't it? I do really love your smile. I think that's okay. I don't want to cause a problem for you and your girl."

"No, Norma Jean, that's fine. No problem. You'd better go catch your plane now." Sammy remembered how he'd felt sad for the young girl. Even though he'd only been around for a couple of years, he'd heard enough stories from his clients of the wrecked lives of those seeking stardom. He had hoped that this wouldn't be another casualty.

"OH! Yeah, I better go. Thanks, Sammy. Wish me luck."

"Good luck, Norma Jean," Sammy quietly called out as she backed out the door and turned to run toward her gate.

The next time he saw her was a week later. She stopped in just as he was opening up the shop. "Hi, Sammy. Remember me? Norma Jean."

"How could I forget you? I have to look at this picture you gave me every day. You know, Norma Jean, I haven't seen a spider in this place since the day I hung this picture." Sammy let his smile grow and then gave her a wink.

"Sammy, that smile is the reason I stopped back. I just needed to see a friendly face," she said with the stress of the past week present in her voice.

"Tough time in New York?" Sammy asked, hoping he wasn't overstepping his bounds.

"Yeah," she said nervously, looking around as if to see if anyone was watching or listening. "It seems that they expect you to pay a pretty high price for stardom. But that's what they told me, Sammy. 'Norma Jean, you're going to be a star.' I don't feel like a star today, Sammy. That's why I stopped by, I just needed a sincerely honest smile. I better go now. I got some things to sort out. Thanks for listening."

"Hey, Norma Jean. Don't let nobody steal your life. That's the only thing you've got and once they take it, ain't no getting it back. Be careful, ya hear?" Sammy smiled as she waved and walked out the door.

Their friendship grew. She made regular stops early in the morning as he opened or at the end of the day as he closed. Whenever she came she always just needed someone to talk to. Even when the whole world knew her, she would show up at Sammy's shop, wearing a wig and glasses or some disguise, seeking a few minutes of peace and quiet and that warm, sincere smile.

He smiled, looking at the second picture taken in 1954. He remembered how nervous he and his wife had been walking into the studio where Marilyn was working on her movie The Seven Year Itch. She had told him that she needed him to be onsite to shine her shoes for an important scene she was doing that day. The studio had even sent a limousine to pick them up. When Marilyn saw him she ran up and thanked them both for coming and said they would have to hurry; the director was ready to shoot the scene. She explained that she would be standing on a grate and a gust of wind was going to lift her skirt and her shoes would have to be perfect.

"Ain't no one gonna be looking at your shoes, Norma Jean," Sammy said nervously.

"Come on, Sammy, let's get a quick picture of you shining the shoes while I'm standing on the grate over here," she said with her now famous giggle, pulling him into a posing position.

Sammy guessed that the picture hanging on his wall was one of the only ones of Norma Jean that could be considered one-of-a-kind. Her famous smile, platinum hair, white dress, and long legs leading down to the white shiny shoes with the black shoe shiner at her feet. The one of a kind picture was signed, "Sammy, the world needs your smile. Marilyn."

He was disappointed when she brought it to him signed "Marilyn." It was an indication that she was forgetting who she was.

The last picture was a beautiful portrait signed simply, "Sammy, thanks for always being there."

He remembered the night she gave it to him. He hadn't seen her in almost two weeks and wasn't sure if she was feeling sick during that visit or feeling blue.

"How you doing, Norma Jean?" He knew the turmoil in her life had been mounting with problems on her latest picture and the divorce earlier in the year. Yet, she seemed to be growing stronger from it all.

"Sammy, I'm really tired, that's all," she said, looking through the dark glasses and scarf that was covering her hair. "You know, I got to thinking the other day that I have known you for over sixteen years. You have always been there with a smile and an open ear. I don't think I would have made it this long without you. I really appreciate you, Sammy. I just came by to invite you and Mrs. Johnson over this evening. You know, I don't think I even know your wife's first name."

"It's Emma," Sammy said, trying to read her mood.

"Can you come over to the new house in Brentwood, Sammy? I'd really like you and Emma to come over. Can you?" She was distant, like she didn't really want an answer.

Sammy knew it would be almost impossible to get Emma to commit to going. She was so shy and the thought of visiting Marilyn Monroe in her house would be more than she could handle, especially on short notice. "Norma Jean, I'm flattered you even asked and it would be a privilege, but I'm afraid we can't tonight. Mrs. Johnson has some other things planned and I am going to make a move that will put my business into the sixties." Sammy felt a big smile come across his face.

"What do you mean, Sammy?" Marilyn asked, a smile coming to her lips. She enjoyed seeing Sammy smile and look excited about something he was going to do. Dark glasses hid the tears in her eyes.

"Well," he continued in an animated fashion, "I'm going to clear off this little shelf in the corner here and pick me up one of those new portable TV sets and place it right over there where my customers can watch it. I'll bet it will even bring more people in. Yes ma'am, I'm making my move into the sixties' way of doing business."

"That's great, Sammy," Marilyn said. "It was kind of short notice, anyway. Maybe some other time I could call Emma and get to know her and then she would feel more comfortable with me. What do you think?"

"That sounds great, Norma Jean. That sounds great."

"Hey, I brought you another picture if you want it. Your wall has certainly filled since the first time I walked in here in 1946. There's a lot of wonderful people on that wall. A lot of sad ones, too, you know. Here's another one for your collection if you have room."

"Of course there's room for you." Sammy smiled as he took the portrait from her and read the words 'Thanks for always being there.' "Hey, you forgot to sign your name on this one."

"That's all right, Sammy," she said as she stood up and kissed her friend gently on the cheek. "You know who it is."

In all the years she had never kissed Sammy. He was touched by the sincerity of the moment. "Thanks," he said quietly.

"I better be going," she said as she walked to the door and then stopped. "Good bye, Sammy. Thanks for always having a smile for me."

"Good bye, Norma Jean," Sammy said, watching her turn and move hurriedly down the concourse.

The next morning Sammy was at the shop early. He set his new television up on the neatly cleaned corner shelf and directed it so people would see it as they walked past his door on their way through the concourse. Adjusting the rabbit ears on his new marketing tool, he turned it on and switched to the local news program, hoping to pick up the sports scores. Tuning it in with a wide smile, he stepped back and heard the solemn broadcaster give the following report.

"This just in from Hollywood. Film star Marilyn Monroe was discovered dead in her Brentwood home this morning by her housekeeper. Her nude body was found draped across her bed with an empty sedative bottle nearby. The initial cause of death is an apparent suicide. Once again, Marilyn Monroe is dead at age thirty-six. Her publicist released this statement, 'A wonderful life has been stolen from us'."

Sammy turned off the television and fell back into a chair. He couldn't believe what he'd heard. Shock turned to pain and anger and hurt as he buried his face in his big rough hands and wept. Could he have done something? Could he have been there?

"Norma Jean, you let them steal your life," he said to himself as he carefully placed the pictures into his worn-out briefcase. He knew he would need them for his presentation at the board meeting. Looking at his watch he realized that the morning had already started to slip away. He had just enough time to take his handwritten page of wisdom, grab his hat, and hopefully make it to the meeting on time.

The McDonald's seemed more lively than usual this morning. The board members, gathered at their normal table, seemed to be sitting a little higher and a little brighter than they had in the past three years since their meetings began. The restaurant was filled with kids, parents, and construction workers getting ready to take their part in another day.

"Do you think he's coming, Joe?" Hoover asked, looking first at his watch, then at Joe and the others.

"He's gotta come," Howard said, half out loud and half to himself. The look on his face seemed to say that the entire group was depending on it. "He's just gotta come."

"He'll be here," Roadie said in a definite voice, taking a cigarette out of the pack, tapping it twice on the table and then sticking it back in the pack that was then placed into his pocket. "He may be a grouchy old man, but you can count on him. He'll be here, won't he, Joe?"

Joe had taken a new seat this morning, the one where Sammy usually sat, freeing up the head of the table for Sammy to speak. He now noticed with Roadie's question that all eyes were on him. He was amazed at the transformation that had occurred in the two short days since he had told this group that they were dead. What he saw looking back at him now was life. This life had been restored by the hope of something that was going to challenge these individuals and break the mundane existence that each had allowed himself to be placed in. In their eyes he could see the magic of the redbuds, and a hope knowing they still had the ability to flower... to be something. Before he could answer Roadie's question, the eyes at the table left Joe and turned to the McDonald's entrance. The silent table was surrounded by the chaos of the morning rush of individuals oblivious to the magic taking place nearby.

"It's Sammy!" Melvin shouted, relieved that he had made it. "I knew he'd make it. I knew he wouldn't let us down."

The board members watched Sammy make his way through the crowd of breakfast eaters. His eyes were fixed on the empty chair at the head of the table. He carried himself to that very spot and then glanced at Joe as if to question and then acknowledge that this was left for him. Joe simply nodded and smiled a smile that said thanks. Sammy then surveyed everyone at the table, their eyes filled with anticipation and hope.

Leo couldn't wait any longer. Standing and giving a yank to his nose he almost pleaded, "Tell us, Sammy, tell us how it really is. What wisdom do you bring to the table?"

Sammy slowly lifted his briefcase and placed it on the table. He slightly adjusted the old blue hat on his head and cleared his throat. Except for the briefcase and different chair, Sammy looked exactly the same as he had every morning for the past three years – solemn, serious, and sad.

"What could this man possibly tell us?" Joe thought to himself. He could hardly believe what he heard next.

"I was the first black man to play golf at the Los Angeles Country Club." As these words left Sammy's mouth, so did the orange juice that Hoover had just begun to drink. The spray from this unexpected statement thankfully missed Leo, sitting across the table, but came too close to the young mother who had just settled down with her crying baby. The near shower was greeted with a stern look from both Leo and the mother.

"Sorry," Hoover said. "I just didn't expect... wasn't ready for... you know... sorry."

"Try and contain yourself, would you, Hoove?" Melvin asked, trying to show respect to Sammy as well as conceal his own smile. "Please continue, Sammy."

Oblivious to his surroundings, Sammy continued.

"I was best friends with Bing Crosby and Bob Hope." This brought everyone forward in their seats; eyes opened wider. "I was present when Bud and Lou wrote 'Who's on First.'" Still more stares. "Lucille Ball would stop and see me every time she was in the airport. I ate dinner at Jack Benny's house. Frank Sinatra said I saved his career. Sammy Davis was at my house many times. If it weren't for Red Skelton I probably wouldn't have a house. Jimmy Cagney visited me regularly for over twenty years just because he liked my smile, and Marilyn Monroe was perhaps the dearest friend I ever had."

It may have been the nervousness of the moment that caused the next response, but the entire Board of Directors let out a howl. The laughter caused everyone in the restaurant to look in their direction and it woke the baby who had almost been showered in orange juice, who responded with a scream that could be heard well over the laughter. Joe felt terrible about the commotion that was going on while Sammy was trying to speak. He couldn't help but laugh because Sammy was so serious about the outlandish statements he'd just made and was able to say them as straight-faced as a master poker player. Everyone's laughter turned to wonderment as they leaned forward and started to look at the pictures Sammy was now pulling from his briefcase and placing on the table. He had a picture to back up every statement he'd made. When he pulled out the final one of Marilyn with the black man at her feet, the table was silenced.

"Is, is that you, Sammy?" Hoover questioned in a tone of disbelief. "Is that you with Marilyn Monroe?"

"That's me," Sammy said, knowing he now had their attention and perhaps their respect. "She brought my wife and I there in a limo that day just to shine her shoes for that movie scene."

"Well, I can sure understand why you're smilin', man," Roadie said, unable to take his eyes off the picture.

"Did she write that?" Melvin asked, pointing to the words, 'Sammy, the world needs your smile. Love, Marilyn.'

"She sure did," Sammy replied.

"Was she writing it about you?" asked Howard, hoping he wasn't stepping out of line.

"Of course she was. Why else would I have it? Are you trying to say you don't believe me?"

"What he is really trying to say," Leo said in the most cautious tone that anyone at the table had ever heard him use, "is that no one has ever seen you smile. That's why it's hard to believe that anyone would tell you that the world needs your smile. Especially if that someone was Marilyn Monroe. That's all we're saying, Sammy. That's all."

Joe was amazed at the tact with which Leo had just made his statements. Joe himself had some questions. He just had to know. "When did you lose it, Sammy?"

Sammy looked again all the way around the table at the friends he never realized he had. Each one was leaning forward with interest. "Lose what, Joe?" Sammy asked, knowing exactly what Joe was asking.

"The smile, Sammy. When did you lose it?"

Sammy began to tell the stories, using the pictures to emphasize his points. He told of all the famous friends he had come to know because they had enjoyed his smile. Everyone listened in disbelief when he finished by telling about placing the portable television in the shop and turning it on to hear about Marilyn's death.

"Is that the day you lost it, Sammy?" Melvin asked, seemingly for the rest of the board.

"That was the day I started to lose it, Melvin. That was the very day."

"She must have been a dear friend," Joe said. "You never got over her death?"

"That's not it, Joe," Sammy said sadly, shaking his head, looking down at the table and then back at him. "Marilyn's death was a sad time, but I could have grown past it eventually. My smile started to leave me the instant I turned that television on. From that day forward I spent my time hearing about the negative and sad things taking place in this world. My smile was being slowly destroyed each time the newscaster would report the deaths, fires, riots, and terror that were going on in the world. The sad thing, fellas, is that I didn't even know it was happening. I didn't realize what had stolen my happiness until I thought back over my life last night while wondering what I was going to tell all of you. It was that television and one very dark day in 1965."

The seriousness of this conversation was being tainted by the screams coming from the stroller, but the young mother seemed oblivious to the distraction, and certainly in no hurry to leave or correct the situation. The cries seemed to be disturbing everyone in the restaurant except the mother and Sammy.

"What happened in 1965?" someone from the table asked.

Sammy continued with his story, raising his voice above the baby's cries. "I had come in that morning and turned on the television set, as I had every day for the past couple of years. A few people had stopped that morning but business was generally slow. I noticed even a few of my regulars walked by without even saying "hi" or looking my way. Sometime right before lunch I was watching the news. The broadcaster was airing some video footage of what he called a riot going on in Watts. Y'all know where Watts is, don't ya?"

Each board member nodded his head in unison and frowned as the baby let out another scream.

"Thought you would," Sammy said, continuing his story. "Well, this caught my ear because my wife was from Watts and a lot of her family was still livin' there. Well, the pictures they were showin' on the TV looked pretty bad."

"I didn't know you had a wife, Sammy," Hoover interrupted uncontrollably.

"Hoove, let him tell the story," Melvin said in a correcting tone.

"That's right, Hoove, I had a wife and she was one of a kind. There was never a more pleasant woman than my Emma. She could always find the good in everybody and everything. That's what made April 11, 1965, such a dark day. I knew if Emma got word of what was goin' on in Watts she'd head down to get her mama out of there until things cooled down. By the time I called home the neighbor lady had already told her the news and she was fixin' to head out. I told her to wait and I'd come and go with her, hoping I could change her mind once I got home. I did something I hadn't done since that picture of Marilyn and me was taken. I closed the shop early and went home. She met me on the front porch and there was no changing her mind. We got off a bus several blocks from the ghetto. I could see smoke coming

78

over the rooftops but she was marching straight in, and there was no turning back. A few minutes later we were standing in the middle of what I still imagine hell must be like. There was screaming and people running in all directions, cars were overturned and explosions were going off. I remember being so scared. Yet, Emma kept pulling me through it toward her mother's apartment.

"As we arrived at the front of the old brick apartment building with windows on the first floor shattered and missing, we both looked up. There was her mama, her hands on her face, looking out from the second floor window in fear and disbelief. Before we could get in, a truck appeared from out of nowhere and a big man jumped out, leaving several other white men sitting in the cab of the truck. He was moving toward us with a pistol pointed right at me. He was calling me names and cursing as if I had done something to him. I saw hatred in his eyes like I had never seen before. 'I'm going to kill you,' he was shouting, and I knew he meant it. I instinctively stepped in front of Emma and opened my coat as if to tell him I wasn't armed. The next thing I heard was the gunshot slamming against my eardrum. If I was hit I couldn't feel it. As a matter of fact, my whole being was numb in that instant. I looked at the man who had pulled the trigger. He was backing up. The hatred in his eyes had turned to fear. He had done something that was beyond even his imagination. He dove into the back of the truck and was instantly gone through the alley."

"My next memory was looking up to see the frozen scream on the face of Emma's Mama. What she had just seen was a life being stolen, a life she had brought into the world. I could tell by the look on her face what I was going to see next, Emma. Motionless. The blast had knocked her ten feet back from where she had been standing. She never spoke again. It had killed her instantly. The shot had just missed me, passing under my arm and beside my chest through this jacket." Sammy slowly pulled the jacket from his briefcase, and to the continuous piercing screams of the infant only seven feet from him, he held it up and showed the bullet hole to the rest of the Board of Directors.

"As I staggered over to her shattered body and saw the life draining from it in a pool on the dirty sidewalk, that was the instant. That was it, Hoover. That was the instant that my smile left my face."

Hoover just lowered his head to hide the tears. The others nervously shifted in their seats, not really sure of what to say next. Leo broke the tenseness, "I wish that lady would do something with that screaming kid," he said under his breath, looking in the direction of the mother and stroller.

Sammy continued, not affected by the increasing noise of the crying baby. "I buried her. Red Skelton was there, you know. I buried her and went to work that afternoon. The first thing I did was turn on the television. For the next thirty years that television drove my lost smile deeper and deeper inside me. With every report of violence, death, war, drugs, scandal, and hate, it was buried deeper and deeper. The sad part of all of this is I didn't know it until I was thinking last night. I haven't wanted to smile in years, but today I once again have the desire. Having the desire to smile is the first step in smiling."

Sammy stood up from the head of the table and reached into his brief-case again. This time he pulled out several pieces of notebook paper and began handing them around the table. When Joe received his it became clear that it was in Sammy's writing, and looking over at Leo's he could tell that each one had been individually written, not copied. Joe was smiling as he thought of Sammy sitting up most of the night writing each of the pages he was now handing out. He looked down at the title and began to read each of the five points listed below it.

THE DESIRE TO SMILE

1. BE AWARE OF EVERYTHING ENTERING YOUR MIND, PAYING CLOSE ATTENTION TO THAT WHICH WOULD HAVE THE CHANCE TO ENTER EVEN UNKNOWINGLY.

2. CHERISH THE TREASURES OF LIFE'S MEMORIES THAT ADD TO YOUR OWN WELL-BEING AND ENJOYMENT, KNOWING THIS IS THE FUEL THAT BURNS TO BRIGHTEN YOUR SMILE.

3. BE AMAZED AND FULL OF WONDERMENT TOWARD LIFE AND THE VERY LITTLE THINGS THAT MAKE IT A SPECIAL CELEBRATION OF FUN AND RELATIONSHIPS.

4. REMEMBER THE PATH OF A SMILE AS IT BEGINS IN THE HEART, MOVES TO THE EYES, AND PERFORMS ON THE LIPS.

5. SEEK TO IMPROVE AND LEAVE A LASTING IMPACT ON THE WORLD WITH YOUR SMILE.

After making sure everyone had a copy, Sammy began to speak again, still struggling to be heard over the continued cries of the infant beside him.

"The desire to smile," he began, "is the wisdom that I have learned in my life. Without it our life is a dark and empty place, but with it we have the power to change the entire world. These five things I give to you as knowledge, and like Joe said yesterday, knowledge doesn't become wisdom until we apply it. I hope that they become wisdom for all of us.

The first point warns us to protect our thoughts and our minds. I had no idea that what I was listening to on that television all day long back in the early sixties would have me feeling like I do today. From this day forward I will focus on what goes into my head in hopes of winning my smile back."

The baby once again let out a scream that nearly caused Leo to fall out of his chair.

"The second point on this sheet came to me last night when I tried to remember where I first found my smile. Remember the janitor I told you about? Clem, he taught me how to smile. He showed me it was all right to be light and carefree. The memory of him and all the other fun things that happened to me had gotten lost – like a lost treasure buried in the quicksand of worry and concern. It's important to cherish the warmth of good memories."

Again a scream and no attention. "I wonder if I should ask the manager to do something?" mumbled Leo, looking toward the counter. "I don't think he'll have time to worry about babies. Look at the bus load of kids coming in. It's really going to get crazy around here."

"Go ahead, Sammy, explain the rest," Melvin said, grateful for the knowledge being shared.

"The third thing is simply to remain childlike." Sammy's thought was again broken by the scream of the baby. "For the most part, children are always happy, especially when allowed to explore. They will always smile while crawling in a yard or looking at a newfound gadget or toy. If we can just keep this sense of wonderment, it will be reflected in our smile. That is one reason I valued the time I got to spend with Red Skelton so much. He was always asking questions, wanting to know more. I spent two hours one day showing him how to pop the polishing cloth to make a loud crack. He was truly interested in it and was always smiling."

By now the baby's screams had caught even Sammy's attention. Joe wondered how long he could go without giving up. Joe noticed that Sammy's face had still not shown a trace of a smile, even through all the discussion about smiling.

"The fourth thing that I learned about smiling is that once the smile hits the lips, it is just a by-product of what has gone on in our hearts. If a heart is hard and cold it will never be able to make the eyes sparkle, and a smile is not complete if it shows up only on the lips. It must also include the eyes."

The baby was now screaming nonstop, "WAAAAAAAA!" To add to the confusion, the bus load of junior high kids had reached the counter and the band director was yelling through a fog horn to "stay in line" and "hurry up" so they could get to their contest. The skateboarders had made their way through the door, and with a large audience had taken the opportunity to show off their skills. The commotion was so loud and distracting that the Board of Directors could hardly listen to Sammy as he started to explain the fifth point.

Sammy tried to continue, "Most importantly. . ."

"WAAAAAAAA!"

". . .if you can. . ."

"Children, stay in line…!"

He tried to talk louder "… smile, then use it…"

"WAAAAAAAAAAA! WAAAAAAAAAAAA!."

BOOM BA BOOM BA BOOM BA

"MISTER, you better get that drum back on the bus!"

"WAAAAAAAAAAAAA!"

". . .to make the world a better place!" Sammy was practically yelling and not being heard.

"WAAAAAAA! WAAAAAAA! WAAAAAAAAAA!"

BOOM BA BOOM BA BOOM BOOM BOOM.

"Back on the bus I said. NOW!"

"WAAAAAAAAAA!"

The Board of Directors were all caught up in the commotion, some covering their ears. Some were standing to get a better look at the band, the baby, and the skateboarders. Joe caught a glimpse of Sammy moving away from the table. He felt bad for him. It was the most he had ever seen Sammy try to talk and now, no one was really listening to him. There was that same sad look on his face. Joe watched as Sammy moved toward the mother and her crying baby. The look on Sammy's face showed no emotion, only a blank stare. Joe felt a twinge of fear for an instant, wondering what Sammy was going to do next. Joe followed close behind Sammy to intercept anything he might say or do, but before he knew it a miracle was happening before his eyes.

In one motion Sammy removed his hat and got down on one knee. He was right over the stroller with the now frantic, screaming youngster. Lowering his hat to his chest and gripping it with both hands, he stared at the infant, tilting his head to the left and then to the right, catching the attention of the other board members who had never seen Sammy without his hat. Sammy's hands were over his heart as if to warm it. From Joe's perspective he could see right into the eyes of his fellow board member. At that moment a sparkle entered those cold, dark eyes, reminding Joe of the early morning sunlight hitting the rushing streams that he and Ernest had walked beside. The sparkle reached its peak and now moved to the lips of what Joe could only perceive as a transformed being. Once the smile reached Sammy's lips and they opened to show the dazzling white teeth behind them, sunlight seemed to flood the entire McDonald's. When the sunlight reached what must have been its brightest, the baby quit crying and the entire restaurant was silent.

Then came a giggle. It originated from the same stroller that only seconds earlier was sending out a distress call that would have made most people run for the bomb shelters. The giggle began as a low, soft gurgle, but the longer Sammy's smile warmed the child, the higher, faster, and louder the giggle grew, until it burst into a full-fledged belly laugh. Nothing is more entertaining or captivating than a laugh coming from a baby. The magical moment caused Joe to chuckle. His shoulders began to shake uncontrollably and the infectious mood spread to the other board members. Sammy smiled, the other six men laughed out loud, and the baby began to squeal with delight; the entire restaurant seemed to explode with excitement and laughter. The board members all stood up and Joe grabbed his leftover sausage. Sammy rose from his squatting position over the laughing baby and was greeted by Leo, who was so taken with his smile and all the laughter that he hugged Sammy and lifted him off the ground. As Sammy turned around, taking in the crowd and the happy scene around him, he was smiling. He was actually smiling.

"Joe, Joe, look!" Sammy said, pointing to his face. "I'm smiling, Joe. I'm smiling again. Thanks, Joe. Thanks."

Joe wasn't sure where all the confetti and balloons had come from, but they were falling all around him. The entire crowd of from the McDonald's was spilling into the parking lot. Joe couldn't believe his eyes, Sammy was actually giving "high-fives" to the skateboarders. The marching band was playing and they were now turning the corner onto Horizons Drive. Joe could see the little picket fence and JoJo, and he knew that Mikey would be incredibly surprised to see him this morning, complete with marching band, balloons, skateboarders, and even the mother and her baby. He sure hoped Jessie was ready for all of this.

JoJo was jumping higher than ever and the blooms of the redbud tree were really starting to open. Joe threw the sausage up in the air and the little dog caught it and once again did his laps, jumped on the porch, and then ran around the wheelchair as the band reached its crescendo. He plopped down in front of his master as the band stopped. The whole event was capped with one quick bark from JoJo and a squeal of joy from Mikey. It had truly been a magical morning.

"Just Joe, what is going on?" Jessie yelled as she came through the door and onto the porch.

Joe felt a twinge of fear, but was betting on Sammy's smile to get them through.

"Jessie!" Joe yelled from the sidewalk as he moved to the front gate. "Jessie, you aren't going to believe it. Can we talk just a second?"

Joe could see tears come to Jessie's eyes; she was biting at her lip just like she had the day they first met. She seemed so nervous. "Jessie, Sammy is one of the Board of Directors. He was telling us about smiling today." Joe had moved through the gate and was walking up the sidewalk to meet her as the board members and the eighty to one hundred band members, participants, and observers looked on. "You see, Jessie, it's magical. Look at the smile on Mikey's face. See how excited he is. Hi, Mikey. See what I mean, Jessie?"

Joe suddenly realized he was talking too fast and in the excitement of the moment he hadn't acknowledged the obvious stress Jessie was under. "Jessie, is there a problem?"

"Just Joe, there's no problem except I can't handle all this. I'm not used to the attention. The kindness. Mikey and I can't or don't know how to accept it. It really is tough raising him, Joe. He needs a lot. More than I can give him. It hurts me so much."

Joe looked at her and recognized her sincerity. He then stepped up on the porch and slowly wrapped his arms around the little boy in the old rickety wheelchair. He just hugged him. He hadn't felt like hugging in years. Sammy's smile had softened his heart. "How you doing, Mikey?"

"Hi, Joe," came Mikey's warm, labored response. "Picture for you, Joe." Mikey handed Joe the drawing from his tray. It was a perfect drawing of him and the other six men yesterday as he was handing them the redbud flowers. "Magic," Mikey said as he pointed to the drawing and then to the people standing in the street in front of his house.

"Yeah, Mikey, magic," Joe said, hugging him one more time and then turning again to the boy's mother. "Jessie, it is magic. That tree, this drawing, that band standing there. Look past what you believe, Jessie, and see it. Watch this." Joe moved back down off the porch to stand beside Jessie in the yard. With a wink toward Mikey and a look toward the street he called out, "Sammy."

Sammy had humbly lost himself in the crowd, a little nervous at what might happen with the boy's mother. Upon hearing his name he moved to the gate front and center. "Yeah, Joe, what can I do for you?"

"Sammy, I'd like to introduce you to Mikey's mother, Jessie."

Sammy stretched his hand out across the fence. Jessie slowly moved toward him, looking briefly back over her shoulder at Joe. As she turned her attention to Sammy and offered her hand, Joe could once again see the glistening diamonds in Sammy's eyes. As that twinkle in his eyes moved down to transform his mouth, Joe saw Jessie's shoulders start to shake. She was laughing. Every face on the other side of the fence began to light up, and before he knew it the instruments were once again raised and the band was playing.

Jessie whirled around. Her smile was warm and friendly as she approached Joe again.

Joe was laughing, too, when he simply shrugged his shoulders and said, "Sammy smiled!"

She pointed her finger toward his face and shook it. With tears in her eyes and the smile still on her lips, she simply said, "You're crazy... thank you." Then she ran for the front porch.

The band was playing full tilt when Joe met his six companions at the front gate. He held up the picture Mikey had given him for the board to see. "It's magic, gentlemen," he said. "Who wants to keep it going?"

"I'll tell you tomorrow how I believe it really is, Joe," came a warm and humble response.

"Thanks, Leo, we'll all look forward to it," Joe said with a grin and a nod toward Sammy that simply said 'thanks.' As they turned to leave, Joe noticed Mikey waving another beautiful picture over his head. "What a day," he thought as he went to receive his masterpiece.

⇐ CHAPTER 6 ⇒

LIFE IS AS WE SEE IT

Joe was holding the Little Ben alarm clock as it started its clanking. "Right on time," he smiled.

He was already up and dressed to go, still feeling the excitement of yesterday and the momentum of today's Board of Directors' meeting beginning to build. Moving into the living room, he stepped up to his desk and began to view his handiwork from the night before. He had stopped at the Wal-Mart around the corner, splurged and bought some frames. He wanted to get the memories of the past three days up on the wall. Mikey's pictures had become almost priceless to him. He put each one in a frame; the picture of the redbud with Joe standing next to it was hung up first.

"That was a magical moment. It was good to remember Ernest and the magic, and then getting to meet Mikey and his mother. He's not a retarded kid. He's a genius." The words echoed in Joe's head as he said them out loud.

Next to the first picture he started a horizontal line with the other two pictures. The moment in time had been captured as he held a redbud branch out and the other six men... his Board of Directors, his friends, looked on. "They were able to see the magic. They looked past what they believed and saw it and now the magic is starting to work."

Underneath the second picture he had framed his original typed page called "Making the Best Use of Your Time." Beside the picture of him and the other men he hung the drawing that Mikey had done of the band, balloons, and people, and right in the middle of all of it he even captured Sammy's smile.

"Ernest, it truly is magic," Joe said out loud and then stopped to look around. He thought he almost felt Ernest near him. "Just my imagination, I guess. That is quite a smile you have, Sammy. It has sparked us all."

Underneath this picture Joe had framed Sammy's handwritten instructions, "The Desire to Smile." For the first time in a long, long while Joe truly felt the desire to smile. "I have more than the desire to smile - I literally feel like laughing, Sammy," he said to himself as he stepped back to take it all in. "Plenty of room for more." Joe hoped that over the next five days he could add five more pictures and five more messages.

"What will be presented to us today? I can hear Leo now, telling us how it really is," he chuckled as he finalized his morning routine in the kitchen. Toast, vitamins, medicine, a smile at two lovely ladies, and out the door to another exciting board meeting.

Everyone was gathered around as Leo set his leather case on the table. Everyone except Sammy, that is.

"Hey, has anyone seen Sammy this morning?" Hoover asked, taking a big gulp of coffee. "I'm ready to get this meeting started. Can't wait to hear what you're gonna tell us, Leo. Just can't wait to hear it."

Leo just smiled and dropped his eyes to the table. Joe could see the tension and seriousness in Leo's eyes as he clenched his case. Leo looked like he hadn't had much sleep and Joe knew that this exercise had been difficult for him. He had seen the same intensity in Sammy yesterday that he saw in Leo today. These board meeting presentations were coming with a price, causing each person to reflect on his life, and in this reflection, they were finding the wisdom that was still there to use.

"Gentlemen, I would like to introduce myself." Each board member looked up to see a sharp young man in a McDonald's uniform and tie, holding a clipboard. "I'm Lanny Smith, the manager here, and I want to comment on what took place yesterday."

"Oh, no," Joe thought, "we got out of hand and he is going to say something about it."

"Hey, man," Roadie spoke up, putting an unlit cigarette back into his pack and then into his pocket. "We're sorry we emptied the place yesterday. Reminded me of my old days on the road with the Angels. We cleared out many a place."

"Yeah," Melvin said with a smile, but that was for different reasons. "Lanny, that was a special day yesterday. We'll try and keep it down today."

"Yeah, Sammy smiled yesterday. You should have seen it," Hoover said, almost coming out of his seat.

"Well, I did see it," said the manager. "That's why I'm stopping by your table. I've been in this place for over four years and have been watching all of you come in and sit at the same table for about the same length of time. Then I watch you get up, head off in different directions, and come back the next day. Just like clockwork."

"Unfortunately, it's the only thing most of us are regular at, if you know what I mean," Hoover inserted with a wink, drawing a chuckle from the board members who definitely knew what he meant.

"Well, I can't do anything about that," Lanny smiled. "But I did want to say thank you and apologize for not getting over here sooner to say hello."

"Well, let me introduce you to the Board of Directors, that's what we call ourselves," Melvin said, introducing each man around the table, who all responded with a warm "Glad to meet you."

"Well, glad to meet all of you," the manager continued and listened as another thanks came his way. "The next cup of coffee is on me today. Say, where is the 'Smiler'?"

"We were wondering the same thing ourselves," Joe said.

"Yeah, he's always the last one here, but he's never this late," Melvin added, "and Leo is ready to get started. You don't want to start without him, do you, Leo?"

"LOOK!!!" said Howard as he stood up out of his seat and pointed to the parking lot. "It's Sammy!"

All eyes simultaneously looked out the window; then each man rose and stared in amazement. Sammy was on a skateboard. He was being held up by the same boys he had grumbled about each morning for a year. Nonetheless, he was on a skateboard and that smile of his was shining through.

'He'll kill himself!" Howard shouted.

"Oh, no, he won't," Joe added. "We're watching a man come to life!"

"Go, Sammy!" laughed Roadie. "I wonder if they can teach me to do that."

"Hey, we have a meeting to run here," Melvin said, trying to restore order as he glanced toward Leo, who was smiling and still nervously clenching his case. Melvin rapped on the window until he caught Sammy's attention. Sammy smiled and then an "Uh Oh" look came to his face as he freed a hand from one of his supporters and held up one finger as if to say, "I'll be right there." Stepping down with one foot on the asphalt and the other on the back of the skateboard, he glanced at the window to make sure he had the board members' attention. He did. They stood in a line, noses pressed against the window. Sammy slowly raised his foot off the skateboard, and then dropped it quickly to the very back tip, flipping the board in the air and catching it with both hands just the way he had seen the boys do it every day since the board meetings had begun. The action caused a gasp and then a cheer from the six men inside the McDonald's. Sammy began to high-five the boys who had accepted him as one of their own this morning.

"Have a great meeting, gentlemen. I know you will. Now I have to get back to work," the manager said, giving a nod toward Leo, who returned it with a nervous smile.

"Thanks, Lanny," said Melvin, sitting back down at the table and introducing Sammy.

"Man, you sure can smile," Lanny said, shaking his hand and then walking away to take his place behind the counter.

"What a great bunch of boys," Sammy said, sitting down to stares of disbelief. "Did you see that little flip of the board I did? I knew I could do that. I just knew it."

He was met with questions of "How," "Why," and greetings of "Unbelievable" from each of the members sitting around the table.

"Sammy, that was something," Melvin said, patting him on the shoulder as he took his seat. "But, we do have a meeting here, you know."

"Sorry," Sammy said, turning his attention to Leo.

The entire table grew silent as all eyes turned toward Leo. The ensuing moments seemed to take an eternity as they all waited in anticipation. Leo just stared at the table in front of him. Occasionally giving a tug to his nose, he slowly removed the leather case from the table and set it on the floor beside him. Melvin wondered if he should prompt Leo to speak since the silence was causing everyone else to fidget nervously. Just as Melvin was ready to ask if everything was all right, Leo looked up and spoke in an ominous tone.

"I'm about to tell a tale of death. . ." he began, causing everyone around the table to lean forward, somewhat surprised that he didn't begin with "how it really is."

"A tale of death so dark and hideous that it may seem unbelievable. But it did happen and I tell you this is how it really is. I have never told anyone the story I'm going to tell you today. Why would anyone want to hear it? It's one of suffering and meaningless loss of life. I'm going to tell you of my time spent in the concentration camps of World War II. Until yesterday I had never known a reason to discuss it." Then Leo slowly turned to face Sammy. "It was your story yesterday, Sammy, and watching that smile come across your face when this whole place erupted with laughter I was moved to hug you. Imagine that, moved to hug you. Who would believe it?" Sammy just smiled and nodded, humbly looking down at the table. "At that moment," Leo continued, directing his attention back to the entire group, "I recalled the suffering that I had so completely suppressed. The thought came to me that if there was meaning and wisdom in Sammy's story yesterday of what joy can do for people, there must also be meaning and wisdom in suffering and loss. This lesson was taught to me many years ago, yet forgotten and never applied. Until now.

"I was born in Budapest, Hungary, in 1922. The war had just ended and the country was trying to rebuild itself. My father was a doctor and had served in the war. Upon his return, my mother and he moved to a settlement on the outskirts of Budapest where a large number of Jews had settled and found work. My parents tried very hard to give a good life to my two younger sisters, my brother, and me. My fondest memories are picnics in the countryside. We had a favorite place to go, by a quiet stream that was far away from the dirt and filth of the city. We laughed and played as a family for hours.

"By 1935 my father had heard of the Germans creating work camps around Munich where Jews were being sent. The stories of what was taking place in these camps frightened my mother, and my father would say that the stories were merely rumors. 'Who would treat people this way,' he would ask, 'even if they weren't Jews? We are still people, and a great people. My Leo, you will be a great man someday. Maybe you will help people to see the good in all humans. You must become a lawyer, Leo, and a judge. You must practice justice and be a great example.'

"He was a fair man and trusted everyone." Leo's eyes grew moist as he stopped, as if to reflect on his father. Taking a sip of his coffee, he swallowed hard and continued. "College was still several years away when the Hungarian government passed a law in 1938 that forbade Jews from becoming lawyers, judges, or holding office. News of this outraged my father. Late one night I overheard him tell my mother at the kitchen table that we must escape to the United States. He had met a man that said he could take all of us and cut through the red tape to get us into the States. 'We must do it for our children,' he said to my mother. 'It will take all the money we have, but it will be a small price to pay.' He said it would be several months before we would be ready to go, but we must make our plans immediately and be ready.

"As the time grew near, he was to meet with the man that would take us from Hungary. I was excited at the thought of going to the United States. He asked if I would like to go with him this one particular morning to meet with the man that was going to give us freedom and allow me to become a lawyer. I jumped at the chance, and knew at seventeen years old, it meant that my father was viewing me as a man. 'This is the morning we receive our important papers and final arrangements for our journey.'

"We walked through the streets of Budapest toward an industrial area where my father had met this man before. During our walk my father removed a ring from his finger. I had always admired it and when I would ask him about it he would always say, 'Never mind, Leo. You will find out soon enough.' He stopped outside the building we were to enter. 'Leo, I am giving this to you as my father gave it to me and his father gave it to him and many fathers before him. This ring is hundreds of years old, my Leo, and it is a symbol of you becoming a man. And a fine man you are. Now wear it, my son, and may it bring you the same good fortune that it has brought to all those that wore it before you - health, and a wonderful family, Leo. That is good fortune. If you have that, you have it all.'

"As I placed it on my finger and looked at it I knew that it was a special day. I will always remember the feeling of my father's embrace as I thanked him for it and promised to wear it until I would have the fortune to hand it on to my son.

'I am giving this man the last of our money today, Leo. Do you understand me? We are risking everything to go to the United States of America, but it will be worth it for you and your brother and sisters. It will be worth it. It is a small risk.' "Inside a dark room at the back of a deserted factory my father confidently knocked on a door. It opened and a man with a dark complection and a scar on his face opened the door and smiled, 'Oh, Doctor, you made it. I'm glad. I'm ready for you. Pointing his finger at me and speaking harshly, he asked, 'Who is that?' Not sure if he was going to let me follow my father into the little room lit only by several kerosene lamps.

'That is my son Leo. I want him to meet the man that is going to show us freedom and allow him to become a lawyer and practice justice. 'Please allow him to come in,' my father answered.

'Oh yes, sure,' the man finally said with a weak smile that showed a missing front tooth.

"Once inside, my father sat at a little makeshift table that he had apparently occupied before. He seemed quite confident in his actions. I, on the other hand, was not and chose to stand as near the door as possible.

'Do you have the final papers that will carry my family to freedom?' my father asked the man with excited anticipation.

'Yes, yes. Everything is set. Do you have the money?' the man asked, casting a cold glance in my direction and then back at my father who was opening up the box that he had carried in.

'You can count it if you like, but it's all there. Everything I have is now yours, but I feel like a free man,' my father said.

"The man put the money under the table and stood up. Reaching into his coat pocket, I anticipated him handing my father the papers he had come to receive. Instead, he brought out a pistol. The shiny blackness of it reflected the lantern light from the table. Before my father could move, the man cursed him and said, 'Jew man, you are dead.' The gunshot sounded through my head. I saw my father falling to the floor and then the man pointing the gun at me. 'Boy, there is no justice to be practiced,' he laughed as he pulled the trigger. The bullet shattered the facing of the door right next to my head. Before another shot could be fired I fell backward through the door and began to run. I heard one more shot, but I ran so fast that he couldn't catch me. I ran and ran and ran. When I finally stopped, I was standing in the middle of a plaza in Budapest. There were statues and people and flying pigeons. It began to rain and I was cold; it was the first time I felt so alone. I looked at the ring on my finger that my father had given me just minutes before. The tears were coming from my eyes like the rain that was falling all around me.

"I stumbled into a police station and finally convinced an officer to follow me to the room, but when we got there, my... my father's body was gone. No blood, the only thing that was still evident was where the bullet intended for me hit the door frame. The policeman didn't seem to believe me and threatened to throw me in jail for lying to a government official. He slapped me on the side of the head and told me to get back to my part of town.

"My mother was destroyed by the news. We were alone with no money, and no place to go for help. I left my schooling to work in a factory to help support the family. Soon news came of the German invasion of Poland; war had officially begun in Europe.

"In the middle of the night the soldiers came through our street and forced people out of their homes. We were allowed to take only what clothes we could grab quickly, and all else was to stay. They told us we would be able to come back for the rest but I knew that wasn't true. We were moved to a section of town close to the clothing factories. The housing was old, run-down buildings and sheds that were overcrowded and filthy. I longed for the freedom to see the countryside again – to sit by that stream in the country – but it would never be again. One evening my sisters and brother and I staggered home after our fourteen-hour day in the factory. Mother had not gotten up that morning, too sick and tired to even move. She was gone when we came home. We never saw her again or had any idea what happened to her. Many suspected that the owners of the factory had her killed to warn others of the consequences of not coming to work.

"These were times that couldn't even be imagined. Yet they were easy, compared to the days that were ahead. I dreamed of taking my sisters and brother out of the country and even escaping to the United States, but it was not meant to be. War was raging now throughout Europe and passage anywhere would be impossible. One day I watched my youngest sister, Yvonne, get her ragged dress caught in a machine at the factory. Before I could get to her, it had pulled her in. Another of my family was lost. I look back on that and sometimes feel she was lucky. The tragedy spared her from the torture that was to come.

"It was May of 1944. Trainloads of Jews from our ghetto were being gathered and shipped north to what we were told were labor camps that were building roads to help Germany in the war effort. One morning my brother, sister and I, along with many others, were stopped outside the factory and marched to a train. There were many whose families never knew what happened to them. We were not allowed to go back to our houses and the only possessions we had were what we had worn to work that day. We were jammed into an overcrowded railcar. I remember my feeling of hopelessness and helplessness. I had no idea what the next days, or even hours, would bring for me and my family. As the train moved north out of Budapest, I was able to see out a crack between the boards on the side of the car. I could hardly believe my eyes as I looked out and saw the field that my family had picnicked in. There was the stream we had enjoyed, and I could see the song birds sitting in the tree that I loved to climb. Just for a moment I thought I saw my family stand and wave toward the train. My mother, father, and Yvonne all waved and looked so happy; then the vision was gone.

"We were on that train for two days. The only food was that which we had taken for lunch the day before, and most had already eaten it. The conditions inside that train were horrendous, seventy people crammed together. I remember looking at my sister and brother as they seemed to age years in a matter of one day. The train was once again slowing. I figured it was making a fueling stop or picking up more workers for the labor camps. I was able to squeeze my way up against the wall again and peer through. This time what I saw was a living nightmare. We were pulling past barbed wire fences and guard towers. I saw a sign that read 'AUSCHWITZ.' I had never heard of this place before but felt an instant unexplainable surge of impending disaster.

"The train had come to a stop and the door was soon flung open. There were soldiers yelling in Hungarian at us to move and move quickly or we would feel a strap. My sister looked at me in utter fear and disbelief as I helped her up from the wet floor. We fell into the line and waited as all the cars were emptied, a long line of Jews from Hungary with no idea what was to happen next. We couldn't even see one minute into the future. We were hurriedly marched into a section of the camp that looked like a parade ground. I saw a man up on a platform and the line was moving in his direction. I could tell as we moved closer that he was giving directions with his finger as to which line a person was to continue in. Some were going to the left, but most were being moved to the right. Too soon it was our turn. My brother was first. The man signaled for him to move toward the left and changed his mind and pointed to the right. My sister was pulled from the line and, with several other young women, rushed to a building beyond the man giving directions. I barely caught a glimpse of her terrified face as she looked back at me before being pushed through the door. The man looked at me, and with what I thought was an approving look, motioned for me to go to the left. Standing in line I saw my brother for the last time. He looked at me with a weak smile and then moved with the rest of the line through a fence toward another part of the camp.

"My group was ushered into a room where we were ordered to remove everything and wait for further orders. We were now standing naked in the cold. 'What kind of place is this?' I wondered to myself. A guard walked in and started looking over the line. He was shouting 'EVERYTHING! EVERY-THING!' and was grabbing watches and jewelry and throwing them into a box. We had become prisoners. The guard came to a stop in front of me and looked down at my hand.

"'EVERYTHING! YOU FOOL, EVERYTHING!' He was glaring at the ring that my father had given me. It had been in my family for many years and now this man was asking me to throw it into a box.

"'NO!' I found myself saying and staring him straight in the eye. 'It is my family's and I will keep it.' Without hesitation he hit me on the side of the head with the butt of his rifle. It was a blow that sent me to the ground.

"'You don't have a family,' he laughed as he tore it from my finger and placed it in his own pocket. 'Now get up before I kill you right now.'

"We moved to the next room, where every bit of hair was shaved from our bodies. After a cold shower we were herded to a room where there was a fire burning. I began to hear men screaming, and the closer I got to the fire the more I could smell the rotten stench of flesh and hair burning. They were branding us. I became number 34557."

Leo pulled up his shirt sleeve to show the men gathered around the table the evidence of truth to the terrible story he was telling them. "It sounds unbelievable," Leo continued, "but I'm telling you like it really was."

Joe looked around the table. Each man was mesmerized by the words of their friend, a victim of the most hideous hatred and greed the world had ever witnessed. Joe felt that each man was relating to the story being told. He returned his attention to Leo, who was rolling his sleeve back down and re-buttoning the button on his cuff. "We believe you, Leo. Please continue if you want."

"In another room we were given striped rags to wear as clothes. I could tell by the smell of mine that I was not the first person to have worn them. Next we were to find shoes to wear out of a pile in the center of a room. We were then brought back into the open yard. There we were made to stand for hours as we awaited our hut assignments. It began to rain, a cold, chilling rain. It reminded me of how I felt in that plaza with the rain falling on me the day my father was shot. I remembered how alone I had felt then, but it was nothing compared to the loneliness at that instant as I stood in Auschwitz.

"There were possibly two hundred men standing in the rain. We had been stripped of everything. We had nothing. They had taken everything, even our names. I was later to find out that there was one thing that they couldn't take.

"After several hours in the rain we were finally moved to huts. As I entered there was a cold glow of an electric bulb at both ends of the building that was maybe sixty feet long and fifteen feet wide. There was a narrow aisle running between bunks that were stacked four high to the ceiling. And then I noticed them... even in the dimness of the light I was struck by every detail. Big, dark spots that shone even in the night... their eyes. I was witnessing my first group of true prisoners in the camp. The guard was yelling and hitting the bunks with his night stick. The men started to crawl out of their bunks, almost animal-like. I thought how they must have just gotten in bed from a long day of torturous work. Our standing in the parade ground had served a double purpose. Long enough and wet enough to exhaust the new arrivals, and timed to disturb the old captives at just the appropriate time. The psychological cruelty of the guards was already apparent to me.

"As the men fell into some kind of order, I couldn't help but think of living skeletons. If they were, in fact, alive. Some screamed in pain as their blistered feet touched the cold ground. There were obvious signs of beatings as I noticed the bruises and bloody faces of most of the men. At the time I guessed that most of them didn't weigh over a hundred pounds. Later I came to realize that most weighed barely seventy-five pounds. As the guard began to move and swing his club, I realized he was just fueling hatred in these men toward us, the new arrivals. He was making room for us to sleep and stealing precious space from those who needed it. As we moved into the hut, he again shouted, 'To bed, pigs.' There was a wild scramble to get into the bunks. I realized the reason why when I saw the last man, who was too weak to move, get hit on the back of the head and then drug by the feet to the door and thrown out into the cold, dark rain. The last thing I saw as the light went out was the guard's gruesome smile as he wished us sweet dreams, followed by a sinister laugh that echoed for several minutes after he left the hut.

"I lay in the cold stillness next to four other bodies crammed into this bunk that consisted of wet straw on top of hard boards. I could feel the insects and varmints begin to move as the night wore on. As exhausted as I was, it was impossible to sleep. Moaning and screams came from nightmares that could not have been worse than the reality of the day that had just passed. My thoughts were on my brother and sister. I could only hope that in some way their situation was better than mine. I also thought of that bullet that had just missed my head years ago and wondered if I would have been better off if it had hit its mark. Morning came, and a loud siren jolted us back to the ugliness of reality.

"The shouting of the guards caused the men to fall quickly to the floor. I noticed some of the poor souls had not moved; obviously they had not made it through the night. The guards then began shoving the new prisoners and directing them to grab the bodies of the dead or near dead and throw them on the cart outside. It was the first time I had ever touched a dead man. I remember thinking how useless this body was without life in it, but in some way I found hope in the situation. I realized that all this flesh and bones I was now carrying to be deposited into a heap was nothing more than the vehicle for life, not life itself. I found this comforting. It was not my body to protect, but the life that was in it. As we tossed the remains up on the pile, I felt the crash of a club come down on my back.

"'Young pig!' a guard growled at me as I picked myself up off the floor. 'Take a good look at that pile, young pig. You will soon be on it.'

"They gave us a few minutes to get ready that morning before going out to the parade ground. Why, I don't know. There was nothing to get ready. I got the courage to ask one of the prisoners who seemed to be fairly open and able to talk if he had any idea where my brother would be.

"'Did he come with you yesterday?' he asked, in a low, lifeless whisper.

"'Yes, we were separated in a line coming off the train...' I responded, watching his glance turn cold.

"'Did he go to the right?' the man asked, knowing the answer.

"'Yes,' I responded, anticipating his explanation.

"He walked me over to the tiny window and told me to look across the camp at the chimneys in the distance. 'That is where your brother is. In that smoke being lost into the clouds. He is better off.' The man's eyes fell to the floor and he walked into the line heading out the door.

"My heart sank as this information permeated my thoughts. My family was gone. I had little hope for my sister and thought, as the man said, that she might be better off in the smoke than in the hands of these animals. I looked again at the smoke as I stumbled with the line of men out of the hut and into what appeared to be a roll call. I couldn't take my eyes off the billow of dark smoke now pouring from the chimney. I tell you, gentlemen, as dark as this whole situation was, I found courage standing there in that prison camp. I found courage when I made the decision that I would live. I would live and try in some way to make the deaths of my family and all those that were dying around me have meaning, and this meaning would show in my life."

Leo fell back into his seat. He had been talking for almost forty-five minutes. His eyes went around the table at each of the men staring at him. They were absorbed in his story. "Yes..." he said, returning a smile to each of them. "Meaning would show in my life."

As silence fell over the group, Hoover nervously glanced around the table. "Let's see if our manager friend was serious about those free coffees."

"I'll give you a hand, Hoove," Howard said, following him.

Joe was amazed at the transformation. It was all happening because their conversation had changed over the past few days. No longer a complaining and combative conversation, it was now focused on sharing. They were starting to share a piece of one another's lives in hopes of making each life better. It was so simple, yet so powerful. What would happen if all the world started changing their conversation? That thought brought a warm smile to Joe's face.

"Thanks for sharing this stuff with us, man," Roadie said in true sincerity as he looked right at Leo. "It must not be easy to talk about."

"It isn't, but I tell you, this is how it really was." Leo smiled as he sat up in his chair, ready to continue.

"We wouldn't expect you to tell it any other way than 'how it really is,' Leo." Melvin smiled and winked.

"All right, here's the coffee," Hoover said, returning to the table. "You know, I really like this place, I think I'll come back tomorrow."

"Leo, are you ready to start again?" Melvin asked, nodding toward Hoover. "You better before Hoover steals the stage."

"Thanks for the coffee, gentlemen," Leo said, as he rose again to his feet.

"For the next eight months I endured Auschwitz. My jobs varied from spreading gravel in sub-zero weather on roads outside the camp, to removing the bodies of those that had been killed in the gas chamber and carrying them to the hot furnaces where they were freed by becoming smoke and entering the clouds. My appearance was similar to that of the other prisoners. But I felt my inner self growing stronger in the suffering and struggle.

"In the winter time, I later found out it was January of 1945, many prisoners were being sent on details and we would never see them again. The population of the camp was growing smaller, and those daily survivors began wondering what was happening. Then one morning the trains arrived. We were quickly moved from our huts to the waiting boxcars. The guards seemed even fiercer that day than in the past, if it were possible. They didn't miss a chance to scream at a prisoner or lay a strap to his back. I remember the sting of a strap going across my back as I was pulling myself into the train. I hurried to my feet and looked down from the car at a guard I had never seen before, who was angrily shaking his clenched fist and yelling 'I should kill you, Jew pig.'

"I couldn't believe what my eyes were seeing. On this guard's finger was my father's ring. I was sure it was, and I wanted to jump back down and rip it off his hand. I felt so much anger and hatred at that moment. Fortunately, I was pushed into the railcar by the other prisoners, who were also hurrying to escape the strap. I was crammed into a corner as the car filled with people.

"We had been a day and night on the train; tempers were starting to flare. No one was sure where the train was headed, but as the sun came up and prisoners started peering out of the cracks at the passing countryside, rumors started to fly.

"'We are headed to Mauthausen,' someone said. Mauthausen was a death camp that had large furnaces. There was a murmur of bleak despair traveling through the car when I first noticed him. Some men were pushing him out of the way as he seemed to be trying to get to the edge to peer through the cracks. The mood on the train had worsened. No one was willing to let go of anything, especially a crack with a view. The man was pushed so hard that he fell to the floor in the soaked straw at my feet. I felt myself compelled to help him up. As he slowly came to his feet and quietly raised his head, his lips curled into a smile and he obviously drifted into some memory of the past. He realized I was watching him and began to speak.

"'I believe we are going past Vienna,' he said warmly. 'I thought I saw a glimpse of a building that I used to see every day on my walk to school.'

"I was amazed at his strength and the tone of his voice. Even though his body had shrunk to the mere outline of a human form, he maintained an inner strength that was apparent in his voice. I asked the obvious, desiring to carry on a conversation. 'Are you from Vienna?'

"'Yes, I'm from Vienna, and I so much look forward to seeing my home again.'

"'I just heard we are going to the death camp of Mauthausen. What makes you think you'll ever see Vienna again?'

"'It is my choice to think that,' the man quietly whispered. 'I have that freedom left.'

"'How can you think that you possibly have any freedom left?' I asked him. Here we were as close to death as one could get, and this poor soul was talking about freedom.

"'Let me tell you how it really is, my young friend,' the man continued. 'Let me tell you how it really is. I have survived these camps and horrors for almost four years. The first day that I arrived at Auschwitz was probably very similar to yours. They stripped me of everything, even my dignity. Did they shave all your hair off?' he asked in a sympathetic way.

"'Yes,' I quietly said, becoming mesmerized by his voice and the whining of the rails below us.

"'All of it?'

"'Yes, all of it,' I answered again.

"'Me, too. I remember standing there naked, all my hair gone, and completely alone amongst all the people around me. For some strange reason, my young friend, I began to smile. I had to fight not to laugh out loud. You know what I discovered at that moment?'

"I just shook my head and anxiously awaited his answer.

"'Let me tell you how it really is,' the man continued. 'They can take away everything that I have, they can take even my dignity and leave me for dead, but there is one thing they cannot take. As hard as they may try, they cannot take away my final freedom. My final freedom is that I have a choice. Even under these cold and dreadful surroundings, I can choose how I will respond to my situation. From that moment on, I decided to respond favorably to my situation, knowing that if I do I will be able to give meaning to my suffering. If we can find meaning in it, we can learn from it, and if we can learn, we can endure. That is all we have left, my young friend, our final freedom to choose how we will respond to our present situation. The way a man accepts his fate, even under these circumstances, enables him to give meaning to his life and his suffering. No one can take this final freedom from us. No one.'"

Leo took a deep breath as he looked around the table. The board members were enthralled. The tale that had been locked inside him for so long was now penetrating the heart of each of his friends.

"Our final freedom, gentlemen. It doesn't have to be exercised only in a concentration camp. It is our choice each and every day. Wouldn't you agree?"

Everyone just nodded in unison and Leo knew they wanted to hear more of the final destination of the train.

"Let me tell you how it really is," continued Leo with a warm smile. "That train ride continued for another day and into the night. I had only a few more minutes of conversation with the man because talking used energy that was needed for survival at that point. But he had told me that he was from Vienna and that he was a psychologist. He had been in the camps for what he believed to be over four years. He knew that one day, all the suffering he'd seen and observations he'd made would help him have an impact on people in a free world. 'That is my 'why' my young friend,' he said. 'He who has a 'why' can create almost any 'how' to live. That is how I survived and will survive.'

"Hours later I was startled out of a standing sleep as the passengers crammed into that car began to cheer. Drowsy, I could not comprehend what was going on, but by the moonlight coming in through the cracks I could see the whole car doing a ghostly dance. Living corpses barely able to stand were celebrating. The journey that we thought was going to end at Mauthausen had taken another course. To reach Mauthausen the train would have had to cross the bridge over the Danube River, but it was now headed for Dachau, a smaller camp with no gas and no ovens. It was truly reason to celebrate.

"At Dachau the conditions were just as bad as the other camps. The food was even less desirable and the attitude of the guards even more abrasive. We found hope in this, assuming it meant the Germans were losing the war and that our freedom was drawing closer. We talked regularly of what it would be like when our rescuers would come, open the front gates, and free us.

"I had lost contact with the man I had met on the train, but his words had stuck with me. About a month after our arrival at Dachau, morale bottomed out again. The smallest acts by prisoners, like relacing their shoes with a piece of rope, were being treated as acts of sabotage. Five prisoners were hung in the parade ground. Later that day some food had come up missing in the mess quarters. The entire camp was given the choice to turn over the guilty persons or be forced to fast for the evening and all of the next day. The camp chose to fast. The night of our fast they pulled all the prisoners out of my hut and hurried us into other huts, seemingly to overcrowd and force morale even lower. I found myself lying on the top bunk with my nose inches from the cold tin roof. It was pitch dark and you could feel the despair in every labored breath. I then heard a voice in a low, serious tone begin to penetrate the night. There in the cold darkness I once again heard the man from the train. He was speaking in a desperate attempt to calm us from the day's fast.

"'Let me tell you how it really is,' the man began, his words echoing through the darkness. 'Even though you are lying there in your bed now, feeling like life has robbed you of everything, consider this one thing. You are still able to lie there. There are many before us that have died, and their days are gone. You still have hope. As long as you are breathing you still have hope of freedom and of one day being reunited with your families. Whatever we have gone through to this point could still be a help to us in the future.'"

"He then quoted a poem," Leo said. "I can't remember by whom, but I certainly remember its meaning. 'That which does not kill me will make me strong.' And then he began to speak about the future. Lying in that hut that night, it was very hard for me to even think of the future. But his words rang clear.

"'I know the future must seem hopeless for you. It is true that our chances of survival are very slim, but look how we have survived to this date. No one knows what the future will bring, but we can only expect that one day the tanks will roll up to that front gate and we will once again taste freedom. The future has a degree of luck, but we will create that luck with our own will to survive.'"

"He gave us something to live for," Leo told the board members. "Even though it was a fleeting hope, it was something to look forward to. He then began to remind us of our past and all that it held.

"'Your past,' the voice continued, 'is yours forever. It is so powerful that it shines even today as a bright, warm light in this cold darkness. What you have experienced, no power on earth can take away from you. Your very existence, in actions and thoughts, has helped to define the course of history, even in the smallest of ways. But in having been, you have lived, and in having lived, you can live.'

"Until last night, I almost let myself forget the next words I heard as I lay in that tomb." Leo looked at Joe. "This is why your words of dead and dying struck so hard the other day, Joe. I wasn't willing to face up to it. But I now remember the words of the man in the hut as he told of opportunities for us.

"'Every life has meaning,' the voice in the darkness said. 'In all circum-stances life has meaning. I ask you, my dear friends, to face present circumstances with courage and dignity. Be an example to others who are struggling– show them the way. Realize that you are wonderful human beings whose calling in part is to face the suffering that you now face, to know the suffering has meaning and that life is worthwhile. Then I will consider my time here with you well-spent.'

"At that moment, a surge of electricity caused the one lightbulb in the center of the hut to come back on. Several of the prisoners started to rise from their bunks. I knew I had to get up and find this voice in the darkness. Stumbling from my top bunk, my blistered feet came to rest on the cold floor. I began to walk toward the lone figure sitting in the chair near the light. Others began to fall in line and move toward him. I grabbed his hand and thanked him for what he had reminded me of, and for the hope he had given to me and the others. It was the most memorable moment in my almost seventy-five years of living, the moment I realized my life had meaning.

"The saddest part of all of this," Leo continued, "is that I had forgotten. Not many years after the liberation, I got so caught up in life itself that I forgot to live. I forgot my life had meaning. I forgot until your words this week, Joe, and your smile yesterday, Sammy. When I saw your smile it was the same feeling I had when that light miraculously came on in that hut more than fifty years ago."

Leo slowly moved his left hand up from the table and, shaking ever so slightly, removed a small box from the pocket of his coat and gently placed it on the table. Carefully sitting back in his chair, he took a moment to catch his breath from the address he had just delivered. Looking up to make sure he had the attention of each of his board members, he slowly opened the tiny box and arranged its contents on the table for each of the men to see.

"YOUR RING!" Hoover yelled, drawing the attention of most of the patrons in the restaurant. The eyes of the men who were gathered around the table, however, remained glued to the treasure placed before them. "How. . .How could. . .How did you. . . Is that your ring, Leo? Is that the ring your father gave you?"

"Tell us how you got it back, Leo," Howard said with childlike curiosity.

"Can you tell us, Leo?" Melvin asked. "Can you tell us about the liberation? Were you a hero? How did you ever find your ring?"

Leo smiled and just shook his head. "Melvin, I was far from a hero the day I got this ring back, but remember the words from the voice in the darkness – you create luck with your own will to survive. I had willed myself to survive and luck surely came my way.

"It was the morning of April 29, 1945. The men in my hut were all startled from sleep by gun shots. We were also puzzled about why the guards had not come in shouting and beating our bunks to begin the torture of another day. Someone had strength enough to move to the window to see what motors were roaring in the distance and causing the ground to shake under our feet.

"'It's tanks,' came the jubilant cry. We all leaped from our bunks with renewed strength. The door of our hut was thrown open and we began to move cautiously outside the hut. We could see some of the guards running and still heard a few stray shots. But what we saw next brought a loud cheer from men who had been barely able to speak just moments before. The Allied tanks were pushing through the gates; the vision that so many of us had played out time and again in our minds was now actually happening before us. There were piles of dead bodies from the past weeks along the edges of the camp. I remember the look on the soldiers' faces as they moved out of the tanks and trucks and started to take in the hideous scene. The stench was more than most of their stomachs could handle. The magnitude of the deaths was overwhelming. It was more devastating than what most of them had seen in their entire service in the war leading up to that point. Then their eyes fell on the living. They saw prisoners starting to filter into the parade ground. Their looks of disbelief reminded me that all of us had grown accustomed to our skeletal-like appearance and even to the stench that permeated the camp. All of a sudden the prisoners began to cheer. They were tasting freedom. Celebration had begun. Those that were able, ran to greet the soldiers. Several of the heroes were hoisted upon the shoulders of the men who had been anxiously awaiting their arrival. It was a site that could only be described as Heaven rising up out of Hell.

"For some reason I turned and ran to the other side of our hut. To this day I can't recall why I chose to move away from the celebration rather than take part in it. I ran past the door of our hut and turned the corner at the end of it. I immediately fell hard to the ground; I had tripped over something. It was an SS guard with what appeared to be the last of his life running out of a gunshot wound in the back of his head. I could hardly believe my eyes. I recognized what I could see of his face. It was the guard who had hit me with the strap as I boarded the train in Auschwitz several months earlier. 'Could it be possible?' I thought to myself. I fell to my knees and grabbed the man's right hand. There it was. My father's ring. My first urge was to take the man's whole hand off to get it back, but as I stared at that ring something came over me. Had all this been for a reason? What? I wasn't sure. But I was alive, and as I slowly slipped the ring off his finger, I felt the hatred that I had for him and others like him slowly slip away. I placed the ring on my finger and realized I had just become liberated, not only from the torture of existence in these camps, but also from the torture of hate and suffering."

Leo nodded in appreciation of the emotion that each man was obviously feeling. White hankies were coming out of pockets and the table began to sound like a flock of geese in 'v' formation heading south.

"That is quite a story, Leo," Joe said, returning his hankie to his pocket. "I had no idea you had gone through all of that."

"Why don't you wear it, Leo?"

"What's that, Roadie?" Leo said, turning his attention from Joe to Roadie.

"Why don't you wear the ring?"

"Probably for the same reason Joe wasn't making the best use of his time and Sammy had lost the desire to smile. If we have the knowledge and don't use it, then it never becomes wisdom. Not long after the liberation I had regained my health to the point of starting a life over again. I was literally given a second chance. But I forgot everything that I had learned from the war and soon, like so many people, became lazy with life and took it for granted. As the years passed I became sour and cynical. I didn't have a son and soon grew discouraged. I put the ring away, and last night was the first time in over thirty years that I even bothered to even look at it. This moment is the first time since my father gave it to me that I have had the desire to place it on my finger."

Leo removed the ring from the box and slipped it onto the little finger of his left hand. As he held it up high and studied it, a smile formed along his tears. "That feels good," he whispered.

"I have something else to show you," he said as he reached into his briefcase and pulled out a book. "The man on the train and the voice in the darkness... I'm speculating, but I believe it's this man. He wrote this book. It is called Man's Search for Meaning. His name is Victor Frankl. I got this book maybe fifteen years ago. In it is the description of that train ride, his talk in that dark hut, and his search for and discovery of meaning in the suffering of the concentration camps. It is said that this is one of the ten most important books in America. I didn't understand it until yesterday."

Leo next brought an old folder from his briefcase. "These are pictures that I have found over the years in books and magazines about Dachau and Auschwitz. I share them with you just to emphasize the suffering and pain that took place. As you look at the faces of each of these victims, try to imagine what's going on in their thoughts."

As each man gazed at the pictures, it was apparent that the faces in them made the story that they had just heard a reality.

"They do seem like ghosts," Howard quietly said, not even realizing he

was speaking. "They look empty and drained of everything: their possessions, their memories, their hope, even a reason for living itself. They look
so empty."

Leo was shaking his head in agreement with Howard. "They were
merely empty vessels, Howard, unaware of what would be placed in them
next and quite unsure if they would be able to hold anything placed in them.
They were empty."

"And this is me," Leo continued, holding up a book with the picture of
a man on it. It showed the man sitting on the ground with a can of rations
in his hand. The inscription below it said 'a liberated prisoner in Dachau,
April 29, 1945.' "This picture was taken on the day of liberation. A soldier
had given me that can of food and I was slowly trying to digest it. But if you
look closely, you can see I was holding my father's ring in my fingers. This
is a reminder to me that I have lived and died and been given a chance to
live again."

The picture and Leo's words had once again brought the white hankies
out of the men's pockets to wipe away the emotion the morning had created.

"Oh, I almost forgot one thing."

Joe hoped that in some way, Leo would be able to capture in writing the
wisdom of the story he had just told. A small smile came to his face as he
saw Leo take some papers out of his briefcase and begin to pass them around
the table. The entire table was silent as each member of the board absorbed
what had been handed to him.

"LIFE IS AS WE SEE IT"

* My final freedom is to choose how I will respond to any situation I may face. I know I can possibly lose everything, but this freedom can never be taken from me.

* When I discover my "why" to live, then my "how" to live will just naturally follow, providing the actions and steps to be taken.

* As long as I have life, I have reason to have hope for a positive future.

* I will create my good fortune in direct proportion to my will to live life to its fullest.

* The past with its victories and defeats can burn brightly to warm me in any situation, realizing that no powers on earth can steal my experiences from me.

* I will always be able to find the courage to survive and prevail the instant that I am able to face up to the seriousness of any situation, regardless of its threat to my existence.

* I will give meaning to every event and emotion, regardless of its initial intent, and in the end I will rest assured that my life had a worthwhile effect on the course of history.

Almost simultaneously, each man finished reading through the wisdom found in Leo's suffering and loss in the prison camp. As they all looked again in Leo's direction, he slowly rose from his seat and stood once again before the Board of Directors. Clearing his throat and looking as if the most important part of his lesson was yet to come, he began to speak.

"And now, gentlemen, let me tell you how it really is. There is an even greater liberation that must take place, and it is to free an even larger group of prisoners than were lost in the tragedies that I have just told you about. When I look at these prisoners of today, I see the same looks of hopelessness and loss that you see, Howard, in the prisoners of Dachau. They are as you said, Joe, of us at this table two days ago, 'dead and dying.' Actually, they are very much alive and should be living. This group of prisoners, gentlemen, is the majority of old people across this country. Their concentration camps are the walls that they have set up for themselves in their own minds. They have resigned themselves to living in a retirement home, apartment, or the spare room of their children's home, spending each day dying in front of the television set. They are worse off than the prisoners that I told you about this morning because their only hope of liberation is death, and then the suffering of age will be done. I choose to help these prisoners. I'm going to start today in the home where I live." Leo was slowly and purposely gathering up his pictures and placing them back in his case. "I know I'll find the same people sitting in the same chairs, talking about the same things, or watching the same shows on TV. This morning I placed a notice on the bulletin board about a discussion to take place after lunch in the piano room. I called this discussion, 'Old Wood Flowers.' I hope you don't mind, Joe."

Joe just smiled and shook his head. The transformation that was taking place around the table was amazing to him. Maybe Ernest had been right many years ago and he would be able to one day help people. "You go right ahead, Leo. That's an excellent idea. You go right ahead."

"And now, gentlemen, I have some liberating to do. Thank you for your interest and attention this morning. And most of all, thank you for your friendship." Looking around the table, Leo adjusted the ring on his finger, picked up his case, and gave a warm nod to each of his friends. Out of respect they rose from their seats to watch this man who had rediscovered his "why" walk out the door.

All were quiet for a moment, and then Joe said, "That was an incredible story." He drew the smiles and affirmations of the others around the table, but there was nothing to add as they stood and absorbed what had been shared.

"Well, I better pay a visit to a little four-legged friend and his master who are probably wondering where I am." Joe once again broke the silence. "Anybody want to walk along?"

Joe's invitation was turned down by everyone but Hoover. The others seemed to want time to themselves to explore the "camp" they had placed themselves in. Joe was glad they were thinking.

"I'd like to walk with you, Joe, if I could," Hoover said in a slightly anxious manner, as if he had something else to say.

"Sure, Hoove, glad to have your company," Joe returned. "Well. . ."

"Joe?" Everyone looked in Howard's direction – "Joe, I'll talk tomorrow, if that's all right. I don't know if I can give as much as we've heard in the past couple days, but I'd like to try."

Joe was amazed. If there was one person he thought might have a hard time taking a stand and telling of his past, it was Howard. "I can't wait, Howard; the floor is yours tomorrow."

⪻ CHAPTER 7 ⪼

FACING THE DRAGON

*T*he captured knight looked in despair at the shackle
*that had been placed on his wrist so many years ago. How long had
he been here? It no longer mattered. It had been a lifetime for him,
and the world he knew was limited by the three-foot chain attached
to his wrist and bolted to the door. He could explore no further than
it would allow. When the heart of a knight is held captive, his spirit
is laid to rest. His captivity was a mystery – to one day wake up in
chains, held there by the insecurity of others and his own lack of
answers. His fate was bound by the shackles of iron that held him
unto this wall till death. It was a pain that left him more than empty
inside; it was a darkness no light could penetrate, and the void
within him made his thoughts as heavy as lead.*

*He surveyed his surroundings. Four iron pins held the shackle
and chain to the wall. He looked at the path that the years had worn
in the stone floor of the dungeon. His world was lit by one torch that
the keeper ignited in the morning when his ration of food was
brought and then extinguished at night by the same keeper. He could
only faintly remember what sunshine was and how it could warm his
skin or reflect diamonds off a stream.*

*When the darkness fell, he could feel the call. Silent, he knew
that something was beckoning him to a battle that must be fought.
This night, like every other night, the keeper removed the torch and
with cloaked head silently assailed the stairs. The darkness once
again landed like a veil. The silent call was louder than ever before.
From deep inside and far beyond the castle wall he could feel the
dragon call. His forehead was wet with sweat. The time had come,
yet he knew little of what to expect or what he should do. That was
what tormented him, knowing the call, yet being unable to answer it.
It was diminishing the last of the spirit that had made him a knight.
Falling to the dungeon floor with his back against the wall, he placed
his face into his hands and began to cry. Through the years, as lonesome and hopeless as his situation had been, he had never allowed
himself to cry. It was not good for a knight to cry; he had learned
that as a child. It was the only thing his father had ever said to him*

before leaving for battle and never returning, but now the tears were consuming him. He could feel the dragon's call.

The battle was at hand.

The dragon's cry had pierced the dungeon walls. Having heard few sounds throughout the years, the knight was taken back. The eeriness of the wailing was banging in his ears. With each piercing screech from the dragon's lair, he begged out loud that it would be the last, but then another would come and yet another, louder still. On the edge of his sanity, the knight rose. In frantic desperation he stretched the chain to its end, blood dripping from the cuts the irons had made upon his wrist. At that moment he knew that the battle could not be won if he continued to be bound by this chain he had allowed to define his world.

Moving toward the wall, he would do whatever it would take. Stone by stone, if necessary, he would tear down this wall and free himself from the bondage of the past. His feet kicked at the bottom and his hands tore at the top, but the wall was solid, his pace was slow, and the battle seemed lost. Again the dragon's devilish cry ripped through the dungeon's darkness. This time it was answered by the knight's own battle cry. Stretched at arm's length again, the chain was pulled taut. He raised his head, and from deep within his courage was renewed as the proclamation left his lips, "The dragon must be slain."

A flash of lightning exploded against the wall, and he stood blinded for an instant. There it lay upon the ground as if it had always been there, a key… the key that had put him here and now would allow him the freedom to choose. Slowly he knelt, picked it up, and brought it to his face. Its gentle glow in this darkest of places gave hope to the knight's heart. He could choose to remain a prisoner or he could use the key and face the dragon's call.

Another scream from the dragon pierced his ears, and he knew the time was growing short. A decision would have to be made or the battle would be lost without ever being fought. How perfectly the key fit into its place and how easily it turned; with a clank the shackle fell to the ground. His action had freed him from his past and now would allow him the choice to free him to his future. Using the key as a light in the darkness, he moved up the stairs that he had watched his keeper ascend so many times throughout the years, thinking he would never make the journey himself. With each step he gained strength and courage to meet the dragon in his lair.

Reaching the top of the stairs, he saw the familiar cloaked figure holding a torch in one hand and a sword in the other. He stood between the knight and the door that he would need to pass through to seek out the dragon. The dragon again let out a scream; this time it sounded more distant. The knight knew his chances were fading unless he moved now. With his first step toward the door, the cloaked keeper moved one step aside and raised his sword, its blade reflecting in the torch light. At the knight's next step, the keeper flipped the sword in the air with ease. With a single rotation, the sword landed perfectly into the knight's hand. He raised it and in the torch light surveyed its detail. The pummel had been made of a crystal stone, probably a diamond. Its cross hilt was fashioned of gold and curled back towards the grip as a protection to its bearer's hand. In the center of the hilt where the sword blade met the grip was a heart stamped into the gold. The blade's sharp edge glistened and its polished steel was engraved with the words "Slay the Dragon" just underneath the grip.

When the knight again turned his attention to the keeper, the cloaked figure had moved away from the door and motioned for him to approach. As the knight's hand touched the latch, he stopped and peered back over his shoulder at the keeper, who had now moved to the top of the dungeon stairs. He lifted his torch and placed it in the holder above his head. Looking down and then moving his covered hands to each side of his hood, he slowly looked up again and in a sweeping motion flipped the hood back; and the entire cloak fell to the floor. To the knight's amazement nothing stood in its place. All that remained was the glow of the torch and the keeper's cloak lying in a pile on the floor. He removed his hand from the latch and moved to the top of the steps. Taking a long look down into the darkness that had been his world, he knew his past was behind him. He picked up the robe and realized that he was now in the present. But the present is only a fleeting moment, and just like the keeper, is gone in an instant. He placed the cloak around the rags that clothed him, and with sword in hand lifted the latch that could free him to his future.

As the door swung open, the clearness of the morning air filled his lungs. He had forgotten how marvelously– fresh air could clear a mind. The sun was just beginning to rise and its soft glow in the east caused his eyes to first squint and then welcome the sight. The scream of the dragon once again brought him back to the reality of his situation and why he had been freed. The key that remained in his hand began to glow again, and as he looked up from it a beautiful white horse stood before him in full battle bard. Placing the key in the pocket of the robe, he mounted his ride with sword in hand as the dragon called again.

Riding to the east, he followed the road that led to the dark forest. There was only one road. He had no choices. As long as the dragon was alive there would be only one road, and it would always lead to this forest. He must slay the dragon. The nostrils of the horse flared as the stench of the dragon's lair permeated the air. Horse and rider swiftly continued forward.

The knight saw no life within the forest. Only the dragon's insistent wail reminded him that his enemy was anxiously awaiting the battle. He looked at the sword in his hand and then over his shoulder, contemplating retreat. To his amazement the road behind him had disappeared without a trace, leaving him no choice but to follow the course he'd begun.

His horse anxiously pawed at the ground as the knight motioned him to move forward. Within the forest boundaries he could feel his heart beating against his chest and echoing in his ears. The dark and dank surroundings engulfed him and he shuddered as he followed charred paths leading to a clearing in the woods. Moving his horse into the clearing, he was less than twenty yards from the dark entrance of a cave. He could hear a hideous laugh which ended in an ear piercing scream. The dragon knew his prey had arrived, and the knight was filled with doubt. At that moment he wished that he were still chained to the wall in the safety of his little three foot semi-circle. He wanted to run, to leave it all, but froze as another scream pierced the air and the dragon's hideous head appeared.

The knight was terrified by the sight. He had envisioned what the dragon would look like, but in his wildest imagination he could not have pictured the fierceness of the creature standing before him. Slime dripped from its huge teeth as it hungered for the knight's flesh. Its eyes were like glass without reflection: cold, dark, and focused on the prey. Twice the height of the knight on his mount, it stared menacingly down on them.

The horse instinctively began to step backward as the dragon moved further out of its lair and into the clearing. The knight was astonished to see another head appear and then another and then another and yet another. When the dragon was completely out of his cave and standing in the clearing, it had five heads in all. The head furthest to the left had deep, stern eyes and the knight felt he recognized it. It was uttering a cry understandable to the knight, "Don't cry. Don't cry. Men don't cry. Don't cry." He hadn't heard that voice in years.

Between the furthest head and the fierce one in the middle was another one on a short neck, accusing eyes staring deep into the knight. Its tongue was lashing out within inches of the knight's face. He could hear it hissing words of slander and hate, "You're a thief, you'll rot in prison... thief... thief... thief."

To the right of the hideous middle head was a mangled and deformed head. Its eyes haphazardly rolled in its head. Its fangs were bent and crooked, and its long tongue hung limply to the side of its mouth. At regular intervals the middle head would lash out and knock the mangled wreck to the ground. It would slowly lift itself back up and address the knight in a slow, gurgled hissing, "You are worthless, you're nothing; you are nothing, nothing, nothing, nothing."

Furthest to the right was a quiet, scared, and nervous looking head. It brought its eyes into contact with the knight and then quickly looked away. Its eyes almost looked warm and caring, as though it wasn't wanting the confrontation to take place. The knight could hear its soft whisper contrast with the starkness of the other four screams. "Shhhhh. We mustn't tell him. It's a secret, he'll get mad, it's a secret, secret, secret...."

"Mother," the knight felt the words leave his lips. He thought he had heard his mother's voice coming from the dragon's head. "Mother, is that you?"

As all the heads began to utter their messages in unison, the middle head again let out its hideous laugh, which turned to a scream that nearly deafened the knight. He realized that the battle he had come to fight was not with the future, but with his past, and these voices from the past could collectively steal his future from him.

The dragon had now grown impatient. His hunger was apparent as the juices dripped from his mouth. Moving closer to his quarry, he unmercifully began his attack. The knight felt fear shoot throughout his being as the four outer heads clamped onto his horse's legs and pulled it out from under him. As the knight fell to the charred ground, the heads quickly devoured the horse; the middle head turned his attention to its true prey. The knight's body was drenched

in sweat and the sword, stuck in the ground, was out of his reach.
He could see the gold heart and the inscription, but it all seemed so
useless now. In an instant the dragon's fangs tore at his flesh. The
knight let out a scream that echoed through the forest and into eternity.

"HOWARD! What is it?" his terrified wife asked, sitting up in bed and staring in disbelief as the moonlight coming in the window cast its white light on the sweat-drenched bed and the pale figure staring blankly at the ceiling.

"Howard!" she called again as she shook him by the forearms. It was not unusual for her to be awakened in the middle of the night by his horrifying nightmare. In their forty-two years of marriage it had occurred almost every night. But tonight's episode seemed different. He had never screamed out before, nor woken up drenched in sweat. He told her it was the same dream night after night. He was a knight locked in a dungeon, tethered to the wall by a short chain, and as hard as he pulled he could not get loose. The dream always ended with the knight falling to the dungeon floor in despair.

Without taking his eyes off the ceiling, Howard quietly asked, "Edith, if you don't mind, would you please get my pills for me and a drink of water?" He continued off into a silent void.

How many times had she heard those words in the past years? She slowly lifted herself off the bed and slid her feet into the worn pink slippers that were always waiting beside the bed. Placing a white robe over her shoulders, she glanced back down at her husband, whose stare seemed to grow more intense as he swallowed hard. She had forever watched her husband battle something from within and had often wondered if the pills he took for depression actually had any effect, but she never questioned his use of them. As a faithful wife she would stand beside him no matter what the circumstance.

She replayed the many conversations of the past concerning children. How much she had wanted them, but he would always say, "Now Edith, let me get this dragon inside of me slain first. I don't want to bring a child into this world if his father can't give him the most important things, love and happiness."

She knew the time to have children had long passed. She wanted to say that he brought all this on himself; the depression, the lack of confidence, the fears and nerves, the need for pills, and the years of searching all the books for answers. She wanted to tell him, but she didn't. She knew it would set him off and drive him deeper into the dungeon he seemed to lock himself in. There had been a glimmer of hope in the last several days as he told her with excitement and enthusiasm of the events taking place at McDonald's. He told her all about making the best use of time, and keeping the desire to smile, as well as the story of the concentration camps. He even told her that life is as we see it. Those conversations had meant so much to him.

"I've never heard good conversation around that board room table," he told her yesterday when she came home from her cleaning job. "But something has changed, and you know what, Edith? I'm going to speak on wisdom tomorrow."

She was amazed at his excitement as he rushed through dinner and then hurried to his desk in search of something. He scurried from room to room, opening and closing the thousands of books on knights, medieval times, kings, and dragons. There were hundreds of artifacts and collections from armor to arrows, leaving each room of the house with narrow paths for movement.

His excitement began to diminish as the night wore on. Edith watched him grow more discouraged as he tried to look outside for the answers that would only come from within. The searching ended a little after 9:00 as he said, "Edith, I don't think I'll be up to the meeting in the morning. I'm not feeling very well now. I think I'm going to go on to bed." He then softly kissed her on top of the head and trudged up the steps without waiting for a response.

And now here he lay here again as he had so many times before, staring up at the ceiling, defeated and depressed, waiting for his pills to come.

He brought his eyes from the ceiling for an instant, glanced at his wife, and then asked, "Is there a problem, Edith? I need my pills. Will you please get them for me?" His voice was slow and remote. In the past she would have responded quickly, assured him there was no problem, and hurried off to get his pills, but tonight she was motionless. He glanced quickly at her and then back to the ceiling, again and again. Finally, she turned with a sigh and began the journey through the narrow path of books to get the pills that she knew would not make a difference.

Howard felt himself sitting up in bed to watch the robed figure move from the room. He realized in the past several minutes that something had changed. He watched as his wife left the room. She meant so much to him, yet he was never able to really show her. He felt a warmth in his heart and a smile on his face. She had always been beside him, before they were married and during the time he'd spent in jail. She was always there. She wanted children but she never complained. He quietly spoke out loud as he took his glasses off the night stand and slowly placed them on his head, "And after forty-two years she's still taking care of her only son, ME!"

"HOWARD!" Edith called, nearly dropping the glass of water as she returned to the bedroom. Her husband began to smile as he watched her glide through the room that looked like a museum. She hadn't seen a smile like that in years and it brought her joy. "Howard, you're sitting up. Are you okay? The dream. . . it must have been. . . you really let out a scream. And the bed is soaked where you were lying. It wasn't your bladder again, was it?"

Laughing, Howard looked at her and said, "I love you."

With tears in her eyes Edith set the glass down on the nightstand. She hadn't heard those words said as if he really meant them in a very long time. "I love you, too. I. . . I wasn't expecting you to be sitting up. Do you feel okay?"

"The dream was different this time, Edith." Looking into the depths of her eyes, he asked, "Do you want to hear about it?"

She just quietly nodded her head as he motioned her to sit on the edge of the bed with him. He took both of her hands in his and in the soft glow of the moonlight explained the dream in exact detail. When he had finished, he squeezed her hand, stood up, and began to pace and talk with an intensity that shocked both of them.

"Edith, I have been having a portion of that dream every night since I was fifteen years old. That is almost sixty years or a total of eighteen thousand times."

"Spoken like a true accountant," Edith said with a smile.

"And in each of those eighteen thousand times," he continued, returning her smile, "it always stopped as the knight fell to the dungeon floor, before a tear was shed. But this time it continued through the tears and leaving the dungeon, and then the dragon's attack on the knight." His face grew stern and the blank stare returned as he pictured again the knight being attacked. What was the final outcome, though? He couldn't exactly remember.

"What does it all mean?" Edith asked.

"I don't know, Edith, but the dream, it. . . it's trying to tell me something. I see now that I can learn something from that dream."

Leaning closer as she touched him lightly on the cheek, Edith paused and then whispered, "I think the time has come to learn it then, Howard. Let's not miss this opportunity."

He looked at her intently, afraid to take the risk as time stood still between the two figures in the moonlight. When Howard began to explain the dream again, the words rolled off his lips, and Edith absorbed every detail.

"... and it ended with the hideous fangs of the dragon flying toward the flesh of the knight. That is when I called out and woke up. The dragon had killed the knight." Twenty minutes later, as he finished his story, he began slipping into his own world again.

"That's not what happened," Edith said, with more emphasis in her voice than either of them had heard in a long while. She clenched her fists and punched the mattress on either side of her, "That's not the ending, Howard!"

"What?" Howard asked, shocked at her outburst. "Edith, it is my dream. That's how it all happened."

"You didn't say the dragon killed the knight when you described it."

"Well, he would have if I hadn't woke up." Howard was looking at his wife in bewilderment. "What is your point?"

"My point is the knight is not dead. That's what your dream is telling you. You woke up, but the dragon did not kill the knight." Edith quickly moved from the bed to a drawer in her dresser. She removed a small stack of books and held them in front of her husband. "I've been reading through the years, too, trying to help interpret your dream. I don't have the thousands of books you have, but I've learned a lot about dreams. That's what these books are about, interpreting dreams. Howard, together we can interpret your dream and maybe we can find what you've been looking for all these years. . . an answer. But the answer is on the inside, Howard, not on the outside. This is the opportunity we have been waiting years for, and if we don't. . . find the answer. . .well. . .then the dragon will have killed the knight."

Edith had decided she wouldn't give him the opportunity to say no. "Howard, what I've learned in my reading is that each element in the dream is describing something about the dreamer. It is you. The dragon's howl that you described is you. The steps, the keeper, the white horse. . . even the dragon, it is all you. And to find the answers we have to piece all the elements together as you personally experience them. You have to become each of the elements and tell how you feel."

Howard was now staring at his wife, wondering what was going to happen next. "You sound like a psychologist, Edith."

"Tell me about that chain, Howard. How do you feel as the chain that was holding the knight to the wall?"

He could tell by her intensity that this confrontation was not going to end until he had risked all that he was and opened himself to the answers they were both desperately searching for.

"Finish this sentence, Howard, As the chain I'm. . ."

He took a deep breath and said, "I'm created by my own doing." He looked surprised. He couldn't believe Edith had gotten him to say it.

"Don't stop, chain," she said with sympathetic sternness. "You're created by your own doing. What else? How do you feel?"

"Useless," came his next words. "I can't believe I can hold anyone to a wall. I'm weak and anyone who wanted to could easily break a link and escape."

"Good," she whispered, sitting in the moonlit room. "What else do you see?"

"The keyhole in the cuff of the chain."

"How do you feel as the keyhole?" she asked in anticipation.

"I'm a darkness. A matter of choice, and choice is dark. Not knowing which one to make. I'm a decision. In this case between freedom and captivity. I feel like half of the solution and when I'm combined with a key, then the decision is freedom."

"Great. Howard, what's next?"

He thought, remembering the path in the stone floor caused by his wandering back and forth at the chain's length, then spoke as he had before. "I'm the path. I feel bland, trodden, I'm a rut, created not by effort but by the lack of effort. Every day doing the same thing. This doesn't take effort, it is laziness that causes the path on the floor... a rut."

"The keeper?" she gently prodded.

"I'm lonesome," Howard continued. "My routine seems so meaning-less. Each morning I walk down the steps with the torch and light the lone light. All because someone told me I was to do this. And then at the end of the day, I extinguish it. But it doesn't matter. No one knows the difference. The prisoner in the dungeon doesn't know if it is morning or night, only that my torch is lit. I would like to do it differently. What would happen if I lit it at night and put it out in the morning? At least I could enjoy being different. But I'm afraid to be different, to do anything out of the ordinary. I persist in leading a life without meaning. I really want to do something different, out of the ordinary, to risk just one time."

"You said in the dream that the dragon's call would always come at darkness. Pretend, Howard, that you are the dragon's call. What do you feel?

He swallowed hard and considered putting a stop to this silly game. It was the caring concern on his wife's face that made him answer. He felt he owed it to her.

"I'm misunderstood," he said. "I come from what seems a great distance, but really I'm very close to the knight. I come from within. I'm perceived to be dark and evil, but I don't feel that way. I'm calling the knight to something better. If only he would respond. I'm heard in the darkness because it is only when a person is quiet that I can be heard. As I land on the ears of those that hear me, something inside them stirs. Depending on the person, I will drive them to further accomplishment or deeper into hiding. As Thoreau said, 'Most men live lives of quiet desperation.' I'm their desperation, but they need only to accept my urgings, not run from them."

Howard sprang to his feet and stormed across the room. When he reached the window, he put a hand on either side of the frame and stared out at the darkness. "EDITH, I can't do this anymore." Angry and defeated, he turned toward his wife once again.

"I don't want to go through with this, Edith. I just want to go back to sleep. This isn't making any sense. And it's not healthy, Edith. You're… you're not a psychologist, so quit trying to act like one. Enough is enough. Let's get back to sleep."

"Did you hear that, Howard?" Edith asked, turning her head and looking around curiously.

"Hear what?" Howard snapped.

"The dragon's call," she answered, looking him straight in the eye and repeating, "It's the dragon's call. Why the tears?"

"What tears?"

"The tears that the knight shed in the dream. I don't ever remember you mentioning tears before."

"I don't know, Edith. What does it really matter anyway?"

"I'll tell you why, Howard. The knight is desperate. He knows this is it. His life could be lost unless he makes a decision and he's afraid. The tears are because he is afraid. Just like you now, Howard, afraid." Edith could see a tear running down the side of her husband's face. She had never seen him cry before. Fighting back her own tears, she knew she had to continue. "The knight was afraid and as the tears began to flow, the dragon's call became closer and more real. Remember the dream, Howard? You told it. The knight rose to his feet. The call pushed him to his edge. That is where you are now. At your edge. The chain was stretched; it cut into his wrist and the blood… the blood was his life, and it was slipping away. Our life can slip away unless we do something. We must take action. In the dream you said he started to tear at the wall, kicking and flailing at it, but it seemed impossible. It was impossible. He could go no further. What happened next, Howard? What did the knight do?" The sharpness of her voice and focus of her stare left no doubt that an answer was necessary.

Through tears Howard managed to answer. "The knight cried out in desperation."

"What did he say, Howard? What was his battle cry? Say it. Tell me. Tell yourself." She heard the frustration of forty-two years escaping in her voice, and all she had held back emerged in a desperate attempt to save them both.

Howard moved from the window and swung wildly, scattering books across the room. He fell toward the bed, catching hold of the tall bed post on his way down. Holding tightly and lunging backward, he felt younger and older at the same time; he could wait no longer.

"THE DRAGON MUST BE SLAIN! ! ! !" he bellowed to the ceiling. His voice was brave and strong. It came from the depths of his being and filled the room, echoing off the books and walls. He quickly brought his eyes from the ceiling to his wife. It was all beginning to make sense.

"It's energy, Edith, the lightning... the key."

Edith smiled, knowing a decision had been made and the shackles had fallen to the floor just as they had in the dream. She waited silently.

"When a decision is made and an understanding is reached there is energy, just like lightning. This lightning brought about the key that was always there. The key is knowledge. I started realizing this knowledge when I listened to Joe, Sammy, and Leo talk at the board meetings. Finding the key in the dream told me that I possess this same knowledge, and if I apply it, it will be wisdom. That's what Joe told us the other day. Wisdom is the good side of growing old."

Howard began to pace purposefully around the stacks of books. He wanted to speak but couldn't find the words. He looked at Edith and saw tears running down her cheeks. "Edith, I feel like I have cheated you out of a life. I, I,..."

"You are the knight." she persisted. "How do you feel?"

"I'm free," Howard continued as he paced around the room. "The shackle has fallen from my arm. My world has now expanded past the rut on the floor. With every step out of the dungeon, I feel more and more courage because I'm taking action. As I now face the keeper standing between me and freedom, I realize that that which dictates our world can also provide opportunity and tools for encouragement. The keeper is symbolic of a day filled with opportunity if only we have the courage to face the day and move through it."

"The dungeon and steps are the past. The keeper is the present and in an instant that which is before you will soon be behind you and gone, vanished like the keeper. When I pick up his robe. . . his robe. . . it is the moment. And in order to succeed and face the battle we must be in the moment, in the now." His pacing stopped and he looked seriously at his wife. "I've never been in the moment. I was too busy fretting about my past or fearing what the future might bring to ever make the most of the present. That is quite a realization, Edith. Too bad it took so many years to reach it. I've spent my whole life running from the clearing and avoiding my battles of change."

"You are not running this time. You are in the clearing and you're going to fight the dragon. It's time to conquer it by understanding it."

Minutes passed as Howard sat deep in thought, struggling to replay the whole ugly scene in his head. Edith knew it was a time to keep silent, and she watched his torment with a patience that is born only of love. Finally, his face showed the dawning of a revelation. Confidently he raised his head and began to speak.

"The dragon had five heads and each one of these heads is a part of me, a part of my past that has shaped my life. The head furthest to the left is my father's influence. The last time I saw him I was eight years old. I was very sick and it was winter. A storm was raging outside. I needed medicine, or so my mother thought. She had been dropping hints throughout the evening. Finally, my father said he would go. I didn't want him to go. I was afraid and started to cry. He kept telling me, as he was putting his boots on, to be quiet, men don't cry. Those were the last words he said as he looked over his shoulder and left. 'Men don't cry.' He never came back. His body was never found. He just vanished in the storm. I always felt guilty, as if I had killed him, and I deeply resented my mother for driving him out the door. I don't remember ever crying after that day.

"The head to the far right is my mother's influence. She was nervous, anxious all the time, always afraid of what my father would do or say. If a tool broke or something happened when he wasn't around, she would say, 'Oh, Howard, you shouldn't have done that. Your father will be mad. Don't tell him. Don't tell him. Don't tell your father. Don't tell him.' Those words haunt me to this day. I resent being secretive, yet it is what I am. I am always afraid to speak out, to make someone mad, and in not speaking out I feel like a coward. Howard the Coward is what the kids in school called me.

"That explains the head next to the one representing my mother. This one is the part of me that I hate the most because it's who I became, an ugly, worthless nobody with a poor self-image and nothing to offer. I was never accepted by my classmates. They called me names and would make fun of me. With each day, the image I had of myself diminished. It did drive me to learn, though. That is the one thing I knew I could do… I could learn, even though I would get made fun of for being so smart and the teacher's pet. The best that I ever felt was the day I graduated from college. Do you remember, Edith, do you remember how happy I was? I was going to be a great accountant. I had a Master's Degree in accounting and business. I was ready to tackle the world. You were so patient, Edith. This low self esteem was why we didn't marry right away. I couldn't let a young woman as beautiful and special as you marry a nobody. I wanted to be someone before I asked you to marry me. I was so excited about my career. Parker and Parker was a very prestigious firm. They recruited me. They actually wanted me to work for them.

"That is the fourth head, Edith. It's the image that stuck in my mind through each minute I spent in that prison. It was John Parker sitting on the witness stand calling me a communist. He was as much a liar as Joseph McCarthy himself, and he was using McCarthyism to frame me for the fraud that his firm was caught up in. I spent two years in that prison for something I didn't do. Falsely accused and used as a cover-up to hide one of the biggest frauds in history. It would have rocked Hollywood if I had just spoken up. But I didn't. I allowed my career to be ruined. I was labeled a communist and went through the horrors of prison all because I did not take a stand."

The room fell silent and Edith sat in awe of what had taken place over the past hour. Now, looking at him, she could see a transformation taking place. Even though he looked tired from speaking, he sat a little taller and braver, having done what he thought was impossible. Yet she knew the task was not completed. There was one more head to understand and one more battle for her knight to face. . . the meeting at McDonald's that was a little over three hours away. She quietly whispered her words of encouragement, "That was amazing, Howard, that you were able to understand the dream. You must feel better from all of it." She struggled to find the right words.

"I didn't just realize it, Edith," he answered, still staring off into the moonlit night. Then turning to her he said "I've always known this, Edith. The battle is not to discover it, the battle is to face up to it. In facing up to the dragon, or my past, then I'm made aware of my responsibility to deal with it, accept it, and move forward. That is the true key that unlocked the shackle from the knight's wrist. . . the key is responsibility."

Edith was studying her husband's face carefully and felt she could now ask, "What about the fifth head, Howard? The one in the middle that stood so tall?"

Howard stood up, walked to the window, and again gazed into the night. "That head, Edith, is me. The me that I never let out. I realize that I have kept my true self hidden in a dark cave, afraid to face it and afraid to set it free. This fear caused me to hate the dragon, to hide from it, and then to seek to destroy it. I can't slay the dragon. If I were to kill the dragon I would kill myself. I believe that is why a person commits suicide, Edith, to kill the dragon. The real battle is to face the dragon, accept it, and co-exist in a peaceful manner. It is every person's responsibility to do this, and up to now I have failed miserably." He lowered his head and again the room fell silent.

"Did the dragon kill the knight, Howard?"

"NO!" he answered vehemently, turning from the window to look intently at his wife. Speaking with more passion than he had ever felt, he answered again, "NO, Edith! In these dark woods the knight lives. The dragon has pulled life out from under me just as the horse was pulled out from under the knight. And in the instant of battle, as I reach for the sword that lay stuck in the ground, I raise it high and with a mighty yell I turn to strike out at the dragon but find standing in its place a reflection of me. No mirror, no glass, I'm standing looking at myself. I lower the sword to my side and let it fall to the ground. The fight is not with a sword; the fight is realizing and accepting that who I am is not what I am. My responsibility is to become who I truly am. In my case I didn't do that until this moment. Now the knight and dragon can co-exist. I can accept my past. I will no longer fear the future and I will live in the moment." The magnitude and emotion of his words had caused his fist to clench and be raised to his chest. "The knight is free, Edith. The knight is finally free."

Tears were streaming down Edith's face as she leaped from the edge of the bed, knocked her books to the floor, and threw her arms around her husband's neck. Their sobs of joy echoed with the ring of freedom, like the shackle falling to the dungeon floor.

Edith noticed that it was getting close to 4:30. "What about the meeting, Howard?"

"The meeting!" he exclaimed. "I forgot about the meeting. I'll just have to tell them that I will speak another day. I don't know what I could take to that meeting this morning."

"You forgot to look at one element in the dream, Howard."

"Forgot? How could I have forgotten anything after all of this?"

"The road," she continued, pressing him. "You said in the dream, when the knight looked back over his shoulder the road was gone. I interpret this to mean that there is no turning back. You must do what you've set out to do. How do you interpret it?"

Howard just smiled, appreciating his wife's persistence and tenacity. "You are absolutely right, My Lady," he said with a smile and a bow. "But what is the wisdom? What do I take to share?"

"Finish the poem," she quietly urged.

"The poem?"

"Finish it, Howard," she persisted. "Go to your desk and finish it while it is fresh in your thoughts."

As Howard pulled the yellowed piece of paper from his desk drawer, he wondered how he could ever finish the poem for a meeting that was less than three hours away. He read again the words that he had written in the prison cell so long ago. . .

Imprisoned in deep despair.

The chain rattled from his wrist.

Strength nor power could he find

In the rage of his clenched fist.

Through darkness alone there he sat…

How could he finish in such a short time what he had not been able to complete in over forty years? He knew the only answer to this question was to just begin. Thrusting his pen forward like a sword, he sat at the desk to begin the battle.

Unable to sleep, Edith decided to spend her time in the kitchen. She caught herself humming a few times. She had not always been able to do that in the past. It had been quiet upstairs in the past two hours since Howard had sat down at the table, but the running around and doors opening and closing upstairs seemed to clearly indicate the writing was done and dressing for the meeting had begun. She fought the temptation to walk up the stairs and check on his progress. Putting the finishing touches on shining the few pieces of silver she owned, she heard Howard clear his throat behind her. The five silver spoons in her hands hit the kitchen floor.

"HOWARD!" she gasped. "Howard, are you going to the meeting? You are dressed to go. . .?"

"Sure, I'm going to the meeting, Edith," he said confidently. "I finished it. I finished the poem. Here, I have just enough time to let you read it, get it copied, and still make the board meeting." Edith was unable to take her eyes off the knight, even when he placed the poem in her hand and moved gallantly across the kitchen. "Well, aren't you going to read it, Edith?"

"OH, yes. Sure. You actually finished it." Edith, slowly pulled her eyes from her husband and toward the paper he excitedly placed in her hand. As she read each word that had finally made the difficult journey to the paper, she could not hold back the tears. Looking at her newly-transformed husband, she didn't know whether to laugh or cry. "It's wonderful. It is your wisdom, Howard. Now go and share it."

Taking the treasure from his wife, he stepped back and clicked his heels. Removing his hat, he gave a sweeping bow and proclaimed, "I shall again return, My Lady," and then he headed for the door.

"I bet he isn't gonna show," Roadie said in a disappointed voice, tapping an unlit cigarette back and forth between his fingers and the table. "I had my doubts when he volunteered yesterday."

"He'll be here. Won't he, Joe?" Melvin asked, hoping for a positive response.

"I'd put my money on it, Melvin," Joe quickly replied, as he began his sandwich flipping ritual.

It was 7:32 and Howard was running late. Even with all the exciting changes that had begun to take place in this group of characters, they still liked their schedule and they still got nervous when someone broke the routine. Sammy had just come in from the parking lot, having completed the skateboarders' first tap dancing lesson. "Those poor kids don't even know who Jimmy Cagney is," Sammy said. "I think I'll have to work with them awhile."

"Hey, while we're waiting…" Hoover spoke up. "If it's okay with Roadie and Melvin I would like to make my presentation tomorrow morning."

"Okay by me!" Roadie said.

"Me, too," added Melvin.

"Great! Hey, why don't you all get here a little early and wear some work clothes?"

"Work clothes!" Leo huffed, "tell me how it really is, Hoover. Why work clothes?"

"Yeah, Hoove, fill us in," Joe said.

"LOOK!" Hoover yelled, nearly causing Leo to drop his coffee. "Look at what's coming in the door."

All eyes followed and then in unison, the entire table stood and asked in various tones, "HOWARD?"

Every head in McDonald's turned to watch the figure coming in the door. The long feather atop his hat bobbed with each step he took. The coat of mail covered the leather and cloth underdress. His leggings of silken purple led to strapped leather boots that resounded with the force of each step he took . Strapped to his side with a thick leather belt and a large hand-crafted buckle was a black sheath holding the sword that probably had seen many a battle.

Howard stopped at the table. No one knew what to say or do. He had made the impact he'd expected.

"Gentlemen, sorry I'm late. I had to have a discussion with a police-man around the corner as to the intent of my apparel."

"What did you tell him?" Sammy inquired.

"I said that I am what I am, and this is part of a very important meeting. Shall we get started?"

As the board members slowly settled into their seats, Joe was amazed at the confidence that this once-timid man was exuding.

"Melvin, with your permission I shall begin," Howard said, nodding in Melvin's direction.

Melvin returned the nod with an astonished look. Howard's attention quickly went to Roadie, who was again fiddling with the pack of cigarettes in his pocket.

"First of all, lad," Howard said, reaching out, snatching the pack of cigarettes, and crushing them without a second thought, "do you really need these?" With a flourish he quickly threw them in the trash.

Joe held his breath as Roadie mumbled, "No. No, I was thinking about throwing them away anyway."

"I thought so," Howard answered with a nod. "Gentlemen, for most of my life I've battled depression. I've tried to win this battle with pills and counseling, but the outcome always seemed hopeless. It is a battle brought on by a dragon, a dragon that lives within me and has called to me each day for as long as I can remember. It was not until last night that I was able to answer this call and stand before the dragon. I now feel that I have begun to win the battle against depression."

Howard went on to mesmerize his audience with every detail of the dream. The interpretation created great discussion among the board members. Each one was able to relate with the knight, the shackles, the dungeon, and the dragon.

126

"My wisdom that I pass on to you, my friends, is that we mustn't slay the dragon. Rather, we must answer its call and stand face to face with it so we can be made aware of who we really are. In discovering this, I was able to face my depression and my responsibility to become the person I really am." The facial expressions around the table indicated that some had fought the same battle and others still had a battle to fight. "I give you this poem as my gift. It was begun in that prison cell many years ago and completed as a free man only hours ago."

Howard moved around the table, handing each man a copy of the gift that had cost him so much. As they began to look at the words, Joe noticed Roadie's panicked reaction before he could hide it. "Howard, if you don't mind, we would be honored to have the author read his poem."

"YEAH!" Roadie responded, "do us the honor."

Joe was relieved as Howard said with his new-found confidence, "It would be my privilege."

Facing The Dragon Within

Imprisoned in deep despair,
The chain rattled from his wrist.
Strength nor power could he find
In the rage of his clenched fist.
Through darkness alone there he sat,
To once again hear the call.
From deep inside yet far away,
The dragon's howl beyond the castle wall.

To this dungeon he'd been bound,
A prisoner of his own past.
"Why me?" he thought this fate to be
Unknowing to each knight cast.
The chains of responsibility
Upon each one must fall.
To step beyond the pathway worn
And meet the dragon beyond the castle wall.

Freedom's key was always there,
Ever present shining bright.
Taking action will unlock the chain

To a journey in the night.
Leaving past to rest and always be
In the moment expecting all.
The future to bring rich reward
By answering the dragon's call.

Clothed in rags yet brave he sat
To the clanking of the bard.
His time had come, his weapon sharp
To fight the battle hard.
One long road no forks nor turns,
Leads to the dark forest grim.
The choice was one, to forward go
And meet the one within.

He knew this was the moment
Perched upon his mount in the clearing.
Bringing memories from his past,
The tormentor began appearing.
With death to his steed the battle began
Quickly bringing this knight to the ground.
Sword drawn to kill, a decision is made
As he recognized the dragon's sound.

It was himself he had fought
And then chosen not to kill.
Miraculously he was set free
With the dragon to exist still.
Traveling beyond the dark forest one will find
Many roads to bright horizons fall.
Giving choices and hope to each princess and knight
Who accepts the dragon's call.

The silence was broken when Hoover spoke. "Richard Burton couldn't have done it better, man."

"That's how it really is," Leo said with a smile. "We answer the dragon's call, we face him in the clearing, we take a closer look at ourselves and are freed when we discover who we are."

All that Sammy knew to do was stand and applaud; the others around the table did likewise. They were soon followed by the tables surrounding them. Then, to the board members' surprise, the entire McDonald's was standing and applauding. Everyone was touched by the reading of Howard's poem, perhaps because each one knew how true it was. After almost five minutes of standing ovation the crowd sat down. All eyes were on Howard as he wiped a tear from his eye and with a graceful swoop of his feathered hat, took a deep bow to thank them for their applause.

"Well," Melvin said, " I guess we could say 'meeting adjourned.' And a great meeting it was. Hoove, you have a hard act to follow."

"I'll do my best," Hoover responded. "Remember, bring your work clothes."

"Hey, I got a piece of sausage to deliver. Anybody want to come along?" Joe looked around the table.

It seemed that everybody was getting busier each day.

"I have another Old Wood Flowers meeting at the home," Leo said.

"Got some arrangements to make," Hoover added, barely able to contain himself..

"Can't do it, Joe. I thought I might visit the airport shoe shine stand. Just to spread a little smilin' to the young boys there," Sammy said.

"Melvin and I were going to go to Leo's meeting, Joe," Hoover added.

"How 'bout it, Howard, care to come along?" Joe asked, standing up from the table.

"Joe, I got a little business deal I want to run past Edith this morning. I'm thinking about opening a day care. Edith loves kids and I thought it just might be the thing to look into. I thought we would call it 'Little Dragons,' what do you think?"

"Sounds great, Howard." Joe said with a laugh, amazed at the changes taking place in the Board of Directors since his 'dead and dying' comment. "Well, I guess I'll see you all tomorrow then. Go get 'em, boys."

☞ CHAPTER 8 ☜

THE VALUE OF WORK

Joe's laugh was full and exuberant as he watched the little dog once again catch the sausage, run his lap, and jump to the porch to rest at his master's feet. Standing beneath the redbud's vibrant color, his laughter seemed to echo off each beautiful flower.

Mikey's smile was brighter than ever as he watched Joe enjoying a good belly laugh. "JoJo funny, isn't he, Joe?" came his bright voice from the porch.

"He sure is, Mikey. He likes sausage, doesn't he?"

"Likes it a lot," Mikey shouted back. "Joobas Joe?"

"Joobas? Oh, yeah, Joobas. They all were busy this morning, Mikey. They all had someplace else to go and couldn't come with me." For an instant Joe thought about what he had just said. Never before had he known the Board of Directors to be busy. For years they were all challenged to find something to do. Now, today they were all too busy. "That's great," Joe said to himself.

"Just Joe!" Joe quickly looked back and saw Jessie step out on the porch. For the first time Joe thought she actually looked rested. She was dressed in jeans and a sweatshirt that had a big red heart on it and the words "Mikey's Mom." Her normally unkempt hair was pulled back in a pony tail and her usually confused expression was replaced with a smile.

"What are you doing, Just Joe, clogging my dog's arteries with that sausage again?" She raised her mug of coffee toward Joe and said, "Hey, I got a cup of coffee here for ya. Would you like to visit with Mikey awhile?"

The whole scene of this wonderful little boy, the dog, a mother doing her best, the big red heart, the flowers on the redbud tree, the picket fence, the blue sky, and the great things happening to the lives of his friends caused a lump to form in Joe's throat. Wiping a tear from the corner of his eye he called back, "I would say it's a perfect morning to do just that."

"Here's the coffee, Just Joe. Do you take anything in it?"

"No, Jessie, this is great. Thanks."

"Good answer," she said as she moved back toward the door. "Go ahead, pull up a chair, and why don't the two of you see how many of the world's problems you can find solutions to this morning?" As she opened the screen door, she teased, "Hey, Mikey, don't let me catch you telling Joe any dirty jokes."

The loving look that passed between mother and son made Joe glad to be a part of the moment. "No jokes, Mom," Mikey said, returning her smile. "Just talk."

The porch grew quiet as the two friends looked at each other, wondering what to say next. JoJo's tail was beating against the spokes of the wheelchair as his eyes went back and forth from his master to their guest. "Beautiful redbud tree, Joe," Mikey said, breaking the silence.

"Very beautiful, Mikey." Joe smiled and looked at the amazing glow of pink coming from the corner of the yard.

"And magical?" Mikey asked.

"Very magical, Mikey," Joe responded, taking a sip of his coffee and studying the tree in wonderment. His thoughts were once again on the old man many years ago. "What is it all about, Ernest?" Joe thought as silence once again fell across the porch.

"How old are you, Joe?" came the timid voice.

Joe's attention left the tree and turned to the young face full of sincere curiosity. Through the wonder in his eyes, Joe saw another little boy many years before. The words seemed to fall naturally from his lips. "Oh, I'm real old, Mikey," Joe said with a smile as he rustled his young friend's hair with his hand.

"Well, are you a hundred?" Mikey asked with all seriousness.

Joe was taken aback as he realized life had come full circle.

"No, Mikey. I'm not a hundred yet, but I have lived a long time and I hope to live a lot longer," Joe said, surprising himself. There had been many days in the past years that he hadn't had a desire to live longer.

"I probably won't get old, Joe," Mikey said matter-of-factly.

Joe looked deeper into the little face staring at him gravely. "Mikey, no one knows if they will get old or not; we just have to do the best we can each day and hope we get old. We just don't know."

"I do know, Joe," Mikey said, without changing his expression. "I have a disease. Probably not going to get very old."

Joe again felt the lump move to his throat and hardly knew how to respond to the little boy's comments. All he could do was ask, "Well, how do you know, Mikey?"

"The doctors said so, Joe," Mikey began to explain. "My disease is called muscular pistrophy, I think. That's why I'm in this wheel chair. The doctor said it will keep my muscles from working right. Just like my legs don't work now and someday it might stop my other muscles from working. And that's why I probably won't get old, Joe."

Joe felt the tears break loose. A moment passed as he absorbed everything that Mikey had just told him. "You are a brave man, Mikey. A very brave man."

"Thanks, Joe."

Joe was putting his hanky back in his pocket when the knife fell into his hand. He stopped for an instant and placed the other hand in his jacket pocket, finding the old brittle chunk of wood. He cautiously looked over at Mikey, who returned his glance warmly.

"Mikey?" Joe said hopefully, "do you believe in magic?"

Mikey's eyes lit up. "Magic like the redbud tree, Joe?"

"Yeah, Mikey, just like it. Magic is a wonderful thing. But what's more wonderful is to be able to see magic. Not everyone can see magic. And that's too bad, because magic is all around us. Do you think you can see magic, Mikey?"

"I think I can, Joe."

Joe remembered the words of Ernest many years ago. "To see magic, Mikey, you must look past what you believe. If you think everything is just the way it seems and can't get beyond that, then you won't be able to see magic. Look past what others say; focus on greater possibilities. Then you will unveil the magic all around you."

Joe could see the wheels turning in his young friend's mind. Mikey was a smart child. He seemed to be grasping what Joe was saying. After a few seconds, Mikey spoke up. "Look past what the doctors say, Joe?"

Joe again felt the lump in his throat. "That's right, Mikey. Look past it and maybe you can find some magic." As the little face lit up with a glimmer of hope, Joe added, "Would you like to see some magic now, Mikey?"

"Yeah, Joe. Show me some magic."

Joe removed the piece of wood from his pocket and held it up in front of his little friend's face. "Mikey, do you believe this piece of wood can turn into a pocket knife?"

"A pocket knife, Joe?"

"Sure. Remember you have to look past what you believe to see the magic."

"I believe it can, Joe," Mikey said, smacking the tray of his wheelchair with excitement. "Show me, Joe. Show me."

As Joe performed the magic, the eyes of his young audience grew larger. He lowered his hand directly in front of Mikey's face. As Joe's fingers slowly started to open, the smile on Mikey's face began to glow; he squealed with excitement.

"I see it, Joe. I see the magic. The wood became a knife. I see the magic."

"Go ahead, Mikey. The knife is yours," Joe said as a warmth spread throughout his body. "You can have it."

Mikey raised his eyebrows in uncertainty as Joe extended his hand further. With an index finger he carefully rubbed the handle of the knife before grasping it and holding it up for close inspection.

"Thanks, Joe. Thanks a lot. I saw the magic. Thanks, Joe." JoJo let out a little bark as if to thank Joe, too, for putting such a smile on his master's face.

"I used that knife to cut flowers from redbuds when I was a boy. I used to give them to my mom. Maybe you can. . ." Joe stopped, knowing that Mikey didn't have the same opportunities to run and cut the branches as he had had. The steps on this porch were his boundary and the porch the extent of his little world.

The porch again grew silent as Joe sipped his coffee and Mikey observed every detail of his new prized possesion. "You know what else is magic, Mikey? You are an artist. You can draw like magic."

"I know, Joe. I like to draw."

"Hey, Mikey, do you know how to draw dragons?"

Mikey looked amazed that a grownup would ask such a great question. "I draw lots of dragons," Mikey said, as he began to move his wheelchair around and laboriously head toward the screen door. "I'll be right back, Joe. I got to get something. I got lots of dragons, Joe," Mikey yelled back through the screen door.

Joe smiled and finished the last of his coffee as Mikey excitedly worked his way back out of the house. "I have lots of dragons, Joe," Mikey said, bubbling with excitement. "Look. Here is funny dragons, and baby dragons, scary dragons, and this is one that flies with big wings. I like this dragon, Joe. He is a brave dragon, he is the leader of other dragons. I pretend he is very friendly and likes to help people. He is my favorite."

Joe picked this one up and looked at it. He was again startled by Mikey's talent. The expression and detail were incredible. "This is magical, Mikey. What is this dragon's name?"

Without a moment's hesitation Mikey answered. "Just Joe."

"Mikey, I believe I've had more tears in my eyes this morning than I've had in the last forty years combined," Joe said, once again pulling his hanky from his pocket and blowing his nose.

"Are you sad, Joe?" Mikey asked.

"No, Mikey, I believe I'm happier than I've been in a long time."

"You can have that dragon picture, Joe. If you want."

"Thanks, Mikey. I want it. I'm hanging all of your pictures on my wall at home and this one will look great." Joe looked down at all the paper and markers spread across the tray of Mikey's wheelchair. It truly was magic.

"Hey! What is this?" Joe asked, picking up one of Mikey's drawings. "This looks like Hoover measuring the front porch. Hey, Mikey, when did you draw this?"

"UH-oh," came Mikey's reply, wondering what he should say next. "Surprise, Joe. I don't know."

"More coffee, Just Joe? OH. . . Oh." Jessie saw the drawing in Joe's hand and knew he would be wondering what was going on. She decided to act fast and get Joe moving. Besides, the phone call said that the delivery would be coming soon. "Hey, Joe, probably time to be going, don't you think? Too much coffee wouldn't be good for you. And Mikey needs to come in and we'll see you tomorrow. I mean, if you want to come around. Not that it's planned or anything. Just if you might happen to be here, we'll see you then." A smile crossed Jessie's face as she saw the gleam in Joe's eyes.

"You're right, Jessie. I better be going. I might stop back tomorrow." He winked at Mikey, who was rearranging the markers and papers on his tray, wondering if he had goofed or not. "Mikey, can I have this picture, too?"

"Sure, Joe," Mikey said, glad for the interest in his drawings.

"Thanks for the coffee, Jessie, and for giving me and Mikey time to discuss the issues of the world this morning."

"Anytime, Just Joe. Thanks for caring."

"Hey, Jessie," Joe said, stepping out on the sidewalk and shutting the gate behind him. "I gave Mikey a knife. It was mine when I was a boy. He promised he would be careful with it. I hope you don't mind."

"Don't mind at all, Joe. He's a big boy. Did he say thanks, though?"

"In more ways than I can begin to tell you, Jessie," Joe said, turning his direction to the redbud. "The tree is beautiful, isn't it?"

"Magical, Just Joe. Magical," she said, putting her hand on Mikey's shoulder as they watched Joe glide down the street.

Joe was standing on the street corner waiting for the light to change as he stared at his newest works of art. The magic of the past few days was almost more than he could comprehend. The bus beside him revved its engine and began to move through the light. Glancing up, Joe saw all the people looking down at him and realized that, one by one, each was returning his smile, adding to the beauty of the day. Then he saw him sitting in the back seat. That familiar long, stringy, gray hair caused Joe to gasp. And there was the scar on the side of his face. The man gave a slow wave, a big smile, and a wink as the bus moved down the road.

"ERNEST!" Joe shouted as the bus pulled away. "Ernest." Joe could hardly believe it. He knew that he'd seen him, but was it possible? Joe felt that after the past couple days anything was possible, but how could it be? Unlocking the door to his apartment, Joe shook his head and quickly went to work hanging the copy of Howard's poem and Mikey's drawings on the wall next to the others. He looked forward to whatever it was that Hoover had planned for them, and the wisdom that would go under the picture of him measuring the porch.

Hoover was like a kid at Christmas as everyone started showing up for the board meeting. He called Sammy in from his skateboarding lesson in the parking lot and acknowleged the stylish bright red overalls that Howard had worn as his work clothes for the day. He was so excited that he couldn't even sit down to eat his breakfast.

Leo, after being asked again to hurry up and eat, set his fork down and laughed, "Tell me how it really is, Hoover. What is the wisdom you are going to teach us today? How to be a nut?"

Leo's comment made everyone chuckle. Sammy, with his smile intact added, "Hoover, you're acting like you're up to somethin', man... what is it? What are you going to tell us about?"

Hoover finally stood still long enough to acknowledge the questions, and taking a deep breath said, "I'm going to tell you about WORK. But I'm going to do more than tell you, I'm going to show you. So hurry up, we've got a lot of work to do."

"I hope this work doesn't include moving you out of your apartment and into Joe's apartment," Roadie said, reaching for an empty pocket where his cigarettes used to be. This caused Howard to smile as he and Roadie exchanged a friendly nod. "He's not moving in with you, is he, Joe?"

Joe just shrugged his shoulders lightheartedly, captivated by the enthusiasm and camaraderie around the boardroom table. He had a good idea where the group was going to end up today.

"Hey, I'm not moving out of or into any place," Hoover said, throwing his chest out a little. "I got that all handled. I was hired to do some small engine repair work at a landscape company. Thanks to your lead, Joe, the guy hired me. I've been working the past two evenings and really enjoying it." Hoover threw a high-five to a surprised Roadie as the rest of the board congratulated him. "So let's get going. I've got a lot planned for today and I'm not real sure how much this crew is capable of doing."

"Hey, Hoover, you just point us in the direction, we'll get the work done," Howard said, brushing a few breakfast crumbs from his new overalls.

"Okay then, let's get out of here," Hoover said, picking up his old brief-case and some rolled-up plans. "Joe, don't forget to bring that piece of sausage." Hoover was standing out in the parking lot before the rest of the board members were barely out of their seats.

"Well, this meeting is adjourned," Melvin said with a smile. "We'd better hurry or he's going to leave without us."

Once the group had gathered in the parking lot Hoover began to speak. "Stay close because I'm going to tell you about something I just discovered while we take a walk over to Mikey's house. Let's go, we'll walk and talk." Hoover had them moving in unison down the street. "Here is what I've discovered. I hate work. Or at least I hated work. It was the dragon I had to face, I guess, Howard."

"And it would be a ferocious one at that, Lad," Howard returned in his best Old English knight's dialect.

"Right," Hoover continued. "From the time I was six years old I was up at 5:00 a.m. and out in the barn helping my father and uncles milk the cows. There was never any choice about staying in bed. The work had to be done and I had to help. No compromises. My family owned a farm outside Urbandale, Iowa. It was hard work in those days, as I'm sure it is even now. But they did it, and no one ever complained. No one except me, that is. I soon realized that my complaining wasn't gettin' me anywhere except in trouble with my dad and his brothers, so I resorted to fast talking. I could always talk my way into the easier jobs and let the others do the harder, heavier jobs. That is how my life as a child went, working harder to get out of work than doing the work itself."

In the short distance they had traveled, Hoover had grabbed the board's attention with his openness and honesty. Melvin tried to comfort Hoover somewhat by saying, "Everybody experiences that, Hoove. But we usually grow out of it."

"That was the problem, Melvin, I never grew out of it. When I graduated from high school I stayed around the farm for the summer. My father was a wise man. He knew I was never going to be a farmer, no matter what he did, but he thought I would make a great salesman. That was his idea of a salesman, anyway. Someone who could talk but didn't like to work. What he didn't realize, as some of you who have sold over the years might know, is that sales is hard work. Anyway, he asked one of his friends that he bought equipment from to give me a job selling farm machinery. I was a hit the first couple of months. I was real good at closing sales but too lazy to do the paper work and follow-up with my customers. Soon there were lots of complaints and late deliveries; I started blaming everyone but myself for the problems. I quit and went to another company. Eventually I got frustrated there and quit. I started hanging around companies only long enough to get fired."

Hoover stopped before making the turn down Horizons Drive. Following his lead, the entire group stopped. Hoover said with disgust, "I counted them up last night. Would you believe I have quit or been fired from fifty-two jobs in the the past fifty-four years? That is a record I am definitely not proud of. So you see, Melvin," he said as he turned down Horizons Drive towards the white picket fence, "I never grew out of it, until this week. I've started my fifty-third job and have decided that I'm going to love this work. I'm going to apply and share the work ethic that my father and uncles tried so hard to teach me so many years ago, and I'm going to start sharing it today."

The conversation stopped right in front of Mikey's house. "Hi, Joe," came a voice from the porch.

"Mikey, this is a surprise. Did you know about this?" Joe asked with a smile, reaching out to pat Hoover on the back.

Mikey was grinning from ear to ear. "Wanted to surprise you, Joe. Look at the stuff, Joe."

As Mikey pointed, the Board studied the orderly pile of lumber in the front yard. The two-by-twos, two-by-fours, and two-by-sixes were in separate stacks; next to them lay six four-by-four posts and two bags of concrete. Arranged purposely behind the wood were the tools. There were three shovels, a post hole digger, a rake, and a wheelbarrow. Next to two saw horses were a power saw, a drill, an electric sander, some wrenches, and a big box of nails. Spread across the top of a make-shift table constructed from two more saw horses and a piece of plywood were seven nail pouches.

"Hoover, this looks like quite a job site," Melvin said as the entire group surveyed the scene from outside the picket fence.

"Yeah, it looks great," Hoover said, scrutinizing every detail.

"Where did you get all this stuff, Hoover?" Howard asked, doing some mental calculations. "There must be a couple hundred dollars in materials alone and the tools and all. . . how did you do it?"

Leo laughed, "I'll tell you how it really is. You are certainly the financial man of this board, Howard. A true chief financial officer."

"Thank you, my friend," Howard returned with a tip of his hat and a bow.

"I just asked," Hoover said. "My first evening at work I was talking with the owner. He was there late and I was fixing a particular lawnmower that they just couldn't get running right. We talked as I worked. The conversation went to Mikey and I told him what I had in mind. Then I started the mower and it ran perfectly. I don't know if he was so happy that I got it going, or if he is a charitable guy, but he said to tell him what I needed and he would donate the wood and let me borrow the tools. So here we are."

"Man, that sounds like one great guy," Sammy said as a camera clicked from the porch.

Everyone turned to see Jessie standing with camera in hand. "I caught that smile, Sammy," she said with unguarded appreciation for what was happening.

"You got you a picture of some 'raccoons' didn't ya?" Sammy quipped.

"Hey, I welcome raccoons in this yard any time." Jessi winked in Joe's direction.

"Hey, Hoove, what are we building here anyway?" Roadie asked with excited anticipation.

"Great question," Hoover replied, as he stepped through the gate and was greeted by a quick bark from JoJo on the porch. Everyone followed Hoover into the yard and up to the table he had set up. He took the plans from under his arm and with a look of concentration unrolled his project for all to see.

"The other day when I was here with Joe I noticed that, although this is a great porch for Mikey to spend his day on, there isn't a lot of room for him to go exploring. I began thinking that if he had a ramp to move off the porch and down into the yard, it might be a better situation for him. I first got his mother's approval, and then I talked to Mikey about it. He thought it was a great idea too, so here is the plan for Mikey's ramp to the world." Hoover stepped to the side so the entire group could see it.

"Hoover, did you draw these?" Melvin asked, obviously impressed with the details.

"Yes, I did." His concentration continued to grow. "I had to do a little research first. I found out that ramps for people in wheelchairs need to be no more than an eight percent rise. The porch is exactly two feet high."

"That means the ramp needs to be at least sixteen feet long," Howard said, not able to control his enthusiasm for numbers.

"Right you are, oh Earl of Arithmetic." Hoover laughed and the others joined in. Howard gave proper acknowledgment with a deep bow and a sweeping of the hat.

"Tell me," Leo said, scratching his head, "are you going to make a habit of that bowing stuff?"

"A group as noble as this deserves a noble gesture, my dear Leo," came Howard's reply as he continued to study the plans on the table.

"I knew you were going to," Leo said.

"Okay. Time's wasting here," Hoover said, bringing everyone back into focus. "I figured we would add another foot to make it even a little easier to move up and down. That means we will need sets of posts here, here, and here for support. We will run a stringer out of the two-by-sixes between the posts and then tie them together with two-by-six joists running on two foot centers. Then it will be a matter of putting a decking on with two-by-fours. The posts will extend up and we will make a railing out of the remainder of the two-by-fours and use the two-by-twos as spindles. With seven of us working on this project, we should be done by noon."

"NOON!" Roadie exclaimed. "No way we can get this done by noon, man!"

"That is a pretty tight schedule, Hoove," Melvin said. "Do you really think we can do it?"

"I don't only think it, I guarantee it," Hoover said confidently as he turned to the second page of his plans, revealing a sheet with large writing on it. "Gentlemen, this is the wisdom I bring to you. This comes from an Iowa farm, heard and observed many years ago but understood and learned only in the past couple days."

WORK

1. Be careful to recognize lack of ambition when it is disguised as frustration.

2. The best work we can do is to help someone, and all the work that we do helps someone.

3. Make your work easier and faster by knowing that time spent planning will greatly reduce the time spent executing the work.

4. Hard work will not kill you; in fact, hard work when enjoyed will help you live longer.

5. Celebrating success will put fun into each task you perform.

"Those are pretty simple principles to follow, Hoover," Joe said. "One thing is for certain, every person probably needs to be reminded of them at some point in time. Maybe even every day."

"I'm not sure about every person, Joe," Hoover said, continuing to study the words on the page, "but I know I need to be reminded of them. That first one about lack of ambition disguised as frustration is what I was telling all of you about on the walk over here. Fifty-two jobs in fifty-four years. And through all those years I felt someone was cheating me and taking advantage of me, so I wouldn't put any effort into my job and would soon be fired. The only person taking advantage and cheating was me. I was taking advantage of the employers who hired me, or of my customers when I had my own business. In the end I cheated myself. Fifty-four years is a lot of time to be cheated out of."

Hoover brought his eyes up from the table and looked around. He could tell that his friends were calculating where they had cheated themselves as well. Knowing it was time to lighten things up, Hoover reared back and let out a holler. With a hearty "YEEEEEH HAAAAAAA AHHOOOOOOOOEY WWEEEEEE!" everyone jumped back from the table. JoJo started barking, Mikey started laughing, and Jessie came running out of the house.

"What was that all about?" she asked, stopping on the edge of the porch.

"That's how my Uncle Bert used to call pigs back on the farm," Hoover explained with a big boyish grin. "My dad said that one time he heard Uncle

Bert calling the pigs on the farm, and he was all the way in Iowa City over a hundred miles away. Do you think that's true, Sammy?" Hoover asked with a wink.

"I don't know if it's true, but if I had to hear that too many times I would have certainly been moving to where I couldn't hear it."

"You know something else my Uncle Bert would say? 'Better to learn it later than never.' So maybe it just took me a while." Hoover raised his hand and gave an enthusiastic high-five to Sammy.

"Now, we gotta keep movin' here," Hoover said, bringing their attention back to the table and the wisdom. "Next is 'The best work we can do is to help someone, and all the work that we do helps someone.' This wisdom is exactly why we are here. I learned growing up that whenever there was a need, the best thing someone could do was step up and fill that need. When I was eleven the neighbor's barn burnt down and it was a big barn. He lost about a third of his cows and most of his machinery in the blaze. By morning neighbors had come from all around to start the cleanup. I remember the atmosphere. I wondered why everyone was so happy. This man's barn had just burned down and his family was going to suffer a great loss. Yet, the farm felt like a fair. There was food, and people were hustling all around. By the end of that day there wasn't a trace of that burnt barn left. The next day at sunup the lumber was waiting. I never knew how or who got it there. It was just there. Then it started. People gathered around and everyone just seemed to fill up the farm. Some were measuring and some were hammering; others cut and hauled materials. In two days that barn was back up and under roof. Then another amazing thing happened. By early afternoon cows started showing up in the backs of trucks. Every neighbor donated a cow or two just to help the family get their herd built back up. A few even delivered extra tractors. Then, as quickly as everyone had arrived, they were gone; the family who could have suffered an incredible loss had gained, instead, insight into the quality of their neighbors and what work can do for the human spirit."

"That is a great example, Hoove," Melvin said. "That's why we are here. That young man has a need and we can fill it. I'm excited about that."

"Don't forget the last part of this wisdom, Melvin. Any work we do can help someone. Sometimes it is just more apparent than others. If we work in a factory we might be making brakes for a car that will protect a family and help them get safely to their destination. If being a waiter in a restaurant was our calling, then delivering that food in a warm and professional way would help customers enjoy their meal and leave feeling better than when they came in. Every job we perform, every task we do, can really be traced to helping someone. If we realize that, we can always be enthusiastic, just as enthusiastic as those neighbors were while building that barn, or as we can be as we build this ramp for Mikey. No matter what the task, we should do it with enthusiasm, knowing we are helping someone."

"That's telling it like it really is, Hoover," Leo said, absorbing every word.

"Okay, one more piece of wisdom here; it will help us get to work on this important project. The third point, 'Make your work easier and faster by knowing that time spent planning will greatly reduce the time spent executing that work.' I know now that's why the neighbor's barn went up so fast. It was planned, everyone knew his role, and they went out and did it. If I heard my dad say this once I heard it a thousand times, 'For every minute you spend planning the job, you reduce the time it takes to do it by the same number of minutes. And planning time is always easier and cheaper than doing time.' When it was planting time or harvest time, my dad and uncles would always eat dinner together. I used to get mad, because all they ever talked about was the work that was going to take place the next day. But I know now that they were actually planning carefully. It was the only way they could have possibly gotten the enormous amount of work done that they had to do."

"Can we apply the same idea here on this project, gentlemen?"

"YES!" came back the enthusiastic, unanimous decision from the board members.

"YES!" came the echo back from the front porch. Mikey was listening intently to every word being said, which caused all of them to laugh and welcome the response from the youngest member of the board.

"Well, let's get started," Hoover continued. "As I see it, we need somebody to take the post hole diggers and dig six holes to put our posts in and then pour the concrete around them. Any takers?"

"Hey, I know how to operate those things," Roadie said. "Last time I used a pair of them I was setting up the stage at Woodstock. Don't remember much about all that but I can use those things. How 'bout it, Melvin, want to give me a hand? This way we can put the biker and the Marine on the tough job."

"You got it, Roadie. I dug a few holes in my day. Let's get started."

"Great!" Hoover said. "You can be the blister brigade. The holes need to be about two and a half feet deep right where I set those stakes. Next we need someone to remove the section of railing to the left of the steps. That's where the ramp is going to come onto the porch."

"I volunteer for that one," Joe said. "I'm not real good at building, but I'll bet I can take apart with the best of 'em."

"I can help with that, too," Leo spoke up.

"All right, men, it's yours," Hoover continued. "That pile of two-by-twos needs to be measured and marked into thirty-inch pieces so they can be cut for spindles to form the railing."

"I volunteer for the task, my Lord!" Howard said gallantly. "With numbers and accuracy there is no finer man than I."

"All right, Sir Howard," Hoover laughed. "As I calculate, we will need approximately forty-eight of them marked."

"Consider it done," replied Howard, picking up a nail pouch and tying it around his waist. He took the tape measure and moved toward the pile of lumber.

"I guess that leaves you and me, Sammy, to man the saw and do the cutting," Hoover said, looking in Sammy's direction. "Are you up to it?"

Sammy's was beaming from the morning's festivities. "Hoove, you are looking at a man who knows how to work with his hands. I'll get it plugged in and the saw horses set up. You just show me where to lay down the first cut."

"You bet, Sammy," Hoover replied as he surveyed the action that was starting to take place. "All right, everybody has their job to do. Let's get this ramp built by noon."

Joe looked at Hoover and cleared his throat to get his attention. Hoover quickly looked at Joe, who returned his glance with a nod toward the porch.

"Oh, I almost forgot!" exclaimed Hoover. "I have a box of nuts and bolts here that needs to be separated, and the washers put onto the bolts so we can bolt the stringers onto the posts when they are ready. Who wants this very important job?"

"Me!" came a very enthusiastic and relieved voice from the front porch. "I can do that job."

"Great, Mikey," Hoover said as he set the box of washers, nuts, and bolts on the wheelchair tray. "All right, everybody, we have some work to do."

Jessie walked out the door to a flurry of activity. With the beautiful backdrop of the redbud's flowers glowing from the corner of the yard, she looked at each of the old men working. They were either whistling, humming, or joking with someone, but every one of them was busy and enthusiastic about the job they were doing. At that moment, the hard heart that she had acquired over the years toward men and old people began to soften. The transformation was evident in the tears she was wiping from her face.

"We need them," she thought to herself. "We need old people so desperately. They know so much and could teach all of us if we would only give them a chance. Old wood flowers, and beautiful flowers they are."

"Look, Mom, nuts, bolts, and washers. This is an important job."

Jessie moved to her son's side and knelt next to him. "That is because you are a very important man, Mikey," she said. "Look, Mikey, at these other important men," she whispered. "They are doing this for you. I know you will always remember this day."

Joe glanced over his shoulder and smiled at the mother and son who were learning a great lesson together.

"MAN, I'm using muscles I haven't used in years," Roadie said, stretching his back after completing his half of the sixth hole. "Feels great, don't it, Melvin?"

"It feels great to be using muscles again, all right," Melvin answered. "I feel alive."

"That is the fourth point on my list," Hoover said, setting the saw down and walking over to the table. "'Hard work will not kill you; in fact, hard work, when enjoyed, will help you live longer.' One thing I always noticed when I sold farm equipment back there in the Midwest; was how many old farmers I would run into. I'll tell you, I can think of maybe a dozen ol' boys who were in their nineties, but looked like they were in their sixties and were still out on a tractor every day. And at that age, they must have started their farming careers when it was really hard work. Like working behind horses rather than a John Deere tractor. I don't know why it didn't sink in back then, probably because I wouldn't let it, but it was obvious that these farmers worked hard and enjoyed what they were doing. As a result they were living long lives."

"How about the hard working executive," Joe began, "who puts in an eighty-hour week. He gives his all to his job and then drops dead of a heart attack at age forty-two. How do you get the wife and kids he left behind to believe that hard work won't kill you?"

"Joe, that is a mystery, isn't it?" Hoover responded. "I certainly don't know a lot about executives. But I'm going to guess that it wasn't the work, it was the stress, and there is a difference. A lot of people believe it is the work that brings the stress, but it isn't. There can be two executives working the same job. One has the work done when it needs to be done. This executive is home on time, able to eat dinner with the family, go to the kid's school events, and take a family vacation each summer. The other executive is the opposite. Works eighty hours a week, bringing home two briefcases each night. Complains that there is never time for exercise or time off and can barely remember the kids' names, not to mention their ages or the date of his wedding anniversary. But it's hard to learn that until it's too late. There is certainly a difference between hard work and working hard. When you strive to enjoy your work, then you are never really working hard. The instant you take the enjoyment out of it, the working becomes hard and stress comes into the picture; unfortunately, the rest could be history."

"Hey, Hoover, you're starting to make some sense," Sammy said. "Now how about making some sense out of these spindles. Howard has them measured. You want to start cutting on them now?"

"Great, Sammy, let's do it."

Roadie was tightening the last bolt that attached the railing to the ramp when he stood up, brushed his knee off, and said, "Just like wrenchin' on my Harley."

"Hey, we're done!" Howard said. "And it is exactly 11:53 and a couple of seconds. We did it, lads! Done before noon. It should be knighthood for all of us."

They took turns congratulating each other with high-fives and cheers. Mikey was clapping and laughing as Jessie came out of the house. "Gentlemen, you are tremendous!"

"Not bad for a bunch of raccoons, huh?" Hoover asked with a laugh, giving a high-five first to Sammy and then to Mikey.

"Not bad at all, Hoover. Thank you, thank you all very much," Jessie said, returning Hoover's high-fives.

Just then a horn beeped in front of the house. "Right on time," Hoover said.

"Hey, it's Lanny, the manager from McDonald's. What brings him here?" Melvin asked.

"I told him we would be done at noon and requested that he send a bag of cheeseburgers with all the trimmings for lunch. He told me it would be no problem. Anything for the Board of Directors," Hoover beamed.

"Hey, Mr. Hoover, here's your order," Lanny called, walking through the gate and followed by another young man in a tie with a notebook in his hand. He set the food on the plywood table and introduced the man with him. "Gentlemen, this is Jim Johnson from the L.A. Times. He's a good friend of mine so I called him about you and what you were doing today. I invited him to come along and meet each of you."

"Wow! We didn't know… I didn't know what we were doing today would be newsworthy," Hoover said, amazed that the L.A. Times was here.

"It is very newsworthy, sir," Jim Johnson said, stepping forward to shake Hoover's hand. "Any time a group of citizens gets together to make a difference in the community, I'm very interested because my readers are very interested. Do you mind if I ask a few questions while you are eating your lunch?"

"We have one more thing to do, Hoover, before eating lunch," Joe said, once again clearing his throat and motioning toward the front porch.

"OH YEAH!" Hoover said. "We need to see if this ramp will work or not. Mikey, are you ready to give it a try?"

Mikey looked at the ramp, then at Joe, and finally up at his mother. Nervously he said, "I'm ready, Mr. Hoover."

"Do you want help, Mikey?" Joe asked, stepping forward and then stopping himself, knowing what the answer would be.

"No, Joe. I can do it." He moved his wheelchair to the top of the ramp, looking down the seventeen feet that led to a whole new world, free from the limitations of the porch that had been the extent of his world in the past. Slowly he moved onto the ramp; time stood still. The eyes of every person standing in the yard were fixed on the little figure moving down the ramp, followed by his faithful companion. As he reached the bottom, his eyes were glued to the redbud. He moved between the two lines that the Board of Directors formed at the bottom of the ramp and then across the grass toward the tree. The only sound was the squeak coming from the slow rotation of the chair's wheels. As he reached the tree, he looked up and touched the flowers on a branch that was within his reach. He then took his new pocket knife out and cut several short branches that were full of blossoms. Putting his knife back in its place, he laid the flowers in his lap and turned the wheelchair back around. With purpose he moved back toward the ramp. This time his eyes were fixed on his mother, who was standing at the top of the ramp with tears of joy streaming down her face. He slowly moved his wheelchair back through the Board of Directors and up the ramp. Stopping in front of his mother, he reached into his lap and lifted the beautiful branches lined with pink flowers up to her. Her trembling hands reached out and cupped his little hands as she received the precious gift.

"I got these flowers for you, Mom," came the angelic voice.

"Thank you, Mikey. They are beautiful," she said as she gave him a hug and kissed his face. Then standing with the redbud branches in her hand, she looked down at the row of dear old men, each with a hanky in hand, and simply said, "Thanks to all of you, too."

Her words were greeted with a chorus of honks that would have scared any goose in the neighborhood. Putting his hanky back in his pocket, Hoover shouted out, "Let's eat! Mikey, bring yourself down here and eat with the rest of these carpenters."

Mikey zipped down the ramp a little faster this time and found his place among the men at the plywood table. The reporter asked them questions as they ate. They talked about Ernest, the wisdom shared to this point, and the redbud tree. They told him about old wood flowering both on the tree and in life. And they told him about Mikey and why they had tackled this project.

"It is magical," Sammy said, flashing a big smile.

"You want to know what's magical?" Jim Johnson asked, setting his notebook and pen down. "The enthusiasm of this group of senior citizens."

"Oh, call us old people," Melvin spoke up. "We don't mind. We've grown to like being old."

"Yeah, go ahead and tell it like it really is," Leo said. "We are old people."

"I mean it," Jim Johnson continued, " I have had the privilege of inter-viewing a lot of famous people, but never do I remember any one person or group with more zest and a more positive outlook than the group sitting around this table. I really appreciate that you are celebrating life rather than dreading it."

"CELEBRATION!" Hoover shouted. " I almost forgot the fifth point."

"Well, go ahead and tell us, Hoover," Melvin said. "The morning just wouldn't be complete without it."

Hoover moved a few of the McDonald's bags out of the way and read the fifth point. "Celebrate your success and it will help to make each task you perform fun." Remember the barn story I told you about earlier this morning?"

"Sure," everyone replied.

"Well, on that second day after all the cows were delivered and the equipment set inside, everyone got in their trucks and headed home. You know what they did when they got home, Mikey?" Hoover asked, giving the boy a chance to speak in the group.

Without hesitation Mikey said, "They went to the bathroom."

The response brought a chuckle from the board and sat Hoover back in his seat.

"Well, how did you know?" Hoover laughed. "That is exactly what happened. They went home, went to the bathroom, got cleaned up real good, put on some good clothes, and then headed right back to the barn they had just raised and had themselves a barn dance. There were mounds of food and pies; the men brought their fiddles and banjos and guitars, and we danced well into the evening. It was a celebration for the project they had just completed. It added to the fun and accomplishment and made the work go faster because they had been looking forward to this celebration all day."

Hoover picked up his briefcase from under the plywood table. "Now here is a smaller copy of the five points we talked about." He handed a copy to everyone, including Mikey, and then pulled a cassette tape out of his briefcase and continued to speak. "We will finish the morning by celebrating the building of the ramp. Jessie, do you have the music box plugged in?"

"I have it right here, Hoover," she said, pointing to the boom box sitting on the edge of the porch.

"Great. Now we are going to have a square dance, and I brought a little Lester Flatt and Earl Scruggs to help us out." As the music began to fill the yard, Hoover started to clap his hands and stomp his feet. "Come on, Mikey, let's square dance." Hoover was moving Mikey around in his wheelchair, his happy laughs and squeals heard even over the loud fiddle music. Howard was drawn to his feet and began to dance a little jig and dosey-do with Hoover. By now every hand was clapping and every foot was tapping. It only took a little coaxing from Hoover and Howard before the entire Board of Directors was up and dancing around inside the picket fence, with the redbud tree in full bloom as their backdrop.

The newspaper reporter and Jessie were both snapping pictures and laughing out loud at the sight. The laughter and joy were evidence of more than a celebration of a ramp being built. Young and old knew it was a celebration of life itself.

When the music died down and they were preparing to go home, all eyes turned toward Roadie and Melvin. Which one was going to volunteer for tomorrow's lesson? Roadie stepped forward and said, "You know I wasn't sure I could do this presentation stuff, because I don't read very well and I write even worse, but I think I can do it. I got an idea. So if it's okay, I'll speak tomorrow."

"The floor is yours, Roadie," Joe said with relief. "Back to our regular time at McDonald's tomorrow."

Everyone took one last look around as they began filing out the little gate. It was as if they didn't want the moment to end. Their waves to Mikey and Jessie were returned with as big a wave and a heartfelt "thank you."

The Board of Directors had learned a great lesson.

⊂ CHAPTER 9 ⊃

INSPIRATION IN EVERYTHING

*T*here were people outside waiting to get in. The music let the crowd know that something different was taking place this morning.

"Joe, hey! Hey, Joe!" Joe turned to see Sammy's bright smile beaming at him from the crowd filling the parking lot. "Man, what is going on... all these people and the music...?"

Joe just shook his head, trying to take it all in. "Hey, you are some of the old men..." came a voice from the crowd that stopped Joe and Sammy outside the door. "You are two of the guys in the paper," the enthusiastic young lady was saying. "Look. Didn't you see the paper this morning? Isn't that you guys dancing in the picture on the front page? Look."

She handed them the paper. They stared in disbelief and then Sammy yelled, "Hey, that's us!"

The picture on the front page of the Los Angeles Times was the seven board members with Mikey in the middle. They were caught in the action of dancing. Mikey's eyes were brighter than ever and Jessie was in the background holding the redbud branches. Underneath the picture was the caption MAKING A DIFFERENCE...

Joe was beaming. He had been wondering whether all that had been happening in the past week was going to make a difference to anyone. And now, here was his answer in bold print on the front page of the Los Angeles Times with a picture to prove it. Their efforts were making a difference. A big difference. His thoughts went to Ernest. "You're still talking to me aren't you, Ernest? Only now you're using the front page of the L.A. Times." Joe looked up from the paper and then handed it back to the young lady.

"Hey, why don't you sign it?" she asked.

"Sign it?" Joe responded with surprise as he looked at Sammy, who gave a shrug that seemed to say "why not?"

"Sure, you know, an autograph," she said, handing back the paper, this time with a pen.

Joe had never given an autograph before. He hardly knew what to write, but the pen just seemed to move in his hand, "Old Wood Flowers, Joe Yamka." He smiled and then handed it to Sammy, who quickly wrote "Keep

Smilin,' Sammy." As he handed the paper back there were requests for more from the crowd gathered around.

"Hey, you two, you're going to be late for a meeting." Joe and Sammy looked toward the door to see the manager, Lanny Smith, come walking toward them, trying to part the crowd. "Come on, the rest of the board is here, you don't want to be late for the meeting. . . Did you see the article, Joe? You guys really impressed Jim Johnson yesterday. Wow! Front page of the Los Angeles Times." Lanny had finally reached them and, guiding Joe by the arm, again parted the crowd and moved Joe and Sammy through the door.

"Is all this commotion for us?" Sammy asked.

"I guess you could say that," Lanny said.

"Well, we're sorry for the trouble," Joe responded.

Lanny stopped in his tracks and looked right at Joe. "Are you kidding? This will be a record-breaking breakfast morning, thanks to you." Lanny opened the door and cleared a path for the two celebrities to come through.

"Hey, Lanny, where is all the music coming from?" Joe's chin nearly hit the ground as the last words rolled off his lips. His question was soon answered. He could see the speakers that were stacked from floor to ceiling. There were little ones and big ones stacked in two identical columns about ten feet apart. Suspended in between the columns was a big screen television showing a clear picture of a sunrise over the ocean. The lights above the speakers would have rivaled any stage production. About fifteen feet away, to the left of the audio-video extravaganza, was a big board with lots of knobs and buttons and dials. Standing at the central board, meticulously making last minute touches, was Roadie.

He looked different this morning. His red bandana was gone and his gray hair was pulled back into a chic ponytail. His ungroomed beard was now neatly trimmed. The Harley Davidson T-shirt was replaced with a clean and pressed blue denim shirt, complemented with blue jeans and shiny black boots. The music coming through the speakers sounded like a live version of Bob Dylan's "Blowin' in the Wind."

Above the big screen TV and between the columns of speakers was a banner which read... "INSPIRATION IN EVERYTHING."

"I think this setup has added to the crowd this morning," Lanny laughed as he looked at Joe and Sammy. "Yesterday afternoon Roadie came by and asked if he could do a little extra setting up for his presentation this morning. Of course I said it was okay and told him he could be here as early as five a.m. Well, he was waiting here with a delivery truck and a couple other "roadies" when I drove up just before five. He started rolling in all of this equipment and as people started coming through the drive-through and stopping at the counter the rumors started to fly that there was going to be a free concert this morning. The more he set up, the more people showed up, and then when the article came out in the paper this morning, more people arrived. The next thing we knew we had a crowd on our hands."

"This is incredible," Sammy said to himself.

"Hey, Joe and Sammy. Let me tell you how it really is," came Leo's excited voice as they walked up to the table. "There's no telling what this group of old birds is going to come up with next." Roadie gave an enthusiastic nod and went right back to his control panel. "Joe, I want you to meet some of the people from the home that I meet with to share the wisdom we've been discussing each morning at McDonald's. We call ourselves, 'Old Wood Flowers.' When I was leaving the home this morning they were gathered in the lobby waiting for me. They saw the picture and article and wanted to come along and meet all of you." Leo could hardly contain himself as he turned to the twenty-five or so elderly ladies and gentleman who were gathered around several tables next to the meeting table. "Folks, this is Joe, the one who told us we were dead and dying; he's also the one who taught us about redbud trees flowering on old wood."

The announcement was greeted by a round of applause that caused the entire McDonald's to join in, making Joe blush. "And this is Sammy, who told us all about smiling. Tell us how it is, Sammy, and let's have one of those smiles."

Sammy obliged, and the audience reciprocated. Leo would have kept the conversation going all morning if Melvin hadn't spoken up.

"Gentlemen, I believe we have a meeting to begin here."

Sammy, Leo, and Joe quickly took their seats. "This appears to be a play fit for a king," Howard said, removing a hat with what must have been a five-foot feather in it.

Hoover ducked as the feather passed by his head. "Wow, this is quite a setup. I hope he's going to play some Hank Williams on the stereo. Hey, Joe, how about this article! We look pretty good and so does the ramp and our friend Mikey. We really got some attention from doing that good deed."

"It's incredible!" Joe said, picking up a copy of the paper. "It's really something."

"I like what it says there about making a difference," Hoover continued. "I don't think I've made a difference in a long time. It really feels good."

Still sitting at the controls, Roadie was slowly and purposefully increasing the volume. The last chorus of "Blowin' in the Wind" reverberated from the speakers as the sunrise on the big screen was reaching its peak. Suddenly a bright flash emanated from both the banner and the TV screen. In place of the paper banner were glowing red letters which appeared to be floating in the air. They spelled out "Inspiration in Everything." On the TV screen were the words "The answer is blowin' in the wind."

As the gasps of the crowded McDonald's subsided, the applause echoed through the restaurant.

Roadie moved to the front of the table where he had set up a microphone. "Thank you. You're a great audience." The voice sounded a lot like Elvis. The entire board just stared as Roadie returned each of their looks with a thankful nod. He looked like a different man standing in front of them this morning. He was not nervous and his usually red and veined face seemed clear and healthy. He hadn't reached for his pocket and the cigarettes that were no longer there even once.

"Quite a crowd you pulled in here this morning, Roadie," Joe said with a smile.

"I'm surprised, Joe. I think the article had a little bit to do with it, though," Roadie responded, covering the microphone so he could not be heard. "Hey, I got everyone's attention, do you mind if I speak through the microphone? I think everybody is wanting to listen."

Melvin spoke up, "Go right ahead, Roadie, it's a great opportunity."

"By all means, ol' noble one," chimed Howard. "Deliver your message to the kingdom."

The board members just smiled as Roadie began to speak. "Ladies and gentlemen, I spent my whole life around rock and roll, and in my sixty-seven years I've had a chance to be around some great people who had a major influence on music. In my youth I was even around one of the pioneers of rock and roll... Woody Guthrie. Even though it was just for a day or two."

"Woody Guthrie?" interrupted Melvin, barely able to hold it in. "He wrote 'This Land is Your Land.' That's my favorite song. Are you gonna play that, Roadie?" Realizing he had interrupted, he apologized and added a final "That really is a great song."

"Yeah, it's a great one all right, Melvin. We'll talk more about it later, man. As most of you probably can guess, I'm not very good at reading and not much better at writing. I don't know why, I just couldn't catch on as a child. Then I got stubborn about it and never allowed myself to learn it, I guess. So you aren't going to get any written things from me today. That's why the stage setup. I'm going to try and communicate the only way I know how. Through music and video."

"Where did you get all this stuff, Roadie?" Joe asked.

"Friends, Joe," he replied. "Roadies stick together, no matter how much time passes. When I said I would do this yesterday, all I needed to do was make a couple calls and I had everything you see here. Even the special effects."

The restaurant grew silent. All eyes were on Roadie, but he seemed as though he didn't know where to start. He raised what looked like a remote control and aimed it at his control board. In an instant the lights above the speakers started to flash red, white, and blue, and two flags appeared from behind the speakers. A rousing rendition of John Phillip Sousa's, 'Stars and Stripes Forever' was so realistic that people seemed to be looking for the brass band. With another flip of the remote control, the big screen lit up with pictures of the American flag waving in a variety of skies and locations. Some men stood and saluted, the ladies from the home clapped in unison, and many cheered as the magic of the music and the moment touched the crowd. The flutes, trumpets, and trombones had never sounded more beautiful. Roadie pointed the remote again. The music stopped as quickly as it had started and the red, white, and blue lights quit flashing. The crowd cheered.

When the cheering stopped, Roadie again began to speak. "There is inspiration in everything. I'm a rocker at heart, but there is no greater music than John Phillip Sousa. We've all heard that song many times. But how often do you let it inspire you, and if it inspires you, how do you keep that inspiration going?"

"I mentioned knowing Woody Guthrie. Actually, I met him when I was ten years old. My family was living in Memphis, Tennessee. My father worked in a factory there and at lunchtime one day this guy was singing songs outside the factory, just to entertain the workers and as part of a union movement that came to town. My father thought he looked like a hobo but the songs he sang were so sincere that my old man asked him if he needed a place to stay for the night. The guy said "yes," so he came home for dinner and spent the night. He repaired our roof the next day to repay us and ended up spending another night before moving on. He said his name was Woodrow Wilson Guthrie and he was from "everywhere," but originally from Oklahoma. After dinner on the second night my father got him to get his guitar out. I can still remember him singing to my brothers, parents and me on the front porch. He told stories about traveling across the country on a train, and how bad it was in the Dust Bowl of the plains and how most of his friends and neighbors packed up and moved to California. That was where the opportunity was supposed to be. He spoke in such vivid detail of the west coast and the east coast and everywhere in between. I was inspired by his stories. He looked me right in the eye and asked if I would like to hear a song he had just written.

"I couldn't believe he was talking to me, and when I slowly nodded my head he began strumming on that old guitar and singing… 'This land is your land/ This land is my land/ From California/ To the New York island/ From the redwood forest/ To the Gulf stream waters/ This land was made for you and me.' By the time he finished singing that song I knew I had to travel this country. I had to see everything he was talking about in that song. Somehow I had to do it.

"For the rest of the evening he talked about inspiration and finding hope in everything around us. Whether it is music, scenery, art, family, good conversation, laughter, or hurt, there is inspiration in everything. He looked at me and said, 'Young fella, if you ever got a question and you are wondering about it, just remember, the answer is blowing in the wind.'

"I'll always remember that instant in time. The answer is blowin' in the wind. He must have told the same thing to Bob Dylan in the early sixties. Dylan would visit Woody Guthrie in a New Jersey hospital where Woody was dying from something wrong with his brain… something called Huntington's chorea. The first time I heard Dylan's song I can't tell you all the emotions that flooded through me. I can picture an old Woody Guthrie there in that hospital looking at this kid of a musician and telling him through cigarette smoke that the answer is blowing in the wind, man.

"It was that answer that three years later had me out on the road. At the age of thirteen I was tired of getting knocked around by my old man and was already wondering what life was all about. Those words kept coming back to me, 'The answer is blowing in the wind.' So I went out to find the wind. I tried to join the Army but at thirteen they saw right through me. I was sleeping in alleys and doing anything I could to stay alive. I was in Nashville and got a job at a recording studio taking out trash and cleaning. Man, I couldn't believe the luck. I watched hillbilly singers and blues guitarists come and go. I worked there for two years and every chance I got, I watched through the door as the guys spun knobs and dials to try and make the music work. At night when I was done cleaning I would sneak into the control room and pretend for hours to be a sound technician. One of the guys caught me in there one night and didn't know whether to throw me out or cheer me on.

"'Hey, can you follow instructions?' he asked.

"I just nodded my head and sat down in the chair like I knew what I was doing. He walked in to the studio, flipped on the lights, and pulled out a guitar. I sat at the board and did everything he told me to do. He started playing this guitar and man, my whole body was tingling. Here I was spinning dials in a recording studio. After about a half hour he came back into the control room and ran back the tape. I tell ya, folks, I hadn't ever heard anything like what that man played in that studio. He listened to the tape for a minute or two and then took it off the reel and said, 'I think we got it, baby.' He put the reel of tape in an old satchel and put out his hand. . . 'Kid, my name is B.B., B.B. King, thanks for your help. You're a natural at spinnin' dials... son.' He picked up his guitar and walked out the door.

"For the next ten years I traveled the road working with any band, radio station, or music hall that would hire me. I was at the Grand Ole Opry, The Chicago Barn Dance, the blues halls in New Orleans, and jazz, and swing bars in New York. And just like Woody Guthrie, I was able to see the east coast, the west coast, and everything in between. The one thing I learned about people who made music is that they can find inspiration in everything. Watch this..."

With the flip of a remote control, the lights above the speakers began to set a mood and a flag came into focus on the TV screen. All eyes were fixed on the screen and the lights, their attention captured by Roadie's words and now his performance. As the flag began to fade into a picture of a black church choir, Sousa's "Stars and Stripes" faded into the rhythmic sounds of Muddy Water's singing blues. For the next ten minutes everyone in the audience was glued to the visual images of the black and white pictures fading in and out on the screen and the medley of blues, jazz, hillbilly, swing music, and ballads coming clearly through the speakers. As the music faded back into Sousa and the flag reappeared, the audience, young and old, jumped to their feet and applauded. Roadie moved from behind the board filled with knobs and dials to the front of the speakers and big screen. Like a professional, he thanked the audience for the response.

"Where did all those pictures come from, Roadie?" Melvin asked, obviously captivated by the presentation.

"I took them."

"You took them, Roadie?" asked Leo. "Tell it how it really is. When did you take them?"

"I was seventeen years old and in Houston, Texas. I was in a bus station trying to get a ride north. A man sitting next to me was looking at a bunch of pictures in an album. He caught me looking over his shoulder and then moved the album so I could see them. They were pictures of nature from all over the country. When he closed the album he looked at me and asked if I had ever taken a picture. Of course I just shook my head. I had never even held a camera.

"He was ready to leave and when he got up he dug into his bag and pulled out a camera. 'Here, you can borrow this one,' he said to me. 'With each click of the lens you can capture inspiration. There is inspiration in everything; you just have to look for it.'

"This is the camera he gave me. I guess I borrowed it for good. I didn't realize it at the time, but the name scratched into the back of it here says 'Ansel Adams'."

Everyone in the audience that knew the famous photographer smiled broadly. "Inspiration in everything, he told me, inspiration in every click of the lens. I figured that means every place we look we should be able to find inspiration. That is what each of the musicians I came across in the forties and early fifties were able to see. Those pictures that I just showed were from my travels around the country. They are pictures of the joy and pain, triumph and defeat, beauty and ugliness of an era that inspired those musicians and artists. They were able to find inspiration in everything, and their music and song was how they tried to get the world to see all of that as well. I believe all their music had a positive intent." Roadie was silent for a moment, perhaps to let the memories of that time in his life sink deeper into his being. "Yeah, man, inspiration in everything."

Roadie looked out across the sea of faces staring back at him. He thought about how long it had been since he had really looked at people. It was a good feeling to be seeing people again. He knew he had their attention and was excited about the next part of his presentation. The words began to flow. "It was spring, 1954, and I ended up back in Memphis. There was a recording studio there, probably some of you heard of it, Sun Records. I was in the right place at the right time and the owner of Sun Records, a guy by the name of Sam Phillips, gave me a job of backing up in the control room. I was back to recording hillbilly singers again. I enjoyed watching a parade of hopefuls come in day after day, buying recording time and hoping to be the next rising star. It was in July of 1954 and this kid was there recording some more hillbilly songs. We were taking a break between sets. All of sudden, out of the studio came this whoopin' and hollerin' and this kid was up shakin' and dancin' around with a big smile on his face. Some of the musicians started to join in and he started singin' a song I'd heard a couple years before down in a blues house in New Orleans. I mean to tell you that studio came alive.

"Sam Phillips come rushing in and said, 'What are you doing?' This kid with sideburns just looked at him and said, 'Just havin' some fun, Mr. Phillips. Hope you don't mind, Sir.'

"'Mind?' he said, 'Man, back it up, try to find a starting place, and do it again.' Then He put his finger in my face and said, 'Son, you better catch this.' We recorded, 'That's All Right, Mama.' Mr. Phillips had me clean it up that night and deliver it to a radio station in Memphis the next day. The station started playing it and by the time the record came into the stores, Elvis Presley was on his way."

Roadie definitely had the undivided attention of his audience. Some listeners showed amazement, others envy and even doubt. Now a picture of a young Elvis was on the screen and "That's All Right, Mama" resounded from the speakers. As pictures of Elvis, his musicians, and kids being caught up in a new era of music flashed to the screen, some of the younger audience members began to move to the music. Before long, the entire McDonald's started to dance, even the elderly ladies. Leo watched them through big eyes. As the last notes and pictures faded, the crowd cheered and applauded.

Joe looked at Roadie as he walked back up to the mike. He was amazed at his showmanship and composure. All he could say was, "That is incredible, Roadie."

Roadie smiled and said, "Yeah, man, and rock and roll was off and running. Elvis started doing gigs around the country, and for the next two or three years I traveled with him and the bands as a roadie, spinnin' knobs. In those early days, if ever there was a person who could find inspiration in everything, it was Elvis Presley. It was like traveling with a big kid. His enthusiasm was bubbling for everything. He'd get excited about gettin' on a bus, and traveling, and coming into a town he had never seen. He was inspired by the kids who were coming out to hear his music and the halls he was playing in. I remember when we were traveling through Texas and the first time he saw a real live cactus. We had to stop and everyone piled out of the old Lincolns and second-hand Cadillacs just to get up next to it. I was a part of that entourage until early 1957. Elvis started making movies then and there were a lot of people around him who made decisions of who would work with him and who wouldn't. For some reason I was one of them who wouldn't. I remember when I was taking my stuff off the equipment bus in San Diego. We had just finished a show in Phoenix and were on our way to Los Angeles when someone decided to stop for the night. We were parked along the beach; it was early evening and the sunset was coloring the western sky over the ocean. Elvis stepped down off the bus, saw me getting my gear together, and walked over.

"'Hey, Roadie.' He was the one that gave me this name. 'Things seem to be changin', man. I'm sorry.'

"'Don't worry about it, man. I was gettin' tired of listenin' to you anyway,' I said with a serious look and then a laugh that I couldn't hold back. He laughed real big and slapped me on the shoulder.

"'Man, would you look at that sunset! I haven't stopped to notice a sunset or sunrise in a long time,' he said, trying to absorb it all.

"I looked over at him as he studied the ball of fire dropping into the water. The sparkle and enthusiasm that I saw in the kid back in Memphis the night of that recording session was fading like the sun at the end of the day. 'Don't lose it, El,' I said. 'Some guy once told me there is inspiration in everything, all we have to do is stop and notice it. Take time to notice it, man.'

"I threw my duffle bag over my shoulder and put out my hand. He looked away from the sunset and shook it. No words were said. I started up from the beach to the highway to hitch a ride. When I reached the road I turned back around to see the lonely figure standing at the water's edge, silhouetted by the last rays of the setting sun."

"Roadie, did all this really happen?" Hoover asked with the innocence of a child hearing about where babies come from for the first time. "You mean you really knew Elvis, Roadie?"

"I knew him just like I told ya, Hoove. When I left that beach, I also decided to leave music. I ended up in San Francisco for a couple of years learning to turn wrenches instead of knobs. I worked as a mechanic and started getting real interested in motorcycles. I loved motorcycles. They were a way of escaping. . . what I was escaping from I don't know, but I enjoyed bikes. In the early sixties I didn't even listen to the radio. That's how much I got away from music. Then one day I was working in the garage and heard two guys talking about a concert coming up.

"'You gonna go hear Dylan, man?' I heard one of them ask.

"'Yeah, man, he's a storyteller, A modern day Woody Guthrie.'

"Well, I had to see this storyteller. There I was back in a concert. But it was different than the last show I had been at with Elvis. The world was changing. They were trying to find inspiration or something in a manufactured way. I was sitting there at that concert in 1963 with a whole different group of kids with a totally different view of the world than those screaming for Elvis just six years earlier. I remember thinking to myself, 'Where is the inspiration in this? Where are the answers?'

"I remember the cheer as this kid walked out on the stage with a guitar and harmonica strapped around his neck. He put his lips on that mouth harp and began to blow. He looked exactly like Woodrow Wilson Guthrie as he sat on that front porch over twenty years before. He started to sing, and I was caught up in the music of a new generation. He seemed to look at me and say, 'The answer is blowin' in the wind.' I knew I had to get back out on the road again. That's exactly what I did and here's what I found." Once again the speakers started to fill the McDonald's with Dylan's "Blowin' in the Wind" and the screen was full of pictures from the sixties: protests, flower children, Woodstock, racial tension, and war. The medley of music took the crowd from Dylan through the Beatles and Motown to Janis Joplin, Jimi Hendrix, and a host of others that had brought a generation through the Vietnam War, into the seventies, and beyond. The music ended with Simon and Garfunkel's "Sounds of Silence" and the video showing the silhouetted 'King' in the setting sun. The response was different this time. They applauded the production, but the message left them uneasy.

"I hated those days," Howard said with a distant and disturbed look. He was more serious than he'd been in a couple of days. "They were full of lies and lost visions. It is a wonder that we survived them."

"You are so right, ol' noble knight," Roadie said, figuring he'd better add a little lightness to the situation and bring Howard back to his medieval self.

Howard quickly stood up and bowed toward Roadie. "Thank you, my dear Roadmaster, for your recognition." Then he sat back down again, seemingly ready to listen further.

"Some didn't make it out alive," Roadie continued. "When I went back out on the road, I was spinnin' knobs again for people like Janis Joplin and Jimi Hendrix. Both of them, just like Elvis, started out excited and inspired about sharing music and the fun of performing and being around people. But it soon captured them and they couldn't find their inspiration in everything that life had to offer; drugs and destruction came into play. I wasn't surprised to hear of their deaths and the deaths of others. When we allow life and all the hardships that life can throw at us to take over, then it becomes impossible to look through the camera and see the inspiration in every click of the lens."

"Tell us how it really is, Roadie," said Leo. "How do we keep from losing our inspiration?"

"It is what you told us the other day, Leo. 'That which does not kill us makes us stronger.' Many people in the sixties, instead of being strengthened by hard times and challenge, were being weakened and seeking inspiration in drugs and hate. Dropping out of life. But your thought holds true, Leo. Because the sixties and seventies didn't kill us as a country, we did become stronger. 'That which does not kill us makes us stronger.' And as we become stronger we have more of an opportunity to find the inspiration in everything."

"Tell us more, Roadie." Hoover spoke up. "What did you do after the sixties?"

"Man, I was one of them that just dropped out. By the early seventies I was running with motorcycle gangs and really didn't care what tomorrow brought. I don't want to get into all of that now; its really pretty sad thinking about what that group was all about. If it's okay, I'll just let you in on one more story."

Joe was amazed at what he was watching. Here was a man who could barely read or write, and up to several days ago didn't look as though he was really able to comprehend anything. But here today, he was magically captivating several hundred people, not only through his music and video presentation, but from his insight and view of life. Joe noticed that Roadie was starting to look at his wrist watch rather nervously as if he was taking too much time. "Hey, Roadie," Joe said. "Go ahead, tell us all the stories you want. What you're telling us is interesting."

"Yeah man, keep talkin'. I'm findin' inspiration in it," Sammy said. Their comments brought applause and agreement from everybody sitting around them; soon the entire audience was clapping.

Roadie thanked them, took another quick look at his watch, and began to speak again. "It was in 1972, I think. I had to get away from the gangs. I was now in my early forties and wondering myself what happened to the inspiration. I headed to the east coast, thinking I would take a little time on the Jersey shore, maybe get a job working in a club in one of the resort towns there.

"It was early morning and the only place I could afford to sleep this particular evening was under a boardwalk in Asbury Park, New Jersey. I had finally crawled out from under my bed around nine o'clock the next morning, stretched the stiffness out, and then walked over to sit on my bike. I was just sitting there contemplating each wave that was rolling in when I heard those all-too-familiar words, 'The answer is blowin' in the wind.' I quickly turned around and saw this skinny kid sitting on a park bench chording his guitar and singing that song with the same feeling I had heard Dylan sing it back in '63." Roadie hesitated for an instant and looked again at his watch. "I was drawn to him. I left my bike and walked in his direction. He was so caught up in the song that he didn't notice me until I was standing right beside him.

"'Got a problem, roadie?' the kid asked.

"Surprised, I answered, 'How did you know my name? That's my name, man. How did you know my name?'

"'Didn't,' he answered, still chording his guitar. 'You just look like a roadie.'

"'I heard Dylan do that song in Frisco, in '63,' I said.

"'It's a great song,' he said, momentarily silencing his guitar and looking up.

"'The first time I heard those words, 'The answer is blowin' in the wind' was 1940. On my front porch. A guy by the name of Woodrow Wilson Guthrie told them to me.'

"'You knew Woody Guthrie?' he asked, stopping completely and looking me straight in the eye.

"'Yeah, well kinda. . .' I told him the whole story because he was so interested in it.

"'Man, that hobo could write words,' the kid said with a faraway look and the same spark of enthusiasm that I remembered seeing in Elvis' gaze back in that recording studio in Memphis. 'You know Woody died just a couple years ago at a hospital not far from here. I wish I'd met him. I read somewhere that Dylan met him. That would be some inspiration, man... meeting Woody Guthrie."

"He looked up and studied my every detail. 'Did it inspire you, man?' he asked.

"We spent the next four hours talking on that park bench. We just talked. It was the first honest conversation I had had in years. This kid soaked up every word. He then said he had to go. Standing up, he continued to play a few more chords on his guitar, told me where he and his band were playing that night, and invited me to come and watch.

"'What keeps you going, Roadie?' he asked. 'Why haven't you ever just settled down?'

"'I don't know,' I answered. I sure don't know where these words came from but I looked at him and said, 'I think maybe I was just born to run.'

"'Born to run, huh?' he said, accompanied by another chord on his guitar.

"'Hey, kid,' I asked, 'what's your name?'

"He shyly looked back over his shoulder and said, 'Bruce. Bruce Springsteen.'"

Cheers came from the younger members of the crowd. Roadie just smiled, looked at his watch, and then moved toward the door. "I'll just finish that chapter of the story by saying I got to be a part of Bruce's road crew through the seventies and into the early eighties. He was different. He seemed able to keep his enthusiasm when stardom came. He never stopped finding inspiration in everything. He could find the inspiration, write about it, put it to song, and then, in my opinion, share that inspiration with others."

"Play some Bruce!" someone shouted.

"YEAH, play some!"

"I'd like to." Roadie smiled, and looked again at the crowd, and then toward the door. "I'd like to. But I would like to say one more thing about inspiration in everything. You want to know what some old people of this country and the sad rock and rollers I told you about from the sixties have in common?" Roadie paused to let the silence drive home the significance of the question. "They both became consumed by life, and in doing so lost their ability to find inspiration. The only thing left was death. But when I look at this picture and this article and hear what I've heard from the people around this table, I'm inspired. I'm inspired by the beauty of that little boy in the picture and the joy on his face, and the moment when he was able to leave the boundaries of that porch and move to cut the branches from that redbud tree and give them to his mother. I find inspiration in that. Yes, ladies and gentlemen, for the first time in a long time, I can see inspiration in everything and I now realize that the answer is not blowing in the wind. The answer is in our hands. It is in our hands to make a difference in this world."

His words were greeted by thunderous applause, and the members of the board gathered around the table were awestruck by what they had witnessed over the last forty-five minutes.

When the applause stopped, Roadie once again looked at his watch and then toward the door. "Well, I guess that's it, thanks for your..." stopped in midsentence as a rumbling started near the entrance. The sea of people began to part for the lone figure dressed in blue jeans and sweatshirt and carrying a guitar.

Somebody in the crowd, half whispering and half shouting, said, "Hey, that's Bruce Springsteen." And then the crowd, young and old, started to applaud as he reached Roadie at the mike. Roadie said, "Thought you'd never get here," as he clasped Bruce's hands and gave him a hug.

Bruce smiled and said, "Let's rock."

Roadie moved to his place behind the board with all the knobs and dials. Bruce took his guitar out, threw it over his shoulder, and then strapped on a harmonica and stepped up to the microphone. Blowing on the harmonica and striking a chord on the guitar, Bruce looked over at his sound man and gave a wink of approval. Roadie turned some lights on above the "stage" and Springsteen began a slow rhythm on his guitar.

"Last night I get this call, ya see. There in the comfort of Beverly Hills and all. It's this guy I knew back in the early seventies on the Jersey shore.

He was a rocker from way back and said he'd like me to do a little favor for him. Now I don't mean to sound anything but appreciative, but I get calls all the time from old friends needing a favor. But I listened... and this guy ya see, he began to tell me all about old wood and how it can still flower. He told me about wisdom and people and inspiration in everything. We started talking about Woody Guthrie and I realized that he wasn't asking for a favor just for him, it was a favor for everyone, young and old.

"Ya see, the reason I like talking about Woody Guthrie is the more I read about him, the more I realize that when he saw a cause, he would try and do something about it. That is what I see here, a cause. We are losing a valuable resource in this country. It is different from any other natural resource we have because it's lost when it's not used rather than when it is used. Using it will benefit everyone the world over."

With guitar still droning a slow, mesmerizing rhythm, the messenger continued. "This resource is our nation's old people and if we don't start using it, it will be gone. And gone with it will be the wisdom that we so desperately need today.

"When I was back on the Jersey shore and first met Roadie, I was sitting there ready to give up the music scene. I was working hard and not getting any breaks. This guy crawls out from underneath the boardwalk and starts talking to me. He listens to my complaining and whining that nobody cares about my future and then he says, 'Let me tell you a story I heard back in Memphis, Tennessee.' Before I could stop him he started to talk."

Bruce changed the chord and smiled at Roadie. "He said this story is about an old man that lived in a village a long time ago. Everybody would come to this old man for answers to their problems because of his experience and wisdom. It seemed he was always right and always willing to help. That is why everybody liked him. Everybody, that is, except this one young man who lived in the village. He was jealous and decided to prove that the old man wasn't always right."

Bruce paused and changed a chord on the guitar; not a person in the crowd moved. He looked around and then continued to capture the audience with his voice. "The young guy, ya see, thought he would catch a sparrow. Just a little bird that he could hold in his hand, and he would come to the old man while everybody was watching him and ask the old man if the bird in his hand was dead or alive. If he said it was dead, he would open his hands and let it fly. If the old man said it was alive, he would crush it before opening his hands and the bird would be dead and the old man... wrong.

"With bird in hand the young man pushed his way through the crowd that had gathered at the town square to listen to the old man speak. He stuck

165

his cupped hands in the old man's face, and with a snarl he said, 'Old man, is this bird in my hand dead or alive?' The old man looked up... and through this thoughtful look and white beard he gently spoke... 'It's in your hands, my son, it's in your hands'." The only sound was the slow rhythm of his acoustic guitar going through several chords.

Then he added, "As it was for me on that park bench and for you who have been fortunate to grow old and you who have not yet gained the wisdom of age... your future is in your hands. Don't waste the opportunity. Old wood flowers."

"This song was written by Woody Guthrie, and I believe it is about the most beautiful song ever written. Anyway..." As his lips went to the harmonica, the restaurant began to fill not only with music, but with a message that cut right to the heart of everyone now leaning forward in amazement that they were sitting in a McDonald's listening to Bruce Springsteen sing. As the last note softly moved across the crowd the words began to rise, "As I went walking that ribbon of highway... I saw above me that endless skyway... and saw below me that golden valley... I heard this land is made for you and me."

By this time the audience could not contain themselves. Their simultaneous clapping seemed to add impact to every word being sung. The voice, guitar, and occasional harmonica note drove home the message. The opportunity in this country is for everyone young and old, but it is in our hands to take advantage of it.

"This land was made for you and me."

Joe was thrilled by the impact of the moment. What had taken place seemed to add further to the magic of the redbuds and the incredible effects of the past week. He began to perceive another message as Bruce continued to play an occasional repeat of the chorus. Joe thought, "if we don't get this place cleared out he may never get out of here, and besides, the two old friends deserve some time together." Out of character as it was, Joe stood up and continued his clapping and repeating in rhythm, "This land was made for you and me."

The other board members followed Joe's lead and did the same; soon everyone was standing. Joe started for the door, hoping that others would follow. And they did, first the board members, then Leo's friends from the home, and then the rest of the crowd. As they reached the parking lot, Joe glanced back over his shoulder at Melvin with a look that said "your turn." Melvin first glanced away but then returned Joe's glance with a nod that said, "I'll be ready."

With the guitar slowly accompanying the harmonica, it seemed like only seconds before the crowd was gone and all that was left was Bruce, Roadie, and the crew behind the counter, dazed by what they had just witnessed. Lanny Smith cleared his throat and they found their way to their stations. He took one last look from around the counter as the last of the notes settled on the restaurant. Two old friends exchanged smiles in silence. Bruce pulled the guitar over his head, set it in the case, and then picked it up and moved toward the door, stopping once again to clasp hands with his old friend.

"Thanks for the use of the equipment," Roadie said with a smile.

"Hey man, it's for a good cause," Springsteen smiled back. Then there was silence.

"I really appreciate you coming down here," Roadie said again.

"Man, what you are doing here is bigger than rock and roll itself. You're saving the world, man, it is in the hands of our old people. . . it's in the hands of our young people, and it's in our hands, Roadie. This is big stuff, man. Let me know if I can help again." With another hand clasp and a hug Bruce headed for the door. Before walking out into the parking lot he turned, "It's like the sign says, man, 'Inspiration in everything'... Old wood flowers... good song title..." With a wave and a smile he was gone.

Roadie sat in the silence. It had been a long time coming, but he felt today that he had finally found the answers that were blowing in the wind.

⮜ CHAPTER 10 ⮞

TAKE ACTION

The setting was different the next morning as the Board of Directors began to take their seats. The crowd from the previous day's event was gone and it was almost back to the regular morning crowd. Leo, Hoover, and Howard were already sitting at the table when Sammy, Joe, and Roadie came in and sat down with their breakfast.

"Hey, what's with this plaque?" asked Sammy, pointing to the wood and chrome sign suspended from the ceiling and hanging over the middle of their table. Inscribed on the metal were the words "BOARD OF DIRECTORS."

"It is in recognition and thanks for your efforts over the past three years and especially in the past week." Sammy turned around to find Lanny Smith beaming with pride, his manager's uniform neat and trim. "I talked to corporate yesterday and they said it would be okay to hang a sign for such an important group as the one I have meeting in our restaurant each morning. You men have had quite a week, haven't you?"

"It has been a week fit for royalty," Howard said, standing and giving a sweep of his hat. "We are honored by your recognition and praise."

His actions brought a smile and a hearty "HERE, HERE" from the rest of the men.

"Hey, I almost forgot to tell you," Lanny said, stopping and addressing the men. "My friend Jim Johnson called late last night. He said he got a call from USA TODAY with questions about all of you and his story. Who knows, you might be famous!"

Joe just smiled, thinking about the possibilities. "What's with the flags?" he asked, picking up the little American flag and stand that had been put on the table at each board member's place.

"I'll tell you like it is, Joe. They were all here when I arrived," said Leo. "I think it's part of Melvin's presentation."

"Where is Melvin?" Roadie asked, obviously still glowing from yesterday's presentation.

"He's been up and down all morning since I've been here," Hoover said. "I think he's in the bathroom now. Good case of the nerves, I think."

"Hey, it's real easy to stay calm after you've made this talk, big boy," Sammy said with a smile and a wink toward Hoover.

"You are so right, Sammy," Hoover said. "The hardest thing about this presentation stuff was thinking about it beforehand. I really had to be honest with myself to realize the knowledge I had not put into action. The wisdom I had not put to use."

"The hardest thing, my dear friend," chimed in Howard, " is to be honest with ourselves. As the great Sir William Shakespeare said, and I quote, 'This above all... to thine own self be true.'"

Sammy nodded at the 'noble knight' and then looked in Joe's direction. "Still dead and dying, Joe?"

"No, Sammy, alive and well. I've never been more glad to be wrong about something than I am right now. This group is alive and well."

"Are we flowering, Joe?" Roadie asked, without the slightest motion to the pocket that used to contain cigarettes.

Joe thought for a moment. He knew the past week had been a rewarding one for everyone, yet he had a fear. Where does it go from here? Are they flowering? Joe didn't think so... yet. He knew there was something missing, but what was it? Then the words he was looking for just seemed to come out. "Let's just say we are budded up, Roadie, ready to flower. And like your friend Mr. Springsteen said yesterday, 'It's in our hands.'"

"You're right, Joe, we've got to keep this going," Sammy said. "But what is the next step?"

"Sorry to keep you waiting, gentlemen," came Melvin's voice as he hurried to his spot at the table and set his cup of coffee down. "If it is all right, I would like to call this meeting to order."

"It is your meeting, oh noble one...."

Melvin sat but then realized he should stand to speak. He slowly rose to his feet and looked at the table of men who anxiously awaited his words. Time was passing. A minute and then two. Melvin was wrestling with the words and didn't really know where to start.

"Just take action," he mumbled to himself.

The old men held their breath in anticipation and concern. The time lapse was uncomfortable for everyone. Melvin continued to mumble things that the others could not comprehend. The color was leaving his face and he seemed to be far from the present. The board members were now very concerned. Leo, fearing that his friend might be having a stroke, nervously cleared his throat and spoke up.

"Melvin, tell us how it really is, man. Are you okay?" Everyone leaned forward, anticipating Melvin's response. He was still distant and mumbling; his hands trembled as he tried to clutch the back of his chair. Leo cleared his throat and asked again, "Melvin, what is the matter?"

Melvin's eyes grew wide and color rushed to his face; he looked out across the table, past the McDonald's to a moment that had long since passed. The muscles in his neck tightened and the veins popped as the words ripped through his throat, "TAKE ACTION!"

The words rang through the restaurant, setting the board members back in their seats and generating stares from the rest of the restaurant patrons.

"Crazy old men!" someone shouted in response.

The restaurant again grew quiet and the board members turned their attention toward Melvin, who now seemed to be back in the present and somewhat embarrassed by the events of the past few minutes. No one spoke as Melvin reached to the floor, picked up a little briefcase, and set it on the table. He cleared his throat and his slight smile comforted everyone around the table.

"I hardly know where to start," he humbly began. "But maybe this will be a good place." He reached into the briefcase and pulled out an old eight-by-ten photograph. The picture was familiar to each man sitting around the table, six Marines raising the American flag.

"That is the flag raising over Iwo Jima," Joe spoke up. "I was in Sai Pan when I first saw that picture. Everyone in the barracks went crazy when we saw it. That was a brave battle. We lost a lot of boys on that beach. I really was touched in Washington, D.C., the first time I saw that monument."

"You're right, Joe," Melvin said, setting the picture back down on the table. "I guess you could say I had something to do with that flag raising."

"You did, Melvin?" Hoover spoke up. "You were there? Were you a hero? Are you one of the men in the picture? Tell us all about it, Melvin."

Melvin just looked at Hoover, appreciating his enthusiasm for the story. "Yes, Hoove, I was there, but I was far from being a hero and I'm not one of the men in the picture. By the time this picture was taken I was back on a ship locked in a cell, my life as a Marine was over."

The board members sat wondering what could have happened that would have put Melvin in a cell and what the story was behind the picture of the Iwo Jima flag raising. None had the courage to ask, however; they waited patiently for the story to continue. Melvin went on, "Gentlemen, I had lived to be a Marine. Growing up in Kansas I had read every story about the Marines and their history that I could get a hold of. When the war broke

171

out I didn't hesitate to enlist, and I knew exactly what I wanted to be. I arrived at Parris Island and endured every minute of the grueling training because I knew it was making a Kansas farm boy into a man. . . a Marine. I can still feel the pride I experienced the day they said to me and my platoon, 'Gentlemen, you are now Marines.' We anxiously awaited our orders and were soon sent to fight the Japanese on Guam.

"We were kids forced to become men. I remember the long journey in that ship to reach the island. All around me were young faces anticipating what the future might bring. On the morning of July 21 we were ordered into the amphibious carriers that would take us to the beach. As we bounced over the waves heading to battle, I wondered more about killing another man than being killed. I wondered if I could do it, take another life. I didn't have much time to think about it. Our carrier hit the beach, and as the door dropped the wave of young men began to move through the early morning mist and waves, running for the beach. I remember the noise of mortars going off around me, and the shells from our ships flying overhead. There were skirmishes all around me. My first devastation came when I saw what was left of one of the boys I had arrived at Parris Island with only months before. Now he lay dead, destroyed by a mortar blast." Melvin stopped, trying to regain his composure and wiping a tear away.

"It was hard to make friends," Joe said. "You were afraid to. You knew that at any moment on those islands, your friendship could end in a brutal death."

"That is so right, Joe," Melvin continued. "I learned that all too soon when I hit that island, and I learned something else about myself as well. At the end of the first day as we lay in foxholes, the blur of shells going over-head and the constant sounds of sniper fire, I realized that I had not fired my gun once the entire day. 'Why?' I wondered to myself. I realized that I was afraid to take action. All the training and everything that I had been taught to do in battle didn't matter if I was afraid to take action.

"Guam was a relatively easy battle as far as battles go. By August 8 of 1944 the Marines, with Naval support, had secured Guam, and my division was to remain on the island for cleanup. We had battled for over two weeks and not one shot was fired from my gun. It was a secret that I kept inside, and the fact that I survived was a miracle. I would help with the wounded and digging foxholes, all the time staying busy or looking busy, but I could not take the action to pull the trigger. I didn't know why, but soon I knew I was a coward. I just wasn't following through on what I knew I had to do."

Melvin's words were making the Board of Directors start to squirm. Each man was beginning to see a personal parallel in Melvin's story. Each one had possessed wisdom, but had failed to take action over the years to make the wisdom a reality in their lives. Joe was thinking this might be the missing element they were all looking for. What was going to help this group make the events of the past week more than just a memory of shared experiences? How could they actually have results and accomplishments continue for weeks and maybe even years to come? This could be it. He hoped Melvin was going to help them take action. Joe spoke up and asked, hoping Melvin would continue, "How did you end up on Iwo, Melvin?"

"I stayed on at Guam until January, 1945; then came orders that we would move to ships coming across from Sai Pan, preparing for another mass invasion on a Japanese stronghold to the north. On the ship, I joined in the talk and bragging of the boys who now looked much older. We all told of our experiences on Guam, each story more embellished than the last. I caught myself recounting incidents that weren't exactly true. I knew I was covering up my inability to take action and was even making myself believe that I had done my part on Guam.

"On the evening of February 18, I lay in my bunk, knowing what the next morning would bring. We had been given our orders and briefings earlier that afternoon. We would be landing on the beaches of a small eight-square-mile island called Iwo Jima. It was crawling with enemy forces and the landing would be a dangerous and critical maneuver. Iwo was an ugly island of volcanic rock and sand, but it was important to capture because of its strategic location to Japan and the airfields that the Japanese had built. So there I lay, knowing that in several hours I would once again be running up a beach, faced with a situation where I would be called on to take action. What would happen? I felt lucky to have survived the battles on Guam but lay there feeling that my luck was about to run out. I would have to take action.

"I did not sleep at all that night and was huddled with several hundred other men as the landing craft moved through the waves to the beaches of Iwo Jima. The big doors of the landing craft dropped and a wave of men splashed into the water. I was pulled along with them. As we hit the beach the thick volcanic sand began to suck us in. Some men sunk up to their knees, making each step slow and treacherous. The mortar shells coming from the enemy entrenched on Mount Suribachi were taking a heavy toll. Many men were falling before they even reached the beach because the Japanese had a clear view from Mount Suribachi; shells were raining down on us. The smoke and haze were settling in, and the screams and agony of dying men all around me made it a living hell. I went to work immediately digging a foxhole that would help support our own mortars. It was like digging in a bag of wheat, and with the shells going off all around us we knew any minute could be our last. My gun lay beside me as I fell into the foxhole, waiting for the mortar launcher to be brought forward. I had no desire to fire or to take action and was only doing what I had to do, not what was needed. There were dead bodies and pieces of bodies lying all around me. These men had taken action, and look what it got them. I planned to stay in that foxhole and await my fate. I planned to do nothing.

"The first day passed and the morning of February 20 arrived. I was ordered to help with the wounded, a job I gladly took because it was behind the action. But I soon grew weary of the hundreds of dead and dying that were assembled on the beach. We were doing what we could to keep people alive, but the situation seemed hopeless. The naval support continued to rock Mount Suribachi and the enemy positions. Word came from the front lines that the enemy was retreating into the hundreds of yards of caves they had dug in the side of the mountain, and that more support was needed on the front line to drive them out. For the first time in three days on Iwo Jima, we were finally making headway; the momentum of the battle was changing in our favor.

"I was ordered with about a hundred other men to move toward the front line and to meet up with Tiger Thomas' platoon. He was a young sergeant from Florida who was quickly making a name for himself. Word came from a command post back on board the USS Texas at the shore: as soon as possible, action must be taken to move a patrol up to the top of Mount Suribachi and to plant an American flag. The flag would be a morale booster for the men on Iwo and would make great press as the government continued to sell the war efforts back in the U.S. This was going to be history in the making. It would be the first flag planted on Japanese soil, and it needed to happen fast.

"On the morning of February 24, the enemy fire that had rained down from the volcano had all but ceased and it was a perfect opportunity to make a move to the top. It was determined that Sergeant Tiger Thomas would take forty men and begin the ascent to plant the flag. A photographer would go along and capture the historic occasion, a guy by the name of Lowery. Somehow I was selected to be a part of the company that was going to make history. The soldier that had not fired a single shot in the war was going off to help plant a flag."

"You shouldn't be so hard on yourself, Melvin," Sammy's said. "You were doing what you could. That counts for something, doesn't it?"

Melvin could only return the comment with a faint smile and answer, "I was doing what I could, not what I should, Sammy. I had a job to do. I knew what needed to be done and I wasn't doing it. I have found that to be the story of my entire life." Those words hit hard with every man sitting around the table. It was obvious from the week's events that they had known what to do but were not taking the action to do it. The table was surrounded by a powerful silence.

"Tell us about it, Melvin," Hoover said softly, breaking the silence. "Tell us about the journey up Mount Suribachi."

Melvin nodded his head and continued. "I was placed in the rear. We met no resistance. It was a journey of death: we passed burned-out mortar stations and the corpses of the men that had manned them. The Japanese that had remained on the mountain were now deep inside in the caves. An occasional sniper shot or blast was quickly taken care of by the men up front carrying flame throwers and grenades. As I reached the summit, several men were making a flag pole out of an old radar post. We were ordered to circle the rim of the volcano and to guard against sniper fire and ambush when the flag went up. I had a sick feeling in the pit of my stomach. I would have to shoot if an ambusher or sniper appeared. The men putting up the flag would be in danger if I failed to take action. I sat on a rock just twenty yards from where the flag was going to be raised. Tiger Thomas was kicking at the stones to make a hole for the pipe to go in. 'Be ready,' he yelled. 'Be ready to take action.' The men with the pole and flag moved quickly to the crest and hoisted the flag. In an instant the Stars and Stripes were flying over Suribachi. Approximately three minutes later, as the soldiers were securing the flagstaff in place and Lowery the photographer was snapping pictures, three Japanese with rifles jumped out of a cave below me and started to shoot. My hand tightened around my gun.

"'TAKE ACTION!' Tiger Thomas started yelling in my direction. 'TAKE ACTION!'"

Melvin's hands were shaking as he told the story to the men gathered around the table. "The gun fire was blazing past me," He continued. "It seemed as though they were just waiting for us to put up the flag.

"'TAKE ACTION, SOLDIER!' Tiger Thomas screamed as he came running through the enemy fire toward my position. 'TAKE ACTION!'"

Melvin's face had that intense faraway look that had worried the others earlier. His words were broken as he continued to shout and tell the story. "TAKE ACTION! I... I... I cou... couldn't. I can't do it. I can't shoot it. TAKE ACTION! Shoot 'em, Sarge. Shoot 'em. TAKE ACTION! TAKE ACTION!"

The words echoed as Melvin fell to his chair weeping. The Board of Directors didn't know what to do next. Some of the people sitting around them found other seats. Lanny Smith moved toward the table but stopped, realizing the scene would be best left alone.

An ominous silence had hung over the group for several minutes before Melvin looked up. His expression had softened. He wiped away the last of his tears and began to speak, this time remaining in his seat. "That moment has haunted me ever since, and each time I try to tell it, the agony is just as powerful as the instant it happened." Taking a big breath Melvin continued, "I didn't take action. My gun was never fired. Tiger Thomas had jumped over the rocks, knocking me out of the line of fire. He then fired the shots that took out the three Japanese, and the rest of the platoon quickly ended the skirmish. When it was over, and I lay there with the barrel of Tiger Thomas' rifle pointed between my eyes, I knew my life was about to end.

"'The only thing keeping me from killing you is that American uniform that you do not deserve to wear,' the sergeant said through clenched teeth. 'But you will die and it will be a slow death, soldier. You will always remember what your inability to take action has done today. It has cost lives. Now get up.'"

Melvin's voice was low and ghostly as he continued. "Six men died in that skirmish. And the sergeant was right. I die each day thinking about it. Six soldiers dead. The flag raising that took place is not the picture you see here. The picture of the first flag raising looked like this one." Melvin pulled another picture from the briefcase. This one showed a much smaller flag and men posed around it ready for action. "That is Sergeant Thomas. This was taken less than a minute before those three Japanese came out of that cave."

"Why two pictures and two flags, Melvin?" Hoover asked.

"Good question, Hoove," Melvin said, his voice still low and serious. "Word got back to command that the flag had been raised and six men had been lost doing it. That made for good press. But when it was further explained that the six men were killed because of a Marine's failure to take action, the press corps was in a tough situation for a story that would sell and keep people back in the states feeling positive about the war. The flag was also a small one and could be seen only from certain areas on the island. One of the commanders knew how morale would be boosted if the flag could be seen, so he ordered another flag to go up in its place and wanted more pictures of it. That's where this famous picture came from. It's the second flag going up... and the rest is history, as they say." Melvin's weak smile and soft voice left a cloud over the meeting.

"I gotta know, man," Roadie said, staring at Melvin. "What did they do with you?"

"Well, Roadie," Melvin continued. "By evening I was under guard back on the beach landing area. Tiger Thomas was going back on a landing craft-later that evening to meet the press, who had plans to make him a hero. Sometime after midnight we were headed to a ship called the Eldorado. What an ironic situation! A hero and a coward sitting across from each other. What separated us was the courage to take action. Tiger Thomas took action. I did not. When we got to the ship, General Holland Smith was there to personally greet Thomas.

"'Congratulations, Soldier,' the general said to Thomas as he stepped onto the deck. 'You led the platoon that planted the first American flag on Japanese soil. You're a hero for taking action, son, thank you.'

"The general never even looked my way," Melvin continued. I was quickly taken below deck to a dark cell. After three days I was transferred to another ship heading back to the states. There was talk of court martial and dishonorable discharge, but the Marines decided it would be better to just let the incident fade without notice. I was discharged immediately. Two weeks after the flag raising I was back on American soil, out of the Marines and dying inside."

"No man sitting here could predict how they would respond in that situation, Melvin," Joe said, trying to comfort his friend. "We don't know until we are in the situation, and then it is still unclear at times."

"Thanks, Joe," Melvin said, standing up, his voice regaining its strength. With a spark of enthusiasm and a glow coming to his eyes, he continued, "I have come to a realization that we might be able to predict it based on past performance. I was suffering through this meeting last night, and it occurred to me that six men died over fifty years ago because of my failure to take action. I feel like I've been given a second chance. I want to make sure that as a group we take action. Just as both those platoons took action raising the flag on Iwo Jima and inspired the men growing weary in battle to continue the fight, we can do the same. There are people around the world, young and old, who can use inspiration. Think about what we discussed here this week. We can't keep it a secret."

"Joe, what was your wisdom?" Melvin asked, clapping his hands and pointing at Joe.

"Make the best use of your time!" Joe said enthusiastically, caught up in the change of atmosphere around the table.

"Exactly!' Melvin said, clapping his hands again. "Sammy, what did you share?"

Sammy slowly got up from his seat and, without saying a word, flashed the best smile of the week as everyone around the table laughed.

"You got it, man!" Melvin said with youthful enthusiasm. "The desire to smile. Let me ask you, how many people do you see each day that have lost the desire to smile?"

"Lots!" everyone shouted.

"Lots is right," continued Melvin. "And what if we were able to help them regain that smile. Someway. . . somehow. . .? And how about you, Leo? What a story of courage and bravery. What did you teach us?"

"Life is as we see it," Leo said, his voice cracking, obviously moved by Melvin's energy and honesty.

"And that it is, Leo. I saw myself as a coward all these years. I now choose not to see myself or my life that way any more. Life is as we see it. And how about you, 'Brave Knight?' Was what happened to you this week a life changing experience or what?"

Howard slowly got up and in a very serious voice said, "I am free. I learned that there is a dragon within us that we cannot destroy, but when we come to understand it, the true self can be set free. I'm free, Melvin. I'm free."

"That is what helped me deal with my situation, Howard. I looked inside myself and tried to get an understanding of my life. My chance to act has come now. I'm not a coward. I can take action. Thank you for teaching me that."

"My pleasure, my lord," Howard said with a bow, returning to his noble self.

"Tell us about it, Hoover. What did you share?"

"The value of hard work," Hoover said, shaking his head and thinking that he had not only shared it with the men around this table but, more importantly, learned it himself.

"That's it, Hoove, the value of hard work." Melvin's enthusiasm was growing and contagious. The men were starting to move to the edge of their seats. "Hard work is action in motion. When we realize that any action worthy of taking is going to be backed by hard work, we can expect great results to come from our actions," he continued. Then, holding up yesterday's newspaper, he said, "This is great results. Look at the smile on that little boy's face and the spring in the step of each of those old men dancing around him. That is great results coming from hard work. And that day proves what you taught us, Roadie."

"Inspiration in everything?" Roadie asked, knowing the answer to his question.

Melvin was more excited than ever as he circled the table. "Inspiration in everything, Roadie. When we are on the lookout for inspiration, we will have a constant source of energy and excitement in our lives. It will be the fuel that will cause us to take action. I was inspired when Mikey rolled his wheelchair down that ramp and across the lawn to the redbud tree. But when he took that knife out of his pocket, cut those branches, and then retraced his journey to give them to his mother, a fire of inspiration ignited inside me. Gentlemen, there are thousands of Mikeys around the world that need the same opportunity to be set free, whether it is with a ramp, a new wheelchair, or just someone to give them some attention. And there are thousands of people like you and me who are held prisoners in their thoughts. They think because they have grown old that there is nothing left. They haven't yet come to realize, as we have this past week, that old wood flowers. That is our call to action, my friends. We must have the courage to act. When we act, all the things we brought to the table this week become wisdom. If we fail to act, then it is just like Joe's friend Ernest said years and years ago when he was asking Joe to get the hornet's nest, 'All of life's experiences become knowledge, but it's not until you use that knowledge that it becomes wisdom.' Gentlemen, we must use the knowledge gained here this week, or it could be lost for good and our lives lost with it."

Melvin's words had a powerful effect on everyone sitting around the table. There was a mixture of emotions; they each knew that what he said was true. It was exciting to have a week like the one they had just finished, but what would next week bring? They wanted to take action, but nobody really knew where to start. Several minutes of silence passed as Melvin watched everyone ponder what to do next. Leo finally broke the silence and said, "Tell us how it is, Melvin. Do you have a plan, and what is the first step?"

Melvin jumped from his seat again and clapped his hands. "Thanks, Leo, I thought you would never ask." He was like a man rescued from the clutches of death. He knew he had a chance to make a difference, to save not only the lives of his six friends, but his own life as well. He thought, too, about how they could help others who have talents and skills and really aren't ready to call it quits. The fire in his eyes and the excitement in his voice made the Board of Directors lean forward in anticipation of his next words.

"This could be it," Joe thought. "This could be the thing that allows the magic of the past week to continue." And then he whispered audibly, "Some old wood is about to flower."

"What's that, Joe?" Melvin asked.

"Just talking to myself, Melvin. Excited about the things you've just told us."

179

"Great!" Melvin said. "Because the first part of the plan begins with you." Melvin pulled some papers out of his briefcase and began distributing them around the table. At the top were the words, "THE COURAGE TO TAKE ACTION." Underneath were the words, "THE OLD WOOD FLOWERS FOUNDATION." These words were followed by a list of step-by-step details that Melvin began to explain.

"Joe, you started this thing with your 'dead and dying speech,' wouldn't you agree?" Melvin asked, looking at the rest of the group, who responded with a series of "yesses" and "it's his fault" tongue-in-cheek answers.

"That's what I thought," Melvin continued. "That's why you play a role in the first step here, Joe. We need you out in every McDonald's, mall, or restaurant possible to tell about redbud trees, Ernest, and making the best use of your time. Let's get copies of the newspaper article; you can tell people how we helped Mikey and how they can do the same for someone else in need. You will start right here in this city, and then before you know it, you'll be traveling all over the country telling people about the Old Wood Flowers Foundation."

Joe was staring at the paper. He felt both nervous and excited, knowing what this challenge meant. What if people didn't want to hear what he had to say? It would also mean breaking his morning routine of coming to this McDonald's and meeting with this group. It had all grown very comfortable, especially after the past week. Joe cleared his throat and looked up from the paper. All eyes were on him. He had been the one that challenged them a week ago, but now the pressure was truly on him. Although each had paid a high price to rediscover and share their wisdom, this was different. Realizing it was time to take action was frightening.

"Joe, do you have the courage to act?" Melvin asked emphatically. Everyone leaned forward and stared.

As he looked into their eyes he knew what the answer must be. "I'll start this afternoon," Joe said as the entire board gave out an enthusiastic "YES!" Melvin reached out and shook Joe's hand, knowing that the rest of his plan would work. "I'll start at the McDonald's on Fifth Avenue at lunch time," Joe continued. "I know some of the old wood that meets there. It will be a great start."

"Leo, the next step is yours, Melvin said, shifting the focus in Leo's direction, causing him to give a nervous tug or two on his big nose.

"Tell me how it is and I'll have the courage to act," Leo said, once again meriting a cheer from the the other board members.

"GREAT!" Melvin said, slapping Leo on the shoulder. "Here's your plan, Leo. You've started the talks at the home, haven't you?"

"I have, and everyone is enjoying them. I'll tell about Iwo Jima and the courage to act as soon as I get back there today."

"That's perfect, Leo, but we need you to take it further. Can you take all the handouts and all the stories and make them into a presentation that anyone can give and add to? We will call it the "Old Wood Flowers Course." All of us will teach it, wherever we are and whenever we can. If we follow through with the knowledge shared here and then teach others to follow through with it, the wisdom will grow and can last forever."

"I'll start on it right away. I know the people at the home will be more than happy to help. We will spread it across the country." Leo stood and gave Sammy a high-five and sat back down, waiting to hear the rest of the plan.

"Hoover and Roadie?"

"Man, just point us in the direction," Roadie said, almost before Melvin could get the words out. "We are ready for anything. Right, Hoove?"

"I'm ready to work. Melvin, just tell us what you need." Hoover could hardly contain himself.

"What you two offer is a vital part of this plan. If we are to have a foundation, then we must have a good cause. Here is what I was thinking a good cause might be for the Old Wood Flowers Foundation. Did you hear that little wheelchair squeak and shake when Mikey rode it down the ramp and across the yard?"

"I heard it, man," Roadie said. "I thought that right wheel was going to wobble off. Nothing a new bearing and a little grease wouldn't take care of. I had the same problem with a side car on a Harley that I owned back in the sixties. I can fix that, no problem."

"That's exactly what I'm talking about," Melvin said. "There are probably thousands of wheelchairs, or hospital beds, or front porches, or whatever that need repair or building. We can start with Mikey's, but one day, because of your efforts, people will be helping special-needs people all over the country."

"We'll start right after this meeting," Hoover said. "Mikey's wheelchair will be as good as new."

"If we are going to fix things, there will obviously be a need for funds, and what is a foundation without fundraisers and contributors?" Melvin looked right at Sammy and said, "Sammy, you got the personality that will open doors. The sincerity of your smile will help get people believing in our cause. Can you do it? Can you help us find the money that will make a difference in thousands of lives?"

Sammy rose. The smile was replaced with a contemplative, serious expression. He looked around the table and was obviously touched by the trust and belief that these people had in him. He took a deep breath that seemed to come from his toes, and then it happened. It obviously began in the heart and traveled to his eyes. They lit up like diamonds. Then it appeared on his lips. The entire table began to laugh as Sammy broke forth in the biggest smile they had ever seen. "I'll do it, and I'll do it with a smile," Sammy proclaimed, returning the high-five to Leo. "I have a few people I'll call tonight. I can't wait to talk to some of my old Hollywood buddies again."

"We'll help too, Sammy," Hoover spoke up. "Just any way we can. We will help."

"If there is going to be some money coming in and going out, we will need someone to keep it all straight and accounted for." Melvin smiled as he and everyone else turned toward Howard.

Howard slowly rose from his seat, adjusted the cape that he'd decided to wear that day, and began to walk around the table and deliver his oration. "My friends, and nobles… your call to such a lofty role is one that humbles me to the innermost depths of my soul. I will proceed henceforth with the greatest of accuracy and precision, knowing that each contributing portion will be accounted for and divided to its most lofty of end results… to aid a fair maiden or prince in need." Howard completed his stroll around the table, placed his hand on his chair, removed his chapeau, took a deep bow, and finished with… "For this position I am most grateful and consider myself a servant to your calling." He then sat down swiftly as everyone gaped in astonishment.

"Does that mean he'll do it?" Roadie asked, not taking his eyes off Howard and requesting an answer from anyone.

"Unfortunately, it does," Hoover said with a wink and a smile.

"Great. Great!" said Melvin, his enthusiasm continuing to grow as the plan was being accepted.

"Tell us how it is, Melvin. What is your role in the foundation?"

"Well, Leo," Melvin answered, "that is probably what I wrestled with the most in putting these ideas together. All of you seemed to fit perfectly in the roles needed to get this plan underway. But for me, well, I'm not sure."

"Continue to lead us," Joe spoke up, almost pleadingly. "We need someone to coordinate and make sure we are sticking to the plan. It was you that was here every morning for the past three years saving this table, and you certainly helped to keep this group together. So why stop now?"

"Coordinator? I don't know, gentlemen. There is a lot more to keep track of than just reserving a table for seven each morning."

"Come on, Melvin," Sammy said. "If you don't do it, then who will? Have the courage to take action."

"Take action?" A distant look came across Melvin's face. He was brought back to the present immediately as the entire table stood up.

In unison they yelled, "TAKE ACTION!" Their cheer caused Lanny Smith to just shake his head and smile.

"All right!" Melvin said, standing and looking around the table. "TAKE ACTION! Come on, the first step is to go see that little boy. We've got some work to do. TAKE ACTION!"

The Board of Directors scrambled to pick up their things. Joe quickly wrapped the sausage, stuck it in his pocket, and then carefully placed Melvin's handout in the briefcase he had begun carrying. They marched to the door like a team with purpose and vision. As Melvin started to open the door, he suddenly stopped and looked back over his shoulder at the board room table that now had the prestigious plaque hanging over it. A warm and grateful smile came across his lips.

"What is it, Melvin?" Hoover asked. "Forget something?"

"No, Hoove, just remembering something. Actually, I want to remember everything."

JoJo was nearly clearing the fence when the men came down Horizons Drive. This morning the corner of the yard was filled not only with a happy bouncing dog, but its equally happy and bouncing master.

"LOOK, JOE!" Mikey yelled out as soon as the men were close enough. "Pop a wheelieeeeee!" Mikey leaned forward and then abruptly let his little body fly back against the seat of the wheelchair. As his little arms pumped at the big wheels, the front wheels came up. He squealed as he traveled ten or twelve feet before being grounded again. His audience first gasped, then cheered and applauded.

"Hey, you guys, don't cheer him on!" Jessie chided as she appeared on the porch. "He's a ham. He'll never stop."

"Hi, Jessie."

"Hi, Just Joe."

"Mikey seems to be enjoying this newfound freedom," Joe said, noticing the subtle changes that had occurred in her as well over the past week. The tired and stressed woman who hated old people now seemed like a warm, loving mother enjoying her son's happiness.

"Can't get him to come in, fellas. Got any suggestions?" Jessie yelled to the men that had helped give her son his freedom.

"Have you tried ice cream?" Sammy asked, causing Jessie to laugh.

"Tried it, Sammy. He puts the bowl on his lap and heads for the door and down the ramp."

"Joe?" Mikey called, grabbing everyone's attention. "Joe... how about a walk around the block?"

Joe glanced at Jessie. He knew the request made her nervous. She had probably never let Mikey go out on his own, or off with anyone besides herself. He could tell she didn't know how to answer, so Joe helped out by answering for her. "Why don't we wait and go some other time, Mikey, when..."

"Just Joe... it's okay if you all want to walk him around the block. It's all right with me. If you want to, that is." Jessie knew she had answered correctly.

Mikey's eyes were gigantic, "All right, let's go!" he yelled.

"Great, man!" Roadie yelled. "We can take a good look at those squeaky wheels and see what it will take to fix them."

"Jessie, we have had an incredible morning," Joe said, glancing up at the redbud tree which had reached its peak in flowering and was now dropping its blossoms in Mikey's hair. "We are TAKING ACTION. . . and our first step is to fix Mikey's wheelchair, and then every wheelchair in this city, and maybe even the entire country."

"Sounds like a pretty big goal, men," she answered, impressed by the glow on each of their faces. "What makes you think you can do it?"

Joe reached up and pulled a small branch from the redbud tree that still held its flowers. "Old wood flowers." he said with his voice cracking.

"It sure does," she said, wiping the tears away. "It sure does. You all be careful... and Mikey, no whistling at the neighbor girls."

"MOM!"

It was quite a sight as the seven old men took turns pushing the wheelchair, each trying to be sillier than the others to make Mikey laugh. Melvin had just taken over for Sammy when Roadie said, "Hey, Melvin, give him a little push and let him ride ahead of us. I'd like to see what's making that wheel wobble."

"Sure, Roadie, one freewheelin' push coming up." Melvin gave the chair a slight push and let it go on its own about ten feet in front of the pack.

"Wheeee!" Mikey said. "Do that again, only bigger." Melvin and the men laughed out loud at Mikey's squeal and request for more. "All right,

Mikey, here it goes again, hold on tight." This time Melvin gave him a little harder push that took him about thirty feet out in front of the pack, causing the squeal to be three times as loud.

"Look, Joe, no hands!" Mikey yelled, trying to hold his hands up and letting out another "WHHEEE!" Each man was bent over with laughter.

Suddenly there was the deafening sound of loud music, its full bass pounding out like the devil's heartbeat. An old car loaded with passengers came peeling around the corner, sheer fright on the driver's face. The vehicle careened off a parked car on the opposite side of the road and headed directly toward Mikey.

In an instant, and with the speed and strength of a young Marine, Melvin propelled himself toward Mikey and lunged at the wheelchair. Transfixed, the six men watched the gruesome scene unfold before their eyes.

"NOOOOO!" Joe's piercing cry hung in the air as he watched the body travel off the front windshield, over the top of the car, and then bounce off the trunk and onto the sidewalk. "NOOOO!" The jalopy hurtled past the powerless men, back across the treelawn, and then vanished down the street. The deadly silence was palpable.

"NOOOOO!" Joe yelled again and ran. He fell to his knees and touched his friend's face. "MELVIN! Melvin."

"Is... boy? Mikey... did I get him out... out of the way?" Melvin gasped.

"You did it, Melvin," Joe said, looking toward Mikey, who was off in a yard with Sammy standing next to him. "Didn't even come out of his wheelchair." His voice cracked when he saw the severity of Melvin's wounds.

"I... I took action... action... I bet I looked like Tiger Thomas... what... what say... Joe?"

Tears were streaming down the faces of the men now gathered around him. Joe had to work hard to answer, but somehow the right words formed, "You're a hero... a hero, soldier." A sob stopped Joe from speaking any further.

Melvin's hand slowly came up and clenched Joe's arm. "Joe... Joe... men..." He was laboring to produce each sound. "Joe... thank... thanks... for... for letting me flower." His last breath escaped from his lungs and the courageous soldier's hand fell lifeless from Joe's arm. The ambulance siren sounded in the distance.

Joe's hand was less than steady as he placed the key in the front door of his apartment. The knob turned and the door slowly opened. He hesitated for just a moment when a strange feeling came over him, he shrugged it off and closed the door behind him. It was probably just the stress of the funeral and the blistering heat of the day.

The room seemed vastly empty as he looked around and let his eyes fall on Mikey's artwork and the six items of wisdom that he had hung on the wall. The final one had not been hung. Since the accident two days before he had not felt like even looking at the wall. Guilt had crept over him as he reasoned again and again that if he had not made the dead and dying speech last week, Melvin would still be alive. At the funeral the faces of the other board members were once again lined with the realization of death and broken dreams. "Maybe Sammy is right," Joe said out loud as he grabbed at his neck and removed the clip-on tie, throwing it at the pictures hanging on the wall. "Nothing good ever happens to people like us."

He stumbled toward the couch, unbuttoning the top buttons of his shirt in an effort to fight the heat, and dropped his daily USA TODAY on the coffee table as he collapsed. Lying with his head back against the cushion, he stared up at the ceiling. "NOTHING good ever happens," he repeated, taking in a deep breath and then blowing it out with resignation.

The knock at the door startled Joe. He got up and moved toward the door as another knock followed the first. "I'm coming," he mumbled. "It better not be a religious fanatic. I'm in no mood for preachin'." Another knock followed. "Okay. Okay, I'm coming. I'm coming. WHO!!!..." Joe's word fell short as he yanked open the door and stared in disbelief. "It couldn't be...," he whispered.

"Hello, JoJo, you've certainly grown into a fine man," came a familiar voice from years gone by. The gray-haired figure moved through the door past Joe and limped his way toward the couch. "This is a nice place ya have here, JoJo. A lot better than that little coal mining shack we used to meet at. Hey, you wouldn't have any of your mother's biscuits around, would ya? HMM. Probably not, huh? Oh well, anyway, how ya been?"

Joe was speechless. What was happening to him was impossible. He began to wonder if it had been him that was laid in the grave that morning, and he was now somewhere else. . . maybe he should have listened to those fanatics.

"Ernest... is that you? Really?" Joe questioned in a childish tone full of uncertainty.

"Well, who else would it be... boy? Who else would it be?" The old man slowly sat down on the couch and then thought to ask, "You don't mind if I set a while, do ya?"

"Ernest, how can it possibly... be...? Ernest, how old are you?" Joe finally blurted out.

"Still asking that same question, aren't you, JoJo?"

Joe smiled as he shook his head and decided to quit trying to figure it all out. He just wanted to enjoy Ernest's company, no matter how unbelievable the situation might be. "Ernest, have you been around the past seven days? Have you had a hand in the events of the past week?" Joe looked on, hoping to get an answer that would help him make sense of what had gone on with the board members, the redbud tree, the wisdom, meeting Mikey, and maybe even Melvin's death. "Have you been around?"

Ernest just gave a big laugh, slapped his knee, and said, "JoJo, I've always been around. We keep our memories with us forever. I've always been there. Sometimes closer than others, that was usually your choice. It all depended on if you wanted to remember me or not. I've always been around, JoJo."

"Did you plant the redbud, Ernest? How did it get there?" Joe sincerely wanted to understand it all.

Ernest continued to smile at the young boy now grown old. "You are still full of questions, aren't you, son? The tree has always been there, too. It is a memory as well, but it's the best kind of memory. It's one that you learned from and grew from. When you decided to use what you learned, that memory and magic of redbud trees became evident to everyone you came in contact with. It's just like the way the wisdom ya have hangin' on your wall became real when each of your friends started to recall and apply it." Ernest slowly got up and shook his leg a little and then limped across the room and stood before the teachings and drawings.

"Think of it, JoJo," he continued as he pointed to the first one. "This wisdom came from your memories. 'Make the best use of your time.' In all that traveling around for those two years after the accident, you gained a valuable insight. But it didn't have meaning, JoJo, until you chose to remember it. And then you shared it and everyone could see it, just like the redbud."

Joe just stared in awe. How did he know about the accident and those two years following?

"And how about this one?" Ernest continued. "'The desire to smile.' That Sammy brought his wisdom to life, didn't he? But he had to remember it first. And once he did... well, that smile was just as magical as a redbud tree." Ernest just paused and let out a big belly laugh as Joe stared on in amazement. "Makes me laugh just to think about it."

"Life is as we see it. We have choices of how we will respond to any situation, and your friend Leo was able to help everyone see that. Again, he had to realize it, then apply it himself before you would ever get to see it." Ernest seemed to stop and take that one in for a moment before continuing.

"Answering the dragon's call... that Howard is a little different, isn't he, JoJo?" Ernest asked, looking at the poem hanging on the wall and the drawing of the dragon above it. "We must look inside and understand ourselves, then accept ourselves and allow our true self to come out. That's what we are seeing in Howard, just his true self, and he is happier because of it. And speaking of happy, how about Hoover? That boy is beside himself. He remembered the value of work, and all of you were able to see his memory come to life in that ramp you built for your little friend."

"Yeah, Ernest, he was happy and beside himself," Joe commented. "Everyone is pretty low right now. With Melvin gone, I don't know what is going to happen next."

Ernest took a deep breath and looked at Joe with a warm smile. He saw the same look on his face the day that little nine-year-old boy was hoping to see the magic outside the coal shack so many years ago. "Have you forgotten what magic is, JoJo?" Ernest asked, looking Joe right in the eye.

Joe felt a lump in his throat as the words tried to come out, "I... I remember what it is, Ernest. I remember."

"So tell me... what is magic, JoJo?"

Clearing his throat, Joe answered, "It's looking past what we believe, what seems to be the obvious, and seeing the possibilities... it's magical when we can see the possibilities... the possibilities of life."

"That's right, JoJo... and when you see the possibilities, then you can really understand what your friend Roadie shared with you... there is inspiration in everything... everything, JoJo." Ernest's voice became very quiet as he limped over and sat in the chair directly across from Joe. "Inspiration in everything... even in death."

The room was silent for several minutes as if both were absorbing the lessons in the conversation. Joe turned his attention back to Ernest. "What do we do next, Ernest?"

Ernest's eyes twinkled as he stood up and made his way over to the desk, picking up the frame that contained the wisdom and plan that Melvin had shared. Walking over to the wall, he placed the frame on the nail that had been reserved for it, and then placed Mikey's drawing of a flag right above it. "JoJo, you will now be able to see the magic of Melvin's wisdom, 'The courage to take action.' Melvin had the courage and he saved that little boy. You can allow his action to save many more people if you will take

188

action yourself. He laid the plan out. Now, do you have the courage to take action?" Ernest let the question reach the soul of Joe Yamka and then continued, "Remember all of this on the wall here is only knowledge. It doesn't become wisdom until you put it into action. Remember the hornet's nest?"

Joe smiled and wiped a tear from his eye as he nodded.

"Put the knowledge to use, JoJo, make it wisdom." The room was silent for several minutes when Ernest said, " Well, JoJo, I thinks it's time for me to get home. I have to go."

"GO?" Joe said with a hint of panic. "Go? Home? Ernest, where's home? What if I need to see you?"

Ernest chuckled as he moved toward the door. "JoJo, I'm always just a memory away. . . Hey, now don't forget to look in your newspaper there," he said as he stepped outside. Glancing over his shoulder, he smiled and added, "Thanks, JoJo," and closed the door behind him.

Joe sat up on the couch. He thought he heard the front door shut. "Ernest!" he called out as he moved to the door and opened it, only to find no one there. He shut the door and rubbed his neck, wondering how long he had been asleep. "What a dream," he mumbled, as his eyes fell on the wall across the room. Mikey's drawing of the flag caught his eye, and right below it hung Melvin's plan. The wall was complete. "How did that get there? It's not possible," Joe said in amazement. And then with a burst of excitement, He shouted, "The paper!"

Joe snatched the paper from the coffee table and unfolded it to the front page. He stared in disbelief. Then a smile began in his heart, sparkled in his eyes, and curled across his lips. There on the front page of USA TODAY was a picture of the board members and Mikey celebrating in the little front yard with the picket fence. The redbud tree blossomed in the background. He could see the smiles on everyone's face. In large, bold letters the headline read "OLD WOOD FLOWERS," and underneath the picture was the caption, "Board of Directors Takes Action."

Tears streamed down his face and his heart raced with anticipation. Joe knew exactly what to do next.

~ EPILOGUE ~

"People taking action." The President's exuberant words brought a cheer from the crowd and caused Joe's thoughts to propel back to the present. A smile of accomplishment, pride, and gratitude formed on his face as the President continued. "People taking action. That is what we are here to celebrate today. We are here to say thanks, not only to the six men on this stage with me, but to the thousands of people who had the courage to take action and make a difference. The movement created by these six men has come to be known as "Old Wood Flowers." The crowd sprang to their feet, cheering and applauding. The enthusiasm of their reaction and sustained applause caused the President to step back and laugh, wondering if he would ever get a chance to continue. He couldn't help but applaud, too, as he turned toward the six men who were the recipients of this response.

The audience of both young and old finally felt, after five minutes, that they had shown their appreciation for the Board of Directors and Old Wood Flowers. They returned to their seats, allowing the President to once again approach the podium. "What this foundation means to each of you is obvious by your reaction. In three short years the Old Wood Flowers Foundation has touched the lives of nearly every person, young or old, in this country. It is a foundation built on helping people, and in the words of Joe Yamka seated here to my right, 'Helping people gives us life.'" Joe nodded and smiled, knowing where those words had come from so many years ago.

"Consider the accomplishments that have occurred over the past three-and-a-half years. The Old Wood Flowers Life Courses have been presented in nursing homes, senior citizens gatherings, and community centers, and are now being introduced into schools and colleges across the country and in Europe." Joe looked at Leo with gratitude as the President spoke of how his efforts had literally touched millions of lives. "There are seven life-changing pieces of wisdom at the premise of this incredible organization, and I would like to remind you of them now." As the President began to state each wisdom, a huge banner was unfurled behind the stage with each teaching printed on it. Slowly and deliberately the President continued, "Old Wood Flowers has reminded us that there is a good side to growing older; there is wisdom. To begin with, we can each

focus on making the best use of our time. We can keep our desire to smile," he continued. "We can remember that life is as we see it, and we must face the dragons within us." With mounting emotion, he concluded, "We can all learn more about the value of good, hard work, and begin to look for inspiration in everything around us. And most of all, we can all start today by taking action." Before the President could finish, the crowd was once again on its feet in a resounding cheer. The Board of Directors looked over their shoulders at the banner and nodded to each other in approval and awe.

The President raised his hand. "Through their efforts, thousands of individuals with special needs, ranging from hospital beds to wheelchairs, have been helped. Through corporate sponsorship and the volunteerism of thousands across the country, we have seen action."

Joe looked over at Roadie and Hoover. Hoover was nudging Roadie, who responded with a wink that said, "Job well done."

"The support of the entertainment industry and performing artists has raised millions of dollars through concerts and benefits for the Old Wood Flowers Foundation," the President continued. "This giving of time, energy, and money has lessened the burden on government-funded programs and has enabled more people in need of help to get help... helping people gives us life." The Board of Directors all turned to look at Sammy, whose now famous smile had been seen on the front of national magazines ranging from TIME to PEOPLE. When Sammy smiled back at them, the convention hall broke into joyous laughter and applause.

The President was obviously enjoying himself. "The principles and focus of the Old Wood Flowers Foundation are not just for the senior citizens of our land, as is evident in the three hundred day-care centers that have been established throughout the country. These centers, known as 'Little Dragons,' not only provide excellent care for children but also offer counseling and educational opportunities for parents and children, with a focus on family values and learning to appreciate ourselves as important individuals." The mention of the Little Dragon Day Care Centers brought applause and appreciation from the crowd and caused Howard to squint through the lights to find Edith, who was seated in the front row wiping tears from her eyes. The noble knight instinctively blew a kiss to his queen. She had become a grandma to hundreds of children across the country.

The crowd grew quiet as a serious look came across the

President's face. He looked up, contemplating his next words. "It gives us life…" he continued, his voice cracking slightly. "Helping people gives us life. Old Wood Flowers has come to symbolize the importance of those in our society that have lived the longest and earned the privilege to grow old." The President then hesitated, gathering his thoughts. He looked back over his shoulder and directly into the eyes of Joe Yamka. The picture of Ernest standing in Johnsons' pasture by the redbud trees flooded Joe's mind.

The President then turned back to the hushed crowd, and the words rolled mightily across the podium to fall on their waiting hearts. "Do you know what a legacy is? It is the passing on of wisdom. It is caring enough to take action, to do something and make a difference. We leave a legacy by caring enough about the people who may not even be born yet, to use our wisdom in a way to make the world better because we were here. We can leave a legacy. No one is too young and no one is too old to apply the wisdom established through this foundation. We must use our own lives to make a difference in our country, our job, our family, and even our own well being and self-esteem. And so it is for all of this, that we thank these six men for their efforts. They have made a difference and inspired each of us to do the same. Gentlemen, please stand as I introduce you. Sammy Johnson… Leo Horowitz… Howard Campbell… George "Roadie" Sparks… Chester "Hoover" Lewis… Joe Yamka… and," he stopped to allow the applause to die down, "the man that should have occupied the chair at the end, the man whose actions taught us to have the courage to take action, Melvin Gross. Thank you. Thank you." In a voice choked with sincere emotion, he closed, "Tonight I challenge the world to have the courage to take action. Young and old, take action and make a difference. Together we can see the magic in Old Wood Flowers."

With a deafening roar the crowd came to its feet again as the President shook each man's hand and then was escorted off the stage and back down the aisle. The Board of Directors followed him down, where they were greeted by the crowd. Joe patiently maneuvered his way through the sea of people to where he knew Mikey and Jessie had been sitting. Mikey was becoming a young man, courageously battling his disease and inspiring everyone. Right beside him stood his mother. How much she had changed, Joe thought. The young woman who had hated old people now played an integral part as executive assistant of the foundation and probably touched more lives than anyone. Joe appreciated her friendship more than ever.

"Joe, that was awesome," Mikey said, as Joe stepped up to his wheelchair. "The President, Joe. The President of the United States shook your hand. I'm proud of you, Joe."

"I'm proud of you, too, Just Joe," Jessie said, smiling through tears. "Proud of all of you."

Joe bent over to hug his young friend in the wheelchair. "Way to go, Joe!" Mikey said, overwhelmed by his hero. Joe just smiled and touched his face. Then he saw it.

"Mikey, where did you get that?" Joe asked, pointing to a picture on his wheelchair table.

"I drew it, Joe. I drew it while the President was talking. But I was listening, too, I promise."

Joe picked the picture up and stared in disbelief. The long gray hair, dark eyes that seemed moist with tears, and that scar cutting through his rugged complexion. Mikey had captured Ernest perfectly.

"When did you see this man, Mikey?" Joe asked, unable to take his eyes from the picture.

"He was sitting next to me, Joe. While the President was talking about you and the other men. Do you know that man, Joe? Do you know him?"

Joe took a deep breath as he looked at Mikey. "Did he say his name, Mikey? Did he tell you his name?"

Mikey looked into the depths of Joe Yamka's eyes, and with a laugh said, "He told me his name was Jooba, Joe. Can you believe it Joe? He said Jooba!"

Joe leaned forward, cupping Mikey's face with his old, caring hands. With the wisdom of many, many years, he nodded his head slowly and whispered through his tears, "I believe it, Mikey. I believe it."

THE DASH

I've seen death stare at me with my own eyes in a way many cannot know.

I've seen death take others but still left me below.

I've heard many scream of mother's cries, but death refuses to hear.

In my life I've seen faces fill with many tears.

After death has come and gone a tombstone sits for many to see.

But it is no more than a symbol of a person's memory.

I've seen my share of tombstones but never took the time to truly read,

The meaning behind what is there for others to see.

Under the person's name it read the date of birth,
dash (-) and the date the person passed.

But the more I think about that tombstone, the important thing is the dash.

Yes, I see the name of the person but that I might forget.

I also read the date of birth and death but even that might not stick.

But thinking about the individual I can't help but remember the dash,

Because it represents a person's life and that will always last.

So when you begin to charter your life make sure you're on a positive path,

Because people may forget your birth and death but they will never forget

your dash.

- Alton Maiden

Alton Maiden played nose guard tackle for the University of Notre Dame between 1992 and 1996. On a trip to Ireland the team visited an old graveyard and Alton was inspired by the great tombstones. When he returned home he put the thoughts that were on his heart down on paper and composed THE DASH. Although Alton never thought the poem would help anyone other than those closest to him, it now inspires thousands.

Books That Inspire

WALDEN POND by Henrey David Thoreau

ESSAYS OF RALPH WALDO EMERSON

MAN'S SEARCH FOR MEANING by Victor Frankel

THE MAGIC OF THINKING BIG by David Schartz

HOW TO WIN FRIENDS AND INFLUENCE PEOPLE by Dale Carnegie

ZEN AND THE ART OF MOTORCYCLE MAINTENANCE
by Robert M. Pirsig

LIFE IS TREMENDOUS by Charles T. Jones

PEOPLE SKILLS by Dexter Yager

LETTERS TO MY SON by Kent Nerburn

CHICKEN SOUP FOR THE SOUL series by Mark Victor Hansen and
Jack Canfield

DON'T SWEAT THE SMALL STUFF by Richard Carlson, PH.D.

SLOWING DOWN TO THE SPEED OF LIFE by Richard Carlson, PH.D.
and Joseph Bailey

TUESDAYS WITH MORRIE by Mitch Albom

WOODIE GUTHRIE by Joe Kline

GLORY DAYS by Dave Marsh

STAIRWAY TO SUCCESS by Nido R. Qubein

THE GO GETTER by Peter B. Kyne

THE CHOICE by Og Mandino

LIGHTEN UP by C.W. Metcalf

NEVER GIVE IN by Stephen Mansfield

GOLF IS NOT A GAME OF PERFECT by Dr. Bob Rotella

OH YEAH…

FIVE IMPORTANT THINGS by Jim Paluch

GREAT THOUGHTS FROM FIVE IMPORTANT THINGS by Jim Paluch

Tapes That Inspire

THE POWER OF OPTIMISM by Alan McGinnis

INCREASING HUMAN EFFECTIVENESS by Bob Mowad

THE SCIENCE OF SELF-CONFIDENCE by Brian Tracy

UNLIMITED POWER by Anthony Robbins

❧ **Want To Inspire a Meeting?** ❧

Jim Paluch's speaking style is an inspirational experience that will make your next conference unforgettable. With a fun, down-to-earth approach, Paluch delivers over 175 talks each year which keeps him in demand as a speaker.

To turn your next meeting into an event and leave
your people energized,

contact JP Horizons Inc.:

Phone: (440) 254-8211

Fax: (800) 715-TEAM

E-Mail: jpaluch@jphorizons.com

JP Horizons' seminars by Jim Paluch

- FIVE IMPORTANT THINGS
- SCORING IN SALES
- BUILDING A WINNING TEAM
- PERFORMANCE MANAGEMENT

- LEAVING A LEGACY
- ROUND TABLE OLYMPICS
- PROFESSIONAL CONSISTENCY
- AN EXPRESSIVE JOURNEY
  TO UNITY

Visit our website at www.jphorizons.com

JP Horizons
INCORPORATED

‿ GREAT THOUGHTS ‿

GREAT THOUGHTS

GREAT THOUGHTS

GREAT THOUGHTS

⌦ GREAT THOUGHTS ⌫

GREAT THOUGHTS

GREAT THOUGHTS

GREAT THOUGHTS

GREAT THOUGHTS

ᘖ GREAT THOUGHTS ᘗ